TURNING GLOBAL RIGHTS INTO LOCAL REALITIES

Sociology of Children and Families

Series Editors: **Esther Dermott** and
Debbie Watson, University of Bristol, UK

This series brings together the latest international research on children, childhood and families and pushes forward theory in the sociology of childhood and family life. Books in the series cover major global issues affecting children and families.

Scan the code below to discover new and forthcoming titles in the series, or visit:

bristoluniversitypress.co.uk/
sociology-of-children-and-families

TURNING GLOBAL RIGHTS INTO LOCAL REALITIES

Realizing Children's Rights in Ghana's Pluralistic Society

Afua Twum-Danso Imoh

First published in Great Britain in 2024 by

Bristol University Press
University of Bristol
1–9 Old Park Hill
Bristol
BS2 8BB
UK
t: +44 (0)117 374 6645
e: bup-info@bristol.ac.uk

Details of international sales and distribution partners are available at bristoluniversitypress.co.uk

© Bristol University Press 2024

British Library Cataloguing in Publication Data
A catalogue record for this book is available from the British Library

ISBN 978-1-5292-2762-8 hardcover
ISBN 978-1-5292-2763-5 ePub
ISBN 978-1-5292-2764-2 ePdf

The right of Afua Twum-Danso Imoh to be identified as author of this work has been asserted by her in accordance with the Copyright, Designs and Patents Act 1988.

All rights reserved: no part of this publication may be reproduced, stored in a retrieval system, or transmitted in any form or by any means, electronic, mechanical, photocopying, recording, or otherwise without the prior permission of Bristol University Press.

Every reasonable effort has been made to obtain permission to reproduce copyrighted material. If, however, anyone knows of an oversight, please contact the publisher.

The statements and opinions contained within this publication are solely those of the author and not of the University of Bristol or Bristol University Press. The University of Bristol and Bristol University Press disclaim responsibility for any injury to persons or property resulting from any material published in this publication.

Bristol University Press works to counter discrimination on grounds of gender, race, disability, age and sexuality.

Cover design: blu inc
Front cover image: Getty Images/DANIEL BUAH/SCIENCE PHOTO LIBRARY
Bristol University Press uses environmentally responsible print partners.
Printed and bound in Great Britain by CPI Group (UK) Ltd, Croydon, CR0 4YY

For my children, Chinua and Chizorom

Contents

List of Figures and Table	viii
About the Author	ix
Introduction	1
---	---	---
1	Tracing the Western Origins of Global Children's Rights Discourses	25
2	From the National to the International: The Makings of the Global Discourse of Children's Rights	41
3	Global Children's Rights Discourses: Imperialistic, Irrelevant and Inapplicable to Southern Contexts?	56
4	Historical Approaches to Child Welfare in Ghana	75
5	From Marginal to Central: Tracing the Deployment of Children's Rights Language in Laws and Action in Ghana	96
6	Exploring the Multiplicity of Childhoods and Child-Rearing Practices in a Pluralistic Society and the Implications for Children's Rights	127
7	The Plurality of Childhoods and the Significance for Rights Discourses: An Exploration of Child Duty and Work Against a Backdrop of Social Inequality	148
8	Implications of the Pluralities of Childhood Conceptualizations and Lived Experiences in the Global South for Studies of Children's Rights	173
Notes	190
References	194
Index	216

List of Figures and Table

Figures

1	Regional map of Ghana	2
2	Map of Accra	3
3	Population by major ethnic groups	129

Table

1	Children's work targeted for regulation or elimination in Ghana	161

About the Author

Afua Twum-Danso Imoh is Associate Professor in Global Childhoods and Welfare at the University of Bristol. Much of her work focuses on constructions of childhoods; children's rights and cultural norms; the impact of historical developments on understandings of childhood and child socialization; and problematizing the binary between the Global North and the Global South in relation to childhood studies. Afua is the lead editor of three edited collections (*Childhoods at the Intersection of the Global and the Local* [Palgrave, 2012]; *Children's Lives in an Era of Children's Rights: The Progress of the Convention on the Rights of the Child in Africa* [Routledge, 2013]; and *Global Childhoods Beyond the North-South Divide* [Palgrave, 2018]) as well as two journal special issues published by *Third World Thematics* (2023) and the *British Academy Journal* (2022).

Introduction

Why this book?

Since embarking on research on constructions of childhood, child-rearing practices and children's rights in the early 2000s, the bulk of my work has been undertaken in Ghana, the country of my birth and where I spent the early years of my life. While there were various factors that underpinned my decision to focus my research on children's rights on Ghana, not least because it was the first country in the world to ratify the 1989 Convention on the Rights of the Child in February 1990 – a fact that intrigued me given everything I knew about the country in that period – I must admit that I was also driven by personal motivations. Leaving Ghana with my family at the age of six, which signified the last time I would live there as a resident, can be identified as one of several reasons behind this country becoming so pivotal to my work over the past 26 years. Researching Ghana, which is an endeavour I embarked upon while still an undergraduate at university in the UK in the late 1990s – though not relating to childhood research – was part of a desire to better understand the country of my birth and the place where I spent many of my long vacations during my later childhood and adolescent years. Beyond understanding, researching this country enabled me to contextualize and make meaning of some of my personal observations, experiences and relationships as a Ghanaian.

In particular, given my interest in urbanization and processes of social change more broadly, especially as it relates to childhoods and family life, the bulk of my research in Ghana has centred on Accra, which is located in the southern part of the country (see Figure 1), and assumed its current administrative role in 1877 when the capital was transferred from Cape Coast.[1] Accra (see Figure 2) is now the 'primate city' of the country (Brydon and Legge, 1996: 26). It is the seat of national government ministries, the locus of most secondary industry, the site of the country's major services such the Korle Bu teaching hospital, the country's main international airport, Kotoka International Airport, the oldest university in the country – the University of Ghana Legon – and the location of the Ghana Broadcasting Corporation and all major press agencies.

Figure 1: Regional map of Ghana

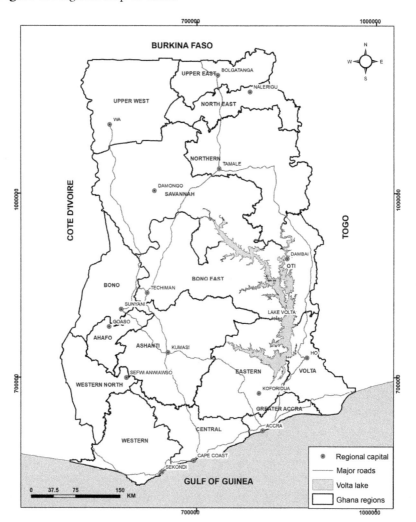

Notes: In December 2018 a referendum was organized in Ghana on the creation of new regions. The resulting outcome led to the creation of six new regions. The changes introduced were as follows: the Northern region became three regions: Northern, North East and Savannah; the Volta region has now been divided into the Volta and Oti regions; the Western region is now split into two: Western and Western North; the Brong-Ahafo region became three regions: Bono, Ahafo and Bono East. All other regions were left intact.

My research, particularly in the early part of my career, focused on communities in Central Accra which, despite their proximity to the financial district of the city, are characterized by poor infrastructure, high levels of pollution, un- or under-employment and large numbers of inhabitants who are illiterate. These are also densely populated areas which result in crowded

Figure 2: Map of Accra

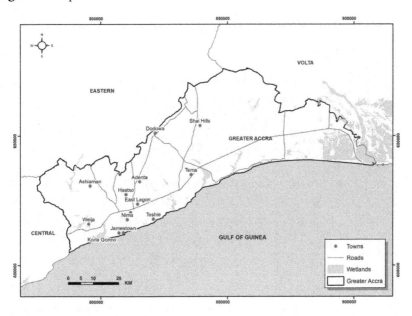

living conditions and inadequate public facilities. In these neighbourhoods most houses, which consist of several nuclear families – sometimes related, sometimes not – living together, with one room allocated to each nuclear unit, lack proper ventilation, pipe-borne water, electricity and toilet facilities (such as pan latrines and Kumasi Ventilated Improved Pit [KVIP] latrines). This forces inhabitants to pay to use nearby public toilets or, alternatively, to defecate in the nearby gutters, or in the case of one of the communities I have worked in, in the nearby sea and lagoons, which exacerbates already high levels of pollution. Louvre windows are fixed in the window frames of houses in these areas, often set behind torn mosquito nets. While old television sets can be found in many of these homes, the device that is, more often than not, blasting sound through windows and open doors is a radio (often battery-operated), blaring out news or music from the numerous private radio stations that exist in the country, such as Adom FM or Peace FM. Mountains of rubbish build up in communal areas, often by the roadside; in one of these communities amidst this heap of rubbish can be found goats and malnourished cows grazing away at whatever they can find. The stench of sewage water from the gutters wafts past your nose as you wander around the streets. Due to the close living quarters in these neighbourhoods people live many aspects of their lives outside, including cooking, eating, playing and engaging in some kind of income-generating activity. Mothers, in particular, set up stalls selling petty goods or cooking local dishes for sale just outside their homes, enabling them to earn money while staying close to home. This enables them to benefit from the help of their older children as well as keep an eye on younger children. While traffic is often heavy in these areas, cars parked outside these houses are few and far between.

The children I have encountered in these neighbourhoods live in homes where resources, in most cases, are scarce. Like adults, they spend the bulk of their lives outside, engaged in numerous activities, including bathing, sometimes in plain sight of others (in the case of young children). As a result of overcrowding, with each house accommodating several members of an extended family or several nuclear families, members of which are all squeezed into one room per family, many children are forced to sleep outside at night due to lack of space in a room, which can be shared by a family of five or more. Many attend, sometimes in a double shift system,[2] poorly resourced state schools most of which are at the primary level. Of those who attend school, many do not do so on a regular basis. A significant number, regardless of whether they attend school or not, engage in some form of work outside the home either by helping their parents, or independently. Even if they do not engage in income-generating work, they spend large parts of their time undertaking numerous chores, which are often allocated on the basis of their gender, including being sent on errands by adults. This leads them to be seen running around the neighbourhood at all times of the day, including scuttling between slow-moving traffic. These children also play in whatever free spaces they find available, which are few and far between, due to the density of these areas, with football being an important pastime for boys. Hanging out with their friends, chatting, playing *ampe*,[3] swimming at the beach (in one particular coastal community), listening to music and dancing to the latest Afrobeats music that is trending on the airwaves at that moment in time are all pastimes in which I have observed children engaging. These are the locations from where I have collected the bulk of the data I have gathered over the years in Ghana.

However, at the end of each research day during periods of fieldwork I travelled about 16 kilometres (approximately 10 miles) from these locations in Central Accra to a suburb near the outskirts of the city featuring: international schools based on the British, French and American systems; expensive four- and five-star hotels which fix their fees in dollars, not in Ghanaian cedis; fine dining restaurants from diverse countries, including China, India, Lebanon, Turkey, Thailand and Italy; shopping malls consisting of boutiques selling expensive imported fabric or ready-made clothes; South African- or Lebanese-owned supermarkets; cinemas; fast-food takeaways; recreational centres which provide swimming lessons to adults and children alike; and well-maintained – albeit small – playgrounds

INTRODUCTION

with mothers, or house helps, pushing young children on swings as they seek to keep them occupied.

In these neighbourhoods I travelled to at the end of the day, large, imposing houses dominated the area, even if incomplete. Surrounding these large structures are high walls with electric fences and iron gates, often with a security guard standing or sitting nearby both during the day and night. As you walk past the houses the loud humming noise from the exterior part of large air conditioners interrupts your thoughts. In such neighbourhoods weekly bin collection services are provided for households that are prepared to pay a fee. Even in times when the national electricity distribution affects all parts of the city leading the Ghana Electricity Company to initiate the process of load-shedding, many of these homes have generators which continue to power their goods, in some cases automatically, in the event of a blackout. Additionally, on the roofs of some houses solar panels are installed in order to give the inhabitants of these homes yet another alternative electricity source. Two or more cars, including a sport utility vehicle (SUV) for use on badly built or underdeveloped roads, can frequently be found in the parking port of compounds. On the roof or the side of many houses in these areas are satellite dishes which enable the inhabitants to access a variety of, primarily American, programmes via South Africa-based cable company, DSTV. The interior of these homes consists of well-furnished living spaces and several bathrooms, some which are attached to its numerous bedrooms as en suites.

The children I encountered in these neighbourhoods have parents who are often well educated, with at least one parent holding a degree and working as a professional of some kind. Many attend expensive international schools or prestigious state boarding schools and after school they have tutors to support them in deepening their learning in various subjects. Such children spend their weekends and free time going to the cinema, going out to eat in a range of fast-food places which, in recent years, have come to include KFC, hanging around in shopping malls, visiting each other at home, or if that is not possible, talking to, or messaging, each other on phones that are increasingly technologically advanced with internet and Bluetooth access. The streets in which they live tend to be somewhat quieter than the neighbourhoods in which I have undertaken the bulk of my research, with less hustle and bustle as the children within these households are either inside playing, watching satellite TV, surfing the internet on one of the laptops to which they have access, chatting on social media, or playing on their Xbox or PlayStation. If they are not at home they are being driven, by either a parent or an employed driver, to different locations for whatever educational, religious, social or leisure activity that has been scheduled for them. Older children may additionally rely on Uber to navigate their way around the bustling city. Afrobeats music may still be heard as you walk the streets of these neighbourhoods, but you are less likely to see who is listening to the music or catch a glimpse of the dance moves they may be deploying as they listen to the latest artist from, primarily, Ghana or Nigeria. On long vacations, some of these children attend holiday clubs that provide sporting or arts and craft activities. With their families, many visit one of the local beach resorts in the country, and on occasion, some travel abroad to countries such as South Africa, the United Arab Emirates, the US or the UK.

In making this journey between my place of residence in Accra and my research sites every day – about 32 kilometres (there and back) – which can take anywhere between 30 and 50 minutes depending on traffic, I never ceased to be struck by the vast differences between these communities and the representations of children identifiable in each area. In between these polar opposite neighbourhoods my journey there and back led me to pass through other residential areas, some of which were similar to either of the neighbourhoods described earlier or which featured characteristics that positioned them somewhat in-between these polar opposite neighbourhoods.

Despite the vast differences between neighbourhoods such as where I undertook research and those similar to the one I stayed in, the lives of children from these distinct neighbourhoods are lived in relative proximity to each other and, as a result, their paths may cross on a regular basis. For instance, at several points in a given day situations can arise whereby a child from a neighbourhood similar to the second one described earlier can be sitting in an air-conditioned car in traffic driving past a child from a community similar to my research sites who may be walking on the pavement, possibly also sitting in an overcrowded minibus which represents a form of public transport vehicle known as the *trotro*, or trying to dodge traffic as they seek to sell their wares to commuters. Their paths may also cross intimately as many of the large houses in the second community I have outlined are maintained, and in some cases, run, by the labour of people who live in, or come from, communities similar to the ones where I have conducted the bulk of my research. In particular, maintaining these homes is dependent on security guards or 'watchmen' remaining vigilant both during the day and night, gardeners maintaining their beautifully landscaped lawns, drivers chauffeuring the family members about, and maids or house helps cleaning the homes, looking after children, washing clothes and utensils, and cooking whatever food that the lady of the house has decided should be cooked that day. In most cases these employees are adults. However, there is evidence to show that in some instances some house helps, in particular, are under the age of 18 (Tetteh, 2011a, 2011b; Omoike, 2013) and, hence, are considered to be children according to the current laws of the country which have been reviewed to ensure they align with the Convention on the Rights of the Child, which was adopted by the UN General Assembly in 1989. While some attend school at the same time as they work for their employers, others do not have the opportunity to do so and, instead, spend the bulk of their day undertaking various forms of housework, looking after children not that much younger than they are and cooking.

Despite the proximity in which they live out their lives, many children residing in more affluent areas, especially those who live with their biological parents, know little, if anything, about the conditions in which children in the deprived communities in Central Accra live. This is something that has been noted in other societies which are underpinned by high levels of inequality. For instance, within the context of Brazil, Rizzini and Barker observed that in the wake of the passage into law of the country's Child and Adolescent Statute in July 1990:

> The worlds of poorer children and their middle- and upper-class counterparts are further apart than ever before: children from various social classes in Brazil rarely meet. A common feature of Brazil's major cities is strictly segregated and divided cities with separate residential areas, recreational areas, and commercial areas for the middle-class and wealthy and for low-income groups. Even when (or particularly when) low-income urban areas (favelas) are geographically next to wealthier areas there is considerable segregation between wealthy and middle-class children and poor ones. In terms of children's everyday lives, they simply do not have the chance to meet and interact with children from other social classes. Rio represents a good example of this division. In the wealthiest part of the city, families live in gated condominiums in which mini cities are built. Residents of these complexes for all practical purposes do not need to leave their complex to obtain goods and services they need. In this situation, children live in supposed safe 'paradises' with all the facilities they need. They often socialize only with peers from the same social class who share their same worldview. (Rizzini and Barker, 2002: 138–139)

Similar to Brazil at the time Rizzini and Barker were writing, the consequences of this segregation of lifestyles for children remain to be documented in Ghana. However, what is evident is that while the lives of children from different status groups may be experienced in relative close proximity to each other, there is not only a distinct segregation in their experience of growing up in this context, but also a lack of awareness, among children of affluent families, of the state of childhoods in poor communities characterized by numerous deprivations.

This is not to say that there are no similarities between the lives of children in these neighbourhoods. In fact, there are a number. Similar values are featured in the socialization process both groups experience, including an emphasis placed on respecting your elders, the importance of children having duties which take the form of engaging in some form of housework, although with varying levels of intensity depending on the socioeconomic status of the family, and the administration of physical punishment as part of an attempt by parents and caregivers to ensure that their children become, in future, 'good', responsible adults (Twum-Danso Imoh, 2013). Added to this, while nuclear family units may be more visible in affluent communities, members of the so-called extended family can often be found living in these homes on a full-time or part-time basis. Hence, collectivist living arrangements are not uncommon in either residential area.

This striking contrast in children's experiences of growing up in the same city based on socioeconomic status is very much evident as one navigates one's way around Accra. However, when I turn to the childhood studies literature to contextualize and further deepen my understanding of children's lives in this context, the depiction of children's lives that is identifiable predominately corresponds with the lives of only one of these groups of children – the children I encountered in my research settings; that is to say, poor children facing deficits and deprivations of some kind. This literature, over the years, has helped me, especially in the early stages of my career, understand, explain and contextualize the economic, social and cultural lives of children whose lives are not only characterized by poverty, but are also so clearly antithetical to the ideal image of childhood represented in global and dominant children's rights discourses and policies. But the questions that have persistently niggled at the back of my mind over the years are: where are the accounts of these 'other' childhoods I was also observing in the neighbourhood I stayed in during periods of fieldwork? Why were their experiences of childhood not analysed in the same way? Where were the narratives of those children whose lived experiences cannot be categorized as lacking or deficient in some way? What did their childhoods mean for how we understand childhoods in Ghana? Very little of the literature on childhoods in Ghana, or sub-Saharan Africa more generally, at least that which is available in the English language, provided me with insights to understand: the lives of these 'other' children; how their realities intersect with dominant global children's rights discourses; and how this may align with, or indeed, differ from, the experiences of the children who were often the focus of my research projects in the early stages of my career.

Instead, the abundance of literature that is focused on sub-Saharan Africa (and indeed, other contexts in the Global South) within the multidisciplinary field of childhood studies, which has grown significantly in recent decades, is centred around childhoods that are characterized by what they lack instead of what they have (see also Punch, 2003; Balagopalan, 2014; Twum-Danso Imoh, 2016). In relation to sub-Saharan Africa these have arguably contributed to portraying African childhoods in a rather pessimistic light. As Ensor asserts: 'The limited corpus of reliable research on Africa's youngest citizens has tended to adopt a negative outlook. Given Africa's turbulent realities, this pessimistic viewpoint is not entirely unwarranted, but [such generalizations] fail to acknowledge encouraging current trends towards brighter possibilities' (Ensor, 2012: 21; see also Abebe, 2022).

In some instances, a pessimistic slant on Africa-centred research has been positively demanded in some academic circles. Punch (2015) refers to the experience of human geographer, Matthew Benwell, who undertook his PhD research on children's outdoor mobilities in a middle-class suburb in Cape Town, South Africa (see Benwell, 2009). As he presented his research in various fora in the years after completing his PhD, he was frequently asked why he chose to not locate his study in a more economically deprived township in Cape Town (in Punch, 2015). For those asking these questions, the fact that a Western researcher could travel to an African country and undertake research which did not involve the most deprived or in need was difficult to understand. This negative slant to studies of Africa is not only unique to childhood studies but can be noted in more general analyses about the region. Cameroonian historian, Achille Mbembe, puts it well when he claims:

> The African human experience constantly appears in the discourse of our times as an experience that can only be understood through a negative interpretation. Africa is never seen as possessing things and attributes properly part of 'human nature.' Or, when it is, its things and attributes are generally of lesser value, little importance, and poor quality. It is this elementariness and primitiveness that makes Africa the world par excellence of all that is incomplete, mutilated, and unfinished, its history reduced to a series of setbacks of nature in its quest for humankind. (Mbembe, 2001: 8)

The motivations underpinning the studies on which these publications are based are numerous. First, influencing social policy either locally or globally has to be understood as a primary motivation behind such depictions of African childhoods. This is due to the centrality of developing interventions to improve the lives of the poor within the discipline of social policy (Highmore, 2002; Twum-Danso Imoh et al, 2022; Pastore, 2022; Twum-Danso Imoh, 2024a). This focus on the poor is not only a feature of the academic literature, but also evident in global social policies and international law. For instance, both the focus of the 1979 International Year of the Child and the Convention on the Rights of the Child, which was adopted ten years later, in November 1989, centred their attention much more explicitly than earlier declarations and initiatives on 'especially disadvantaged groups – addressing the rights not only of children living in "average" situations within the family, but also of those experiencing exceptional circumstances such as war, abandonment or abuse' (Boyden, 1997: 175). Balagopalan (2014: 4) adds to this when she asserts that the 'near unanimous global ratification of the UN's Convention during the 1990s brought intense focus on the marginal child in the South'. Technically, given its global remit and universalist undertones, it can be argued that this focus on children in especially difficult circumstances within the Convention applies to contexts in both the North and South. However, in the years following the adoption of the Convention attention has been particularly given to children living in difficult circumstances in the South. This is evidenced by the strategies and policies of international organizations and agencies. Notable examples are recent United Nations Children's Fund (UNICEF; 2018) and Save the Children (2019) global strategy documents, which centre around the lives of poor, deprived and marginalized children almost exclusively in the South despite the 'global' vision behind their respective strategies. This focus may be changing for some organizations. For instance, in August 2020 UNICEF launched its first-ever domestic emergency response in the UK in its 70-year history as part of an attempt to support and feed poor children whose economic situations had been compounded by the COVID-19 pandemic (UNICEF, 2020). While the focus on the South in academic or policy discussions about children's rights is seen as justified by some authors, many of whom are based in the Global North (see, for example, Hanson and Nieuwenhuys, 2012), this has also been problematized. Pupavac, for example, has asserted that the focus on children in the South reproduces 'the colonial paternalism where the adult–Northerner offers help and knowledge to the infantilized South' (Pupavac, 2001: 103; see also Burman, 1994).

Second, the focus on deficit childhoods in the academic literature can be linked back to the objective of challenging Eurocentric assumptions about childhood and child development underpinning the notion of a global childhood which is embedded in universalizing agendas of international child-focused treaties such as the Convention as well as that of many international agencies and organizations (see Twum-Danso Imoh et al, 2023). The driving force behind this body of literature is to highlight the difference and, hence, incompatibility, between children's lived realities in diverse contexts in the South and dominant global children's rights discourses, articulated by key pieces of international law, which are widely recognized to have emerged within the societal and economic upheavals that characterized Western European and North American societies from the 17th century onwards (Burman, 1994, 1996, 1999; Boyden, 1997; Aitken, 2001; Balagopalan, 2002, 2014; Burr, 2006; Twum-Danso, 2008, 2009; Ansell, 2016; Twum-Danso Imoh, 2016, 2019, 2020). This historical context has been foregrounded in much of the literature on children's rights, especially with the intention of illuminating the extent to which such dominant discourses, based on their origins, are in sharp contrast to understandings of childhood and child development in societies in the South which have historically followed different trajectories (Burman, 1996; Boyden, 1997; Aitken, 2001; Ansell, 2016). Therefore, the global diffusion of rights that has emerged within the specific historical circumstances of Western Europe and North America is seen as problematic as these rights are perceived to be incompatible with the 'so-called communitarian and consensual communities of the South' (Kaime, 2010: 638). This incompatibility, it is argued, leads to a situation whereby children (and their families) who fail to conform to a particular model of childhood are either stigmatized, made invisible or become seen as delinquent or deficient in some way (see Burman, 1994, 2016; Boyden, 1997; Aitken, 2001; Ansell, 2010; Hopkins and Sriprakash, 2016). As a result of these concerns there has been a proliferation of publications foregrounding the lives of children living in marginalized and especially difficult circumstances or whose lives are impoverished and characterized by 'lacks' in discussions about children's rights in the South in order to counter dominant children's rights discourses underpinned by universalizing agendas (see Punch, 2003; Balagopalan, 2014; Hopkins and Sriprakash, 2016; Twum-Danso Imoh, 2016).

Foregrounding childhoods characterized by lacks: consequences and limitations

These outputs emphasizing the dissonance between childhoods in the South and the principles underpinning dominant global children's rights discourses, which proceed to be consumed not only by academic colleagues, but also by students and members of the public more generally, lead to a situation whereby the knowledge that is produced, at least in English, about the intersection between dominant children's rights discourses and the lived realities of childhoods in contexts in the South, ends up being partial and one-dimensional with a specific focus on childhoods defined by deficits or 'lacks', or childhoods that are distinctly at odds with dominant children's rights discourses (Punch, 2003, 2015, 2016; Balagopalan, 2014; Abebe and Ofosu-Kusi, 2016; Twum-Danso Imoh, 2016; Barra, 2022; Pastore, 2022; Twum-Danso Imoh et al, 2022).

This raises a number of concerns. First, if, for instance, I search for literature on children in Brazil, I will find a lot of health-related literature on vaccinations and child health more generally, but beyond that, the literature centres largely on the challenges of education for poor children and the lives of street and working children. While this is certainly a limitation of the literature available in the English language, it has also been argued by Brazilian academics themselves that a similar bias exists in local academic discourses. According to Fulvia Rosemberg:

> Writing on childhood by academics, activists and Brazilian governmental agencies shows the same bias as writing from the northern hemisphere about the southern hemisphere: the focus is to treat social inequality from the point of view of the dominated rather than the dominant. Thus, what is problematic are the poor, the blacks, the indigenous, i.e., others. Rarely is the issue framed from the reverse point of view: what it means to be white, of European origin, to belong to the economic and political elites, to speak a dominant and hegemonic language. We do not examine the effective strategies we use to maintain their (our) dominant position. (Rosemberg, 2005: 144)

Consequently, if I read most of the available articles about children's lives in Brazil, including those produced in Portuguese if I had the ability, I will increase my knowledge about particular groups of children in that country, most notably those who are marginalized and living in difficult circumstances in one way or another, but I will not have a deeper insight into the full range of childhoods in Brazil and how they are further intricately shaped by intersecting variables such as race, economic status, education, geographical location, gender, ability/disability and sexual orientation.

This is problematic for me as an academic who primarily has, for the bulk of my 16-year career, taught around global childhoods and international children's rights at institutions where the majority of students on my undergraduate units have been White and have had relatively little knowledge, or experience, of contexts in the Global South. What this means for me when I teach my undergraduate or postgraduate students about childhoods in Brazil is that I will then be obliged to focus on the lives of street children, child workers and the education of children living in poverty in the context of my teaching and the examples I offer. Importantly, I will also primarily only be able to share with my students literature that focuses on these particular childhood experiences. Thus, many of my students will then leave my course with the impression that 'all' children in Brazil are poor and/or living on the street and are experiencing childhoods that are so clearly antithetical to dominant children's rights discourses that they will have no doubt in their mind about the inapplicability of related global policies and norms in such contexts. Not only that, but they will also additionally leave the class with the view that these childhoods are so vastly different to their own contexts that they cannot be compared. I have had students who have reached the conclusion, after engaging with this literature, that (and I am paraphrasing) *childhoods are so different there compared to here and so we just need to accept that education is not valued in the same way there and, instead, children need to work over there to survive so we should not be imposing our own values on them.* For others they feel pity for the children who experience such deficits in their childhoods while at the same time feeling a sense of

INTRODUCTION

relief that childhoods in their own context are not afflicted in such desperate ways. It can be argued that this mixture of pity and gratitude felt by some students can result in feelings of superiority about their way of life compared to those they associate with contexts in the South. Sociologist Alan Prout puts it well when he asserts, in relation to images of children in the South publicized by the mass media, that:

> The consumers of images of children in distress are mostly located in the wealthy regions of the world but the children represented in them are not. While poverty, exploitation and malnutrition are to be found outside South America, Asia, and Africa, it is these places that are most often represented through pictures of unhappy, hungry, exhausted, and exploited children. ... Images of the child victims of famine, natural disasters, poverty, war, burdensome work, and cruelty have ambiguous effects. Their purpose is to make an emotionally powerful appeal to the rich or the relatively rich, for financial aid, appealing to their consciences in the hope of credit card donations. *However, in evoking the pity of the wealthy they also reinforce their sense of superiority.* (Prout, 2005: 13; emphasis added)

Although Prout's focus is on the media, his point can also apply to classroom contexts as through continuous depictions of the suffering of children in Southern contexts, which I, as an academic, end up peddling to my students, Northern students, especially those who do not have access to other images of, or narratives about, Southern childhoods, end up with the impression that this is the only story of childhood that exists in contexts in the South.

The contributions of these outputs to how students perceive Southern contexts, especially those located in sub-Saharan Africa, do not only have implications for how they think about the subject of study on the academic units on which they are registered, namely, childhoods, but it also has an impact on assumptions they make about the fellow students they meet from that continent. Nigerian novelist, Chimamanda Ngozi Adichie, illuminates the impact of this one-dimensional knowledge production about Africa on African students when they venture beyond the continent for the purpose of pursuing higher forms of education and meet their peers from the Global North. In her Technology, Entertainment and Design (TED) Talk, filmed in October 2009, she recollects her encounter with her American roommate when she first arrived as a student in the US at the age of 19:

> What struck me was this: she had felt sorry for me even before she saw me. Her default position toward me, as an African, was a kind of patronising, well meaning, pity. My roommate had a single story of Africa. A single story of catastrophe. In this single story there was no

possibility of Africans being similar to her, in any way. No possibility of feelings more complex than pity. No possibility of a connection as human equals. (Adichie, 2009)

This is what Adichie calls the effects of 'the danger of the single story' because it is based on stereotypes and, as she goes on to say, 'the problem with stereotypes is not that they are untrue, but they are incomplete. They make one story become the only story' (Adichie, 2009). The problem here is that if all the information an individual hears about Africa (or indeed, another context in the South) is negative, then how can they engage with people from that continent as equals when they meet them at university, at their place of the work in their own context in the Global North, or as they travel to visit or explore professional opportunities in the South?

At the same time as observing the impact of this paucity of balanced literature about Southern childhoods on my predominately White students, I also, over the years, have noted the interactions I have had with international students from the South – Latin America, Asia (South Asia in particular), Africa – or with home/British students whose heritage can be traced to these contexts in the South. In these interactions such students express that they sometimes feel uncomfortable with this overemphasis on one particular childhood in contexts they know well as it does not resonate with their own experiences of growing up in whichever Southern context from which they originate. As one Latin American student told me recently following a guest lecture at a different institution to the one I work, since embarking on the programme for which she was registered in the UK, she has felt uncomfortable about the focus on the dissonance between childhoods in the South compared to global children's rights principles and the normative notions of childhoods in the North which are foregrounded in class discussions as well as in the literature. This left her uneasy as, based on her own childhood and adult experiences, she did not see this sharp distinction between 'Western' and 'non-Western' ways of life as her experience of growing up had been very 'Western' despite the fact that, hitherto, she had only lived in her country of origin in Latin America.

In addition to these, I have been struck by the number of international PhD applicants from sub-Saharan Africa who have approached me with the desire to undertake doctoral research which takes as its starting point the principles of the Convention on the Rights of the Child, with the view to exploring how they can identify solutions or strategies which will contribute to ensuring that childhoods in their context can better align with global norms. The desire of these applicants, some of whom did proceed to embark on doctoral studies, was not as a result of their lack of awareness of the socioeconomic characteristics or cultural norms of their society and how these continue to shape, and inform, the lives of primarily poor children

INTRODUCTION

living in rural or urban areas. In fact, in some cases it is because of this acute awareness (and even experience) of the conditions of these children's lives that informed the applicant's decision to embark on a PhD focusing on exploring an aspect of dominant children's rights discourses. They sought to deepen their understanding of dominant children's rights principles so that they could contribute to addressing the plight of poor children living in difficult circumstances in their contexts and transform their lives in the hope that this will also have knock-on effects, in due course, for the development of their society.

For me, over the years these interactions with these different groups of students or prospective students have made me feel increasingly uncomfortable about the state of the literature within the multidisciplinary field of childhood studies. While I have taken steps to address it in my teaching practice by drawing on the limited, and increasingly outdated, literature that provides somewhat of a more holistic analysis (for example, Hecht, 1998; Hollos, 2002; Rizzini and Barker, 2002) as well as my own data from projects which have sought to include children from different social and economic backgrounds (see Twum-Danso Imoh, 2016), this strategy has been limited. The resulting outcome is that the lack of literature on childhoods other than those living in poverty or at the margins of societies in the Global South makes it difficult to share more balanced and holistic lived experiences and perspectives that demonstrate the plurality of childhoods and multiplicity of children's rights possibilities or realities in a given context. While the lack of literature on the plurality of childhood experiences in contexts in the South has led to fruitful and very interesting class discussions that interrogate the reasons behind this, when students come to write their essays, which require a reliance on academic literature, they are still limited in their ability to draw on, or engage with, appropriate literature that goes beyond, and enables them to discuss, and elaborate on, childhoods which are not defined predominately by what they are seen to 'lack'.

The second concern raised by this focus on childhoods characterized by 'lacks' is that it results in a determination to view cultures of childhood in contexts in the South as homogeneous and static instead of as fluid and unstable, a focus which, arguably, conventional anthropological studies over the decades have contributed to reproducing. Such concerns about the insistence of foregrounding the features of 'traditional society' when talking about Africa have also been noted in relation to broader debates about the continent. Both Mbembe (2001) and Beninois philosopher, Paulin Hountondji (1996), talk about how the dominant literature about Africa, much of which is anthropological, insists on focusing on African societies as though they are stuck in a time warp and are incapable of change and transformation regardless of the processes of change that continually affect their structures and systems. Mbembe explains it thus:

In addition to being moved by the blind force of custom, these societies are seen as living under the burden of charms, spells, and prodigies, and resistant to change. Time – 'it was always there,' 'since time immemorial,' 'we came to meet it' – is supposedly stationary: thus, the importance of repetition and cycles, and the alleged central place of witchcraft and divination procedures. The idea of progress is said to disintegrate in such societies; should change occur – rare indeed – it would, as of necessity, follow a disordered trajectory and fortuitous path ending only in undifferentiated chaos. (Mbembe, 2001: 10)

Focusing so much on culture or the 'traditional' aspects of societies in the South results in overlooking the impact of social transformation on children's lives (Balagopalan, 2014; Naftali, 2014; Twum-Danso Imoh, 2019; Liebel, 2020). In relation to the limitations of using the notion of 'traditional society' to explain contemporary childhoods, Kesby and colleagues (2006: 187), in relation to Zimbabwe, claim that focusing on traditional models of childhood which emphasize the work in which children engage, instead of exploring the activities that dominate the lives of many children living in this context today that relate to play and school, 'fails to conceptualise all childhoods in contemporary Zimbabwe as hybrid creations of the nation's complex historical geography'. Drawing on the work of Cowan and colleagues (2001), Liebel also makes the following point:

While the Western or mainstream culture is allowed and even expected to develop, activists and academics become consumed with the 'preservation' of indigenous and minority cultures which are then expected to stay stagnant to be seen as successfully preserved. The preoccupation with the preservation and perceived authenticity of indigenous and minority cultures ignores the reality of today's interconnected world and limits the possibilities of these communities by painting 'traditional cultures' as in general opposition to international human rights, commerce and communication technologies deemed to be purely 'Western'. (Liebel, 2020: 140)

He then points to the example of female genital cutting and states that adopting a cultural relativist position risks overlooking the point that the practice does not have unanimous support within practising communities. This is evidenced by the fact that some of the most vocal voices against this practice within countries over the years have been people or groups from practising communities (see Twum-Danso Imoh, 2012b). In particular, Liebel (2020) underscores the vested interests and power dynamics that underpin the culturalist positions put forward by group members.

INTRODUCTION

What all of this means is that while the contributions of such publications foregrounding childhoods characterized by deficits or deprivations are both valid and invaluable, they are limiting due to that fact that they do not offer us holistic insights into the multiplicity of ways that dominant rights discourses intersect with local realities in such contexts. Specifically, they overlook the fact that at the same time as human rights and children's principles have been evolving over the past 500 or so years, so have many societies in the South, albeit unevenly – namely, as a result of their own transformations and upheavals (many of which have been intricately tied to the upheavals taking place in Western Europe and North America in particular). Mbembe captures the implications of these interactions between European and African societies for the analysis of African history:

> The peculiar 'historicity' of African societies, their own raisons d'etre and their relation to solely themselves, are rooted in a multiplicity of times, trajectories, and rationalities that, although particular and sometimes local cannot be conceptualized outside a world that is, so to speak, globalized. From a narrow methodological standpoint, this means that, from the fifteenth century, there is no longer a 'distinctive historicity' of these societies, one not embedded in times and rhythms heavily conditioned by European domination. Therefore, dealing with African societies' 'historicity' requires more than simply giving an account of what occurs on the continent itself at the interface between the working of internal forces and the working of international actors. (Mbembe, 2001: 14)

Therefore, these interactions with European societies, much of which relate to the transatlantic slave trade, missionary engagement, trade, colonialization and its attendant capitalist forces, urbanization and the intensification of global forces in recent decades, have had an impact on these societies and, consequently, have shaped emerging understandings of personhood, childhood and rights (Stephens, 1995; Kesby et al, 2006; Twum-Danso Imoh, 2019, 2020). The resulting outcomes of these interactions mean that instead of focusing almost exclusively on the extent to which dominant children's rights principles with their emphasis on the individual are inapplicable, or struggle to be realized in African contexts, we need to *additionally* explore those experiences of childhood in contemporary sub-Saharan Africa which have varying levels of synergy with dominant children's rights discourses and interrogate the reasons behind this.

Colonization, and its legacy, is one factor that needs to be considered when trying to understand developments that led to new understandings and attitudes about personhood and rights in large parts of the South as it led to the introduction of policies which were enforced by a powerful state machinery onto Indigenous people in these areas. While such policies and laws did not lead to sweeping changes among all sections of society in a given context, it must be acknowledged that some transformations in local behaviours and practices were observed as a result of colonial rule, many of which affected the conceptualization of childhood and child-rearing practices among some sectors of the population (see Twum-Danso Imoh, 2020). In Africa these factors are part of what Ali Mazrui (1986) has termed Africa's 'triple heritage', which he argues is the resulting outcome of the combination of the values of so-called traditional society, Islam and European values as represented by colonial rule and missionary activity, the legacies of which continue to intersect and shape the lives of groups in now-independent countries across the continent. As I have stated elsewhere:

> These developments that are a feature of the historical fabric of many countries imply that any analysis of childhoods in former colonial territories is difficult to fully comprehend unless they are considered within a broader historical view, which takes into account not only tradition and social norms but also colonialisation and the impact of missionary activity in their contexts. (Twum-Danso Imoh, 2016: 459)

A noteworthy example highlighting the need to incorporate a historical analysis in studies of childhoods relates to the 1989 Convention on the Rights of the Child. Since its earliest days the Convention has been widely critiqued for its Western bias, which, it is argued, has led to a perceived dissonance between its vision of childhood and the realities of children's lives in various Southern contexts. However, a consideration of these historical developments allows us to uncover attitudes and behaviours among certain sectors of the population in these same contexts which may correspond with the vision of the Convention in a number of respects (see Stephens, 1995; Hollos, 2002; Kesby et al, 2006; Twum-Danso Imoh, 2016, 2019, 2020). Therefore, the experience of colonialism and missionary education and its impact on specific groups of people in formerly colonized territories may have led to a situation whereby clear distinctions between what is 'Western' and what is 'traditional' may have become somewhat blurred among certain social groups in a given context. Therefore, in trying to understand human and children's rights in sub-Saharan Africa, analyses and discussions must not only draw on social norms and traditions dating back to pre-colonial society, but they must also consider other historical developments that have impacted many societies on the continent, some of which were initiated in the 15th century and remain influential due to their enduring and pervasive legacy.

The third area of concern about the childhood studies literature relates to the implications of the disproportionate focus on the dissonance between global children's rights principles and childhoods in the Global South for the study of children's rights in the Global North. Specifically, implicit in these arguments is the notion that the bulk of childhoods in the Global North and the cultures that underpin these, by contrast, correspond with these global ideals much more closely and, therefore, are more compatible than Southern cultures. As Freeman states:

> It is standard, when culture is discussed in the context of human/ children's rights, to confine discussion to cultural practices in Africa, Asia, or other parts of the developing world. So the emphasis tends to be on female genital mutilation, child marriage (particularly forced marriage), and issues like child soldiers. It is as if the norm were the practices of the developed world, though there are cultural practices in this part of the world too which may be considered to be against the human rights of children. (Freeman, 2011: 384; see also Hopkins and Sriprakash, 2016)

Thus, this focus on the oppositional norms and cultures of contexts in the South and their impact on the realization of children's rights norms leads to a failure to subject to similar intense scrutiny the cultures of communities in Western European and North American contexts. Consequently, it results in a failure to interrogate the extent to which there are dissonances as well as synergies between these so-called Western cultures that shape childhoods and children's lives and dominant global children's rights principles which emerged within the context of liberal traditions. In this way Western childhoods become not only normalized but also invisible and, hence, not subjected to systematic analysis or significant scrutiny. This is clearly problematic given the existence of communities located in Western Europe and North America whose culture or 'traditional' ways of life can be seen as antithetical in many ways to dominant children's rights or human rights norms. Notable examples can not only be drawn from Indigenous communities in North America, Australia and New Zealand, but also from Amish and Mennonite communities who can be found in North America, and from Gypsy, Roma and Traveller communities who are located, primarily, but not exclusively, in parts of Europe.

In relation to the latter, it is important to note that while much of the media and public discourse focuses on Eastern European Roma who are relatively recent migrants to numerous countries in Western Europe, the umbrella term Gypsy, Roma and Traveller refers to a much larger group of people than Eastern European Roma, including those who self identify as English Gypsy (also known as English Romanichal Gypsy) who, although, sharing a similar heritage with Eastern European Roma, which can be traced back to India 1,000 years ago, have been part and parcel of British society since the 16th century when mention of them was first included in official records in England (Foster and Norton, 2012; see also Clark and Cemlyn, 2005). Despite the significant social changes that have had impacts on their nomadic way of life in recent decades, which have, in turn, affected the levels of mobility in sections of these communities in the UK, the bulk of the evidence suggests that the language and traditions of this group remain indicative of their origins in the Roma migrations from Asia. In particular, they remain highly communitarian and collective communities in which family relationships and loyalty are prioritized over the needs of the individual (Levinson, 2008). Due to social norms and cultural values, knowledge in traditional Romani society is passed on orally, with family members, especially the elderly, being seen as the main transmitters of knowledge due to the fact that they are seen as repositories of traditional customs and stories. As a result, the home is seen as the main learning environment in which children gain knowledge alongside adults by watching, listening, copying and developing skills in everyday activities (Bhopal, 2011). Due to this value system, learning approaches for the young foreground early responsibility and work alongside adults instead of school-based education leading to the development of a sense of autonomy in children at an early age (Levinson, 2008; Bhopal, 2011). By working alongside parents and other family members children gain expertise in the skills that are deemed to be essential by their community (Levinson, 2008). The aims of this form of learning go beyond developing a knowledge/skills base; it also connects children to their social and communal identities. This learning paradigm foregrounded within Gypsy, Roma and Traveller communities leads to challenges within the formal education sector as while the two forms of education are not mutually exclusive, 'they do not complement each other in a way that allows for a smooth transition between the learning contexts' (Levinson, 2008: 247). This has resulted in children from these communities in England and Wales being recognized as the 'group most at risk in the education system' (Clark and Cemlyn, 2005: 146), with many dropping out of school or making the shift to so-called 'home education' by the age of 12 or 14, which involves spending large amounts of time working alongside adult men if they are boys, or helping to take care of the house and younger siblings if they are girls (Derrington and Kendall, 2007).

The key point that I am seeking to make here with the example of Gypsy, Roma and Traveller children is that a study of their lives demonstrates that there are cultures, social norms and ways of life within contemporary contexts in the North that do not correspond with dominant children's rights ideals. We do not need to cast our eyes to the Global South to identify such oppositional cultures to dominant children's rights norms. If we do not subject cultures such as the one described here, which can be found within the locales in which Northern childhood researchers are based, to the same scrutiny or systematic analysis as we do to those elsewhere in relation to children's rights then we create a situation whereby cultures labelled as 'Western', especially those which are not middle-class-related – are erased from our purview. It further reinforces the argument that culture is something found elsewhere – in the South or 'non-West' especially – and not in the villages, towns and cities of countries in the Global North or the so-called 'West'.

Towards a more holistic approach to the study of children's rights

These concerns illuminate the need for a more holistic approach to the study of both childhoods and children's rights in the Global South. Specifically, they demonstrate that there is a need for researchers to start exploring, more comprehensively, the lives of multiple groups of children and how their lived realities of childhood interact, or intersect, with dominant children's rights discourses. The objective of such an approach leads to multiple possibilities of rights realization in the lives of diverse groups of children and what that means for how both power and inequality operate in that society.

To achieve a more holistic approach to the study of children's rights in the Global South it would be necessary, as an essential requirement, to provide insights into not only the dissonance that can be identified between the everyday lives of many children and dominant children's rights discourses, but it will also be important to illuminate the existence of other attitudes, discourses and lived experiences relating to children's lives which indicate an openness and even an enthusiasm for dominant rights discourses as articulated in international laws such as the Convention on the Rights of the Child (Shepler, 2005, 2012; Cheney, 2007; Kaime, 2010; Naftali, 2014; Twum-Danso Imoh, 2019, 2020). The identification of multiple experiences of childhood highlights the diversities or pluralities that coexist, and influence, with varying levels of intensity, conceptualizations of childhood, child-rearing practices and the treatment of children, which, in turn, has implications for the lived realities of children growing up in these contexts, including in relation to their experiences of rights.

Book scope and aims

It is this plurality of childhoods and children's lived realities and its intersections for dominant children's rights discourses that this volume seeks to explore. Focusing on Ghana in particular, the first country in sub-Saharan Africa to gain independence from European colonial rule and the first country in the world to ratify the UN Convention on the Rights of the Child in February 1990, this book will examine the various ways dominant children's principles and policies intersect with the lives of diverse groups of children with the view to not only illuminating the dissonance that exists, but also the synergies that can be identified. Additionally, it will consider the factors that underpin this intersection, including culture and social norms, the legacy of British colonial rule, the widespread influence of Christianity as a consequence of missionary endeavours (much of which was centred around the development of school-based education), urbanization and the intensification of global economic, social, cultural and political processes, including international social policies and the power imbalance and inequalities that exist. Given the tensions and conflicts between these competing factors, the volume will also reflect on the stability, changeability and inconsistencies of the intersections between global rights discourses and understandings and experiences of childhoods within these contexts.

The volume is based on six research studies undertaken in Ghana between 2005 and 2023, which have explored: how constructions of childhood and child-rearing practices intersect with dominant children's rights discourses, specifically the Convention on the Rights of the Child, with a focus on norms such as reciprocity, respect and responsibility (Study 1; fieldwork period: 2005–2006); children's perceptions of physical punishment and its implications for dominant children's rights discourses and principles (Study 2; fieldwork period: 2009); the impact of social change on child-rearing practices and parent–child relations (Study 3; fieldwork period: 2013); gender identity acquisition among children and its implications for how they understand power imbalance between genders and concepts such as gender-based violence (Study 4; fieldwork period: 2015); the impact of British colonial rule on constructions of childhood in the Gold Coast (now Ghana) and its legacy for that society today (Study 5; fieldwork period: 2018); and the efforts of government officials and non-government organization actors to realize children's rights in Ghana in the decades since the country ratified the Convention (Study 6; fieldwork period: 2022–2023).

These six studies underpinning this volume have drawn on a range of primarily qualitative methods to collect data from children and the key adults in their lives in urban, peri-urban and rural areas of southern Ghana – notably in the Greater Accra, Eastern and Central regions. Specifically, the methods utilized in these studies, categorized according to groups, can be outlined as follows:

- *Methods with children*: participatory workshops (centred around activities such as risk and activity ranking exercises, drawing, community mapping and body mapping), focus group discussions, diaries, essays, photo elicitation, semi-structured interviews and structured interviews.
- *Methods with adults*: focus group discussions, semi-structured interviews, structured interviews, life history interviews, surveys and expert interviews.

INTRODUCTION

Moreover, I have conducted archival research in both the UK and Ghana as well as content analysis of laws and policy documents. For all the studies conducted ethical approval was obtained from the University of Birmingham (UK) where I completed my PhD in 2008, the University of Sheffield (UK) where I was employed from 2008 until early 2020 or the University of Bristol (UK) where I am currently employed.

Book structure

Given the linkage between dominant children's rights discourses and policies and the development of understandings of childhood from the 17th century onwards in Europe and North America, Chapter 1 outlines developments in reconstructing the conceptualization of childhood from the medieval period to the early 20th century within this context. To demonstrate how a middle-class discourse around child saving, which eventually evolved into the language of children's rights, became national within European and North American contexts and proceeded to become embedded in global discourses around children's rights, Chapter 2 focuses on the process underpinning the internationalization of these ideas about childhood which were intricately linked to developments that were associated with the economic and social upheavals relating to Western European societies. This close association between dominant children's rights and the social, cultural and political history of European countries has resulted in arguments about the imperialistic nature of children's rights and its applicability in contexts with different understandings of childhood and, indeed, what it means to be human. Thus, the aim of Chapter 3 is to explore these critiques of dominant children's rights discourses and to subject these critiques themselves to scrutiny in light of the historical and social transformations that have affected Southern societies in the last few hundred years. Given that this volume seeks to explore these issues within the context of Ghana, Chapters 4 and 5 are structured as contextual chapters. Chapter 4 provides a historical overview of approaches that sought to ensure children's welfare (or in some cases compounded the challenges facing children) in Ghana, starting with a review of pre-colonial approaches which were centred around the family and community, followed by colonial government and non-governmental strategies, and concluding with post-colonial governmental approaches and policies. In discussing welfare approaches adopted in each of these periods, the chapter also discusses the various ways in which children's welfare was also adversely affected by community or governmental priorities. In relation to the former it specifically focuses on child pawning and *trokosi*, a form of ritual servitude. While Chapter 4 illuminates approaches adopted to address children's welfare, it also makes clear that underpinning these strategies, especially those in the latter colonial and early post-colonial periods, was

23

a distinct lack of the language of children's rights to frame policies and programmatic interventions. Hence, Chapter 5 is centred around tracking the development of the language of children's rights within governmental approaches to ensuring children's welfare, interests and wellbeing. Bearing in mind that much of this development took place during a period of authoritarian rule, the chapter also reflects on the impact this political context had on the emergence of children's rights language in government policies and programmes. This chapter ends by exploring the impact of the legal and policy developments in Ghana on attitudes and lived experiences of the public. In particular, the chapter discusses that while some of these ideas have been imbibed by sections of the public, for others they continue to have little impact, leading to resistance and the persistence of children's rights violations such as sexual abuse and physical punishment. Having situated the discussion within the context of Ghana, Chapter 6 seeks to build on the themes explored in Chapter 3 by illuminating the plurality of childhoods and family life in Ghana both historically and in the present day with a focus on child-rearing approaches and transitions from childhood to adulthood focusing specifically on two puberty rites practised by different ethnic groups in Ghana – *Bragoro* and *Dipo*. Chapter 7 continues the discussion by using the concept of child work as a lens through which to explore the pluralities of childhood experiences and the factors that underpin this diversity with a specific focus on social inequality. The final chapter, Chapter 8, reflects on what this coexistence of different understandings of childhood and children's lived experiences in Ghana means for researchers and students of children's rights.

1

Tracing the Western Origins of Global Children's Rights Discourses

Introduction

Today, the notion of children's rights is perceived as global and universal by sections of the population in many societies in both the Global North and the Global South. It is now recognized as a concept that is supposed to have meaning in the lives of those regarded as children, now widely defined in the legal framework of diverse countries as all those under the age of 18. This increased visibility of children's rights is now evident in diverse parts of the world regardless of the socioeconomic and cultural context in which childhoods are experienced – to such an extent that a violation of children's rights in many countries is quick to be spotted and flagged up for intervention by many adults and children alike. Despite the prevalence of this notion, at least within policy, practitioner and, increasingly, media and public discourses, the notion of children's rights that are foregrounded in dominant discourses in a range of countries can be traced back to the specific circumstances that underpinned the evolution of Western European societies from what was perceived as their 'primitive' past to their so-called rationale, 'civilized' modern present. Specifically, these transformations were characterized by social and economic upheavals which accompanied the modernization and industrialization of Western European and North American societies (see Twum-Danso Imoh, 2020). Although the concepts of human and children's rights have evolved over time, there remains a linkage between this historical legacy and contemporary understandings of children's rights that are reflected in dominant human and children's rights discourses and policy making within global institutions.

Therefore, in a discussion about dominant children's rights principles, even in contexts which are historically, culturally and socially distinct from those from which they emerged – Western Europe and North America – it is still important to start by casting our attention back to the historical developments that took place in these regions and explore their implications for shaping the way:

- understandings of childhoods changed;
- the impact these transformations had on constructions and reconstructions of children's capabilities, their needs and, indeed, their rights; and
- how these have shaped societies in the South, especially from the early 20th century onwards.

The development of the 'modern Western' conception of childhood

To fully appreciate the transformations that evolved in Western Europe and North America and the impact they had on understandings of childhood and the lived experiences of children, especially in the 18th and 19th centuries, there is a need to outline conceptualizations of childhood that existed prior to these periods. While historical accounts can provide us with glimpses of societal understandings of childhood going back to Ancient Greek and Roman periods (see Sommerville, 1982), the 20th century was pivotal in the development of a mass of evidence by historians that centre around childhoods and children's lives in the medieval and early modern period in Western Europe. This is largely as a result of the seminal work of French social historian, Philippe Ariès (1962: 125), who boldly concluded, in his study which focused on French medieval iconography, that 'in medieval society the idea of childhood did not exist; this is not to suggest that children were neglected, forsaken or despised'. While it did not take too long for the flaws in Ariès' work to be illuminated and his argument critiqued by other historians of the period (see, for example, Pollock, 1983; Shahar, 1992; Heywood, 2001; Orme, 2001), his work has undoubtedly had a significant impact on the study of childhood, to such an extent that there is hardly an article or book about childhood or children's rights that does not launch its argument, regardless of its disciplinary framings, without reference to Ariès as its starting point. His influence is well noted even by his critics, such as Colin Heywood, a fellow historian, who states:

> As a historian one must surely acknowledge the role of Ariès in opening up the subject of childhood, profit from his many insights into the past, and move on. A more fruitful approach is to search for these different conceptions of childhood in various periods and places, and to seek to explain them in the light of prevailing material and cultural conditions. (Heywood, 2001: 15)

Even authors writing on childhood and children's rights in non-European contexts find it necessary or, at least, useful, to refer to Ariès, if only as an entry point to their analysis, including the author of this very volume.

The influence of Ariès' work, which crosses disciplinary boundaries, at least in the humanities and social sciences, can largely be attributed to the fact that, despite its various weaknesses, it threw into sharp relief the extent to which childhood was historically and socially situated. The recognition of the variable nature of childhood that can be attributed to Ariès' work revealed that while all societies have a *concept* of childhood, its *conception* could vary over both time and space. This distinction between the concept and conception of childhood is one developed by David Archard, a critic of Ariès' claims. In particular, Archard (1993: 22) explains that 'the concept of childhood requires that children be distinguishable from adults in respect of some unspecified set of attributes. ... A conception of childhood is a specification of these attributes'. Thus, for Archard, while all societies have a concept of childhood, different societies and cultures will have different ideas – that is, conception – about the beginning and ending of childhood focusing on key factors such as the achievement of a particular chronological age such as 18, leaving the home of your parents to set up on your own and provide for yourself, especially in the case of boys/young men, a rites of passage ceremony, which is normally held at puberty, or the capacity to marry and bear children. As Archard asserts (1993: 27), 'the adoption of one conception rather than another will reflect prevailing general beliefs, assumptions, and priorities'.

If we apply Archard's framework on the concept of childhood versus the conception of childhood to European medieval society the historical evidence, some of which was analysed, not least in part to counter Ariès' assertions, provides detailed accounts of the extent to which medieval European societies possessed a concept of childhood. Orme (2001), for instance, insists that childhood was regarded as a distinct phase of the life course and that, as with modern society, not only did parents treat their children both as children and as adults, but they also treated them with care. Orme adds that in these societies children required and received specialized food and clothes, different in quantity and sometimes in kind, from those of adults. In fact, a 15th-century dictionary has a special word for a 'child's cap'. Rhymes and games were either invented by children themselves or designed for their use. Importantly, even when these were similar to those of adults, 'they could still be used separately by children and in distinctive ways' (Orme, 2001: 10). Moreover, childhood was both recognised by the state and the Church. In terms of the state, Heywood (2001) notes that medieval law codes contained concessions to the minority status of children, by, for example, protecting their inheritance rights. Further, evidence shows that during this period the concept of the age of majority existed and ranged from the ages of 12 to 21. The achievement of this age signified the right of young people to assume responsibilities that were associated with adult status, including administering their own affairs and property (Orme, 2001). In relation to the Church, its acknowledgement of the *concept* of childhood is illustrated by the fact that by 1200, there existed a clear distinction within the structures of the Church between children and adults. While adults could confess to a priest, receive holy communion, pay tithes/Church dues, initiate marriage proceedings and be anointed if sick, children were not eligible to participate in any of these rites or practices until they reached puberty as this signified their sexual and mental maturity (Orme, 2001). Therefore, the work that has emerged primarily as a counter to that of Ariès leads to the conclusion that medieval European societies certainly had an understanding of childhood as a phase in the life course.

However, the evidence also shows that *the conception* of childhood in this period was distinct from later understandings of childhood that came to dominate political and public discourses in Europe by the beginning of the 20th century. In particular, the conception of childhood in medieval Europe also shows that there was less of a distinction between adults and children, leading to children living, playing and working in the adult world, alongside adults. Children over the age of four or five could start working and by the age of 12 apprenticeships were compulsory (Hoyles, 1989). Gambling was a pastime opened to those we would now call 'children' as well as adults, and games we now consider 'childish' such as hide and seek and fiddle dee dee were played by adults as well as those we now deem to be 'children' (Plumb, 1972). The institution of the school provided learning to all males regardless of age and was more dependent upon the ability to pay rather than the age of the pupil (Twum-Danso, 2008). Hence, what this meant was that classes in a school could comprise a 24-year-old man as well as an 11-year-old boy. As Plumb states:

> These circumstances meant that in the 15th century it was customary for men of all ages – 'children', adolescents, young and old men – to be in the same class, learning the same lessons. In Eton for example there was only one schoolroom and in France, as late as the 17th century it was possible to find a 24-year-old man in the same class as an 11-year-old child. Furthermore, 12-year-olds went to Oxford and Cambridge although by the 17th century the age of entry was usually 15. (Plumb, 1972: 158)

For Plumb (1972), this detailed evidence emphasizes the extent to which the worlds of children and adults were deeply interconnected. This further illuminates the point that the distinct nature of childhood was not recognized in the same way that it came to be acknowledged by the latter decades of the 20th century.

By the end of the 17th century attitudes towards children started to change. The conception of childhood in Western Europe became narrower, more rigid, and intrinsically became intertwined with concepts such as modern education and biological age (Firestone, 1971; Archard, 1993; Twum-Danso, 2008). This process of refining the conception of childhood continued to evolve from this period until the 20th century when the features of what most people now take for granted as being key components of the phase of life known as childhood were consolidated in Western Europe and the Americas. In the intervening period, there emerged specialized games, toys and literature for children. For instance, literature that had been previously read by both adults and children alike was now designated as children's literature due to improved literacy among adults, which resulted in their reading tastes becoming both more sophisticated and, arguably, less imaginative (Sommerville, 1982). Examples of the literature that became seen as aimed at children were fables, fairy stories and nursery rhymes that appeared in medieval sermons and romances such as Robin Hood and the Seven Wise Masters. By 1800 the publishing industry had established the principle that 'children's books do not have to make sense to adults, that children's minds are not simply smaller versions of adult minds' (Sommerville, 1982: 146). That these were now aimed at younger readers was signified by the fact that they were printed at a cheaper rate. In relation to toys, while there is an acknowledgement that they existed in the medieval period, it is argued that many were simply child size replicas of adult objects and were not used beyond the ages of three and four (Firestone, 1971). However, this started to change in the 18th century. By 1780 numerous toy shops manufacturing sophisticated gadgets specifically for children such as rocking horses and mechanized toys could be found in London (Sommerville, 1982). In addition, alongside books, games and toys specifically for children, there also emerged new ideas relating to what was considered to be suitable activities for them. Gambling, for instance, became an inappropriate activity for this group.

Two men were particularly influential in this period of change: John Locke and Jean Jacques Rousseau. Of the two, Rousseau has been particularly credited with pioneering the ideology of the innocence of childhood on which the modern Western conception of childhood is based (see Twum-Danso, 2008). This is because although Cambridge Neo-Platonist philosophers, such as Ralph Cudworth and Richard Cumberland, had asserted the innate goodness of the child in the 1680s, the idea did not gain currency until the emergence of Rousseau's landmark novel, *Emile ou Traite de l' Education* (1762), the story of a boy and his tutor. This book came to be seen as a catalyst for many of the changes that took place. In his book, Rousseau strongly criticized those 'seeking the man in the child without thinking of what he is before being a man'. In this new ideology 'childhood' has its place in the order of human life and, therefore, 'the man must be considered in the man, and the child in the child' (quoted in Archard, 1993: 22).

Emile came to be treated as 'the dividing line between the dark age of childhood and the beginning of an enlightenment concern' (Sommerville, 1982: 127). The impact of Rousseau and his ideas on understandings of childhood and attitudes to children are evident:

> If the philosophy of the Enlightenment brought to 18th century Europe a new confidence in the possibility of human happiness, special credit must go to Rousseau for calling attention to the needs of children. For the first time in history, he made a large group of people believe that childhood was worth the attention of intelligent adults, encouraging an interest in the process of growing up rather than just the product. Education of children was part of the interest in progress, which was so predominant in the intellectual trends of the time. (P. Robertson, 1976, cited in Jenks, 1996: 65)

These changes resulted in the child and his distinctive status of childhood being not only recognized, but also respected; he[1] became categorized as a special creature with 'a different nature and needs, which required separation and protection from the adult world' (Plumb, 1972: 159). This is perhaps most notably signified by a change in sexual attitudes which saw the emergence of the practice of avoiding sexual references in the presence of children becoming entrenched in society. More affective relations started to develop between many parents and their children within specific social groups, and the former became concerned about protecting their children's innocence and their exposure to what had, in this period, become perceived as 'the vulgarities' of adult life (Firestone, 1971; Plumb, 1972). Sommerville (1982: 147) describes the change in attitudes thus: 'parents were made aware that some things are suitable for children and other things are not; they were further encouraged to accept amusement as good in itself. It was part of the child's right to a happy childhood.' These changes were linked to the development and widespread acceptance of the concept that childhood was an innocent stage in the life cycle and that it was the duty of adults to preserve it (Plumb, 1972).

One major area where the impact of Rousseau was especially felt was the formal education sector. As Firestone (1971: 92) aptly puts it, 'if childhood was only an abstract concept, then the modern school was the institution that built it into reality'. Schooling was transformed. No longer was it open to men of all ages and centred on scholarship. By the beginning of the 19th century schools were divided into classes and boys of the same age were moved from class to class, resulting in the eventual exclusion of adults from this sphere of society.

Life in schools became very particular and centred on discipline. Rather than focusing on individual sporting activities as before, new attention was paid to games and sports, which developed team spirit; literature in schools was censored to ensure that children were not exposed to inappropriate content. In fact, it is believed that in the 19th century the headmaster of Harrow forbade novels in the school in case it corrupted young minds (Plumb, 1972). Gambling and alcohol were also banned in schools. Even the food changed, becoming plainer than that for adults. Finally, there was the emergence of the school uniform. In the 18th century this consisted of a sailor's uniform or the Scottish kilt and bonnet, but by the early 20th century uniforms had become more specific and sophisticated, consisting of short trousers and pullovers in plainer colours such as grey, blue and black (Plumb, 1972).

The key role of the school in the construction of childhood meant that girls of any status and working-class boys were initially excluded from this emerging conception of childhood. According to Ariès (1962: 59), the 'particularization of children was limited for a long time to boys'. For children of both genders from the working classes and girls of the upper classes, the old way of life, which is said to have made no distinction between children and adults in dress, work, education (or lack thereof) and activities, continued for a long time. Upper-class girls immediately moved from swaddling clothes to the style of dress worn by adult women by the age of nine or ten. Furthermore, girls from this social background did not attend school; rather, they stayed at home, shared the same activities as older women, and they were betrothed to a husband soon after they reached puberty, sometimes at the age of ten or 12 (Firestone, 1971). The portrayal of lower-class children regardless of gender tells a similar tale. They graduated immediately from infancy to adulthood. According to Plumb:

> The picture of working-class children of Victorian London or Paris shows them still dressed as adults, usually in their parents' worn-out and cut-down clothes ... we know that they drank, gambled, and rioted sexually and in fact, participated in every form of adult life ... indeed, they physically had no escape from it. (Plumb, 1972: 163)

This exclusion of the lower classes and upper-class girls from the 'new' conception of childhood led Firestone (1971: 91) to conclude that this was due to the fact that the end of childhood in the early modern period 'marked a graduation to adult male power, marked by the adoption of adult male regalia'. As girls of all classes and lower-class boys were never to achieve this level of power, there was no reason for them to pass through this rite of passage, after all, 'there was nothing for them to grow up to' as the role of both groups, at the time, was always to serve upper-class men (Firestone, 1971: 91).

This exclusion of the poor from the modern conception of childhood disappeared in all classes by the end of the 19th century. Social legislation was key to the changes that took place during this period. In Britain, for instance, questions had started being raised by the beginning of the 19th century about whether mines and factories were appropriate places for children to spend large parts of the day. While the first law introduced to regulate children's employment in factories was passed in 1802, arguably the first effective legislation against the employment of children in the factory industry was the Factory Act of 1833 (Hendrick, 1997a, 1997b). This prohibited the selective employment of children under nine years and limited the working day to eight hours for those between the ages of nine and 13. This law is especially significant as it is seen as marking the beginning of a change in the perception of children in legislation and social policy. As the century went on, more detailed laws were passed outlining more stringent regulations relating to children's employment in, primarily, factories and mines, leading to the eventual removal of children from these environments. For example, the Factory Act 1847 made provisions that ensured that by 1 July 1847 children aged between 13 and 18 could only work 63 hours per week. The Act also stipulated that by 1 May 1848 the number of hours that this age group could work in factories had to be reduced to 58 hours per week (about ten hours a day). The Factory Act 1853, which mainly focused on mills, went even further, and stipulated that children aged nine to 13 could only work between the hours of 6am to 6pm in summer months and 7am to 7pm in the winter.

In the years following the introduction of laws prohibiting children's labour in certain industries, attention started to be paid to the appropriate training required by children which led to steps being taken to ensure that all children spent the bulk of their time in school. While in Britain there had long been laws outlining the provision of formal education, the instrumental policy that illuminates the impact of the changes to childhood that were being constructed at this time was the 1870 Education Act in England and Wales. The law made the provision of schooling for those aged five to 12 the responsibility of local authorities who were authorized to use public funds to improve existing schools. It was seen as significant in the transformations that took place at the time as it demonstrated a commitment to the provision of education on a national scale by stipulating the need for the establishment of a system of school boards to facilitate the building and management of schools in areas where they were needed. This law was further strengthened in 1880 by another Education Act which made school attendance compulsory for all those aged between five and ten. While these laws were increasingly making schooling compulsory, it is important to note that it was not until 1891 that fees for primary school attendance were abolished, making basic education free for the first time in the country. Further legislation in 1893 and 1899 extended the age of compulsory school attendance to 11 and 12 years, respectively.

Added to these laws on employment and education were a range of others regulating children's lives in some way. Thus, in the latter decades of the 19th century laws were passed: banning children from pubs and forbidding them to gamble; setting a fixed age for consent; stipulating the prevention of cruelty to, and neglect of, children; introducing the school feeding of 'necessitous' children; outlining the process for school medical inspection and treatment; and establishing a juvenile justice system. Thus, by the early 20th century, the major pieces of legislation and institutions needed to realize this conception of childhood had been firmly established in England and Wales at least.

Squeezing all children into a mould: the role of middle-class activism

The changes that took place which started to encompass the lower classes cannot simply be attributed to legislation. These new ideas about childhood were actively produced by, and gained the support of, middle- and upper-class elites who, drawing on, largely, the teachings of Christianity, led the process of ensuring their spread throughout society (Hendrick, 1997a, 1997b). For instance, as mentioned previously, by the early decades of the 19th century in Britain certain groups had become concerned with questions about whether mines and factories were appropriate places for children. Many of those expressing concern were appalled by the scale of the exploitation of children working in these industries. Consequently, they raised concerns about the physical and moral dangers associated with child labour, such as the damage to children's bodies as a result of the long hours they worked, the debilitating temperatures and polluted environments prevalent in these industries, the physical punishment they experienced at their place of work, and the negative impact the lack of education and religious instruction had on children (Hendrick, 1997a). Beyond this, they were concerned about the intensity of the industrialization process and the worsening social and economic conditions that resulted (Hendrick, 1997a).

A good example of a British reformer from the 19th century, a period when many of the transformations that had started to occur in the 18th century were consolidated, is perhaps Anthony Ashley Cooper (later the Seventh Earl of Shaftesbury), who became a Tory MP in 1826 and had a keen interest in the welfare of children (see Twum Danso, 2008). In 1840 he contributed to the establishment of the Children's Employment Commission, which published parliamentary reports on working conditions in mines and collieries. He later became the Chairman of the Ragged Schools Union, which established hundreds of schools for poor children around the country.

These schools provided inspiration to other later British reformers such as Thomas Barnardo who taught in Ragged Schools before opening his own. Through his work with the Children's Employment Commission, Cooper, who by this time had become the Seventh Earl of Shaftesbury, was instrumental in the factory reforms that were initiated in much of the 19th century. In particular, he was largely responsible for the Factory Acts of 1847 and 1853, both of which had stipulations that had an impact on children's ability to work in this sector. These efforts of elites were not only visible through politics, legislation and philanthropy. Novelist Charles Dickens, for example, played a significant role in the change of public attitudes that eventually took place through his novels, most notably *Oliver Twist* (1837) and *Bleak House* (1852–1853).

Such campaigners were not only driven by philanthropic motives in their efforts to introduce a new conception of childhood in their country. The evidence shows that they were also motivated by fears of the criminality and delinquency of the thousands of young people, namely those from the working classes who, by the middle of the 19th century, had nothing to do now they were no longer able to work in factories and mines (Boyden, 1997; Hendrick, 1997a, 1997b; Wells, 2015). As Boyden (1997: 192) states, 'the fear was that childhood innocence, if not properly directed and trained at home and in school, could give way to riotous and immoral behaviour'. In fact, this fear was so powerful that contemporary discussions foregrounding the importance of school-based education were, at the very least, driven partly by a desire to ensure that children who had been removed from working in factories and mines would not end up hanging around the streets all day (Boyden, 1997).

The resources and the social position of many of the reformers involved in discourses around childhood and children's position in society meant that they were able to advocate for, and push through, many of the aforementioned changes in all spheres of children's lives and overcome much of the resistance that resulted. Both Hendrick (1997a, 1997b) and Sommerville (1982) illuminate the extent to which these transformations were part of a struggle that occurred, which had as its objective the goal to ensure that this particular conception of childhood applied to the lives of all children regardless of social status. For example, by making education compulsory (and ensuring that inspectors were out in force to monitor adherence to this law), many children were now spending significant parts of their day out of the home. This enabled them to come under the scrutiny of emerging groups of professionals who were central to fostering and maintaining this new idea of childhood – teachers, social workers, youth workers, correctional offers, paediatricians, nutritionists and development psychologists, among others who all played a role in ensuring that all children fitted into this mould (Firestone, 1971; Hendrick,

1997a, 1997b). The implementation of these measures meant that through their everyday involvement in children's lives, middle-class professionals were able to transmit certain class-based conceptions of childhood to significant numbers of children (Hendrick, 1997a, 1997b). In this way it became possible to normalize and universalize the conception of childhood within national boundaries in Western Europe and North America. The key point is that even in Western societies, from which the modern conception of childhood emerged, significant numbers of children had to be squeezed into this new conception constructed by middle- and upper-class reformers who were very often influential members of society and had resources and access to those with decision-making powers. This is important as it demonstrates that although we often critique the 'Western' nature of children's rights, its middle-class origins deserve as much scrutiny given that for many children and their families in these very contexts this understanding of childhood did not correspond with their value systems or realities.

The example of schools is especially notable. Given the role they were supposed to play in 'civilizing' children, especially those from poor communities, schools were carefully constructed sites that sought to create a new construction of childhood by requiring the child to cast aside any previous knowledge obtained from elsewhere (such as those derived from parents and community or the world of work) and, instead, display a state of ignorance which would be filled in over time by knowledge gained from teachers in the form of experts, or books. The requirement that children set aside prior knowledge from parents and community was part of a process of institutionalizing the separation of children from society and underscoring the fact that the correct place for them to be was in the classroom as opposed to the streets, the factory, the mine or even the home (Hendrick, 1997a). This role of the school has led Hendrick to argue that:

> But the classroom and the ideological apparatus of education were crucial because they demanded – indeed, could not do without – a truly national childhood, one that ignored (at least theoretically) rural/urban divisions, as well as those of social class (Hurt, 1979, passim). Schooling, as has just been shown above, did more than merely declare a particular definition of childhood. By virtue of its legal authority, and on a daily basis through teachers and school attendance offices, it was able to impose its vision upon pupils (many, perhaps the majority, of whom were unwilling to accept this 'reconstruction' of what they should be) and upon their parents (many of whom showed a similar reluctance) (Hurt, 1979). This construction was intended to directly involve *all* children and was meant to be as inescapable as it was visible, for in denoting them as 'pupils,' the school was a constant and

omnipotent reminder of who they were. (Hendrick, 1997a: 46–47; emphasis in original)

These efforts to initiate a change in the role children should play in British society were contested and resisted, especially within lower classes for much of the 19th century as the inclusion of working-class children into the newly constructed notion of childhood arguably made them economically useless and a burden on their families who struggled to survive without their wages. For instance, at the 1902 Trades Union Congress the Gas Workers' Union's resolution to prohibit the employment of children under the age of 15 was carried by only 535,000 votes to 514,000 votes (Hoyles, 1989). Further, following the introduction of compulsory education for children school strikes were initiated across the country in response to what children considered to be their imprisonment in schools and the restrictions on their ability to earn a living (Hoyles, 1989). Importantly, this resistance was not only evident among working-class sections of the population. It was also noted among sections of the middle and upper classes earlier on in this period of change and transformation. For example, the extension of the period of study in schools, its increasing centralization on children and the introduction of corporal punishment as a form of discipline, led to rioting at Winchester and Eton in the 18th century where the pupils occupied the school for two days and hoisted a red flag. At Rugby, pupils set fire to their books and desks and withdrew to an island. Such riots in public schools continued until the last major one at Marlborough in 1851 (Hoyles, 1989). Among the working classes school strikes persisted well into the 20th century. These developments and struggles demonstrate that the understanding of childhood that prevails today came into being gradually and over time and was not even a universalized concept within European and North American societies until well into the 20th century.

Therefore, by the early decades of the 20th century a new conception of childhood had not only emerged but had been consolidated and universalized across many societies in Western European and North America (and among certain groups elsewhere such as Latin America). Sommerville describes the change in attitudes:

Parents were made aware that some things are suitable for children and other things are not; they were further encouraged to accept amusement as good in itself. It was part of the child's right to a happy childhood; the widespread acceptance of such a right was seen as a milestone in the history of childhood. (Sommerville, 1982: 147)

In this conceptualization of childhood, childhood was now conceived as a special time of life, separate and distinct from adulthood (Plumb, 1972;

Weisberg, 1978). The child became categorized as a special creature with 'a different nature and needs, which required separation and protection from the adult world' (Plumb, 1972: 159). These separate characteristics of children centred around them being innocent, physically weak, vulnerable, mentally immature and dependent, as well as foregrounding their lack of sound judgment, inexperience and incompetence (Verhellen, 1994; Ncube, 1998). As a result of these features associated with this phase of life the prevailing belief that emerged foregrounded the idea that children required protection from the vices of the adult world, which included being protected from exposure to issues relating to sex and from participating in forms of work that were not seen as appropriate for this group. The world of children, instead, became characterized by activities relating to learning, especially that which took place in schools, and play as an activity in and of itself.

This difference between the status of childhood and that of adulthood was central to the construction of children's rights at this time. The idea of the different nature of childhood was critical to the understanding that children had different needs and, therefore, required assistance on top of those that all others required to ensure their protection from the harsh realities of their societies (see Boyden, 1997; Liebel, 2012). Cunningham (2013: 370) supports this when he argues that reformers and philanthropists were deeply convinced by the romantic belief that childhood should be a happy phase of life. For this group, it then followed that 'if these happy childhoods were to be achieved, childhood had to be sharply separated from adulthood, and its characteristics and needs had to be recognized'. As a result:

> Childhood and adulthood, in this thinking, became almost opposite of one another. If adults were burdened with responsibilities, children should be carefree. If adults worked, children should play ... if sex was part of life of adults, it should play no part in that of children ... and if adults had to live in towns, children were entitled to contact with nature. (Cunningham, 2013: 370)

Therefore, the separation between adults and children was critical to the development of children's rights discourses. In keeping children 'protected' from the adult world, the child-saving movement of the time, followed by later government policy, led to many poor children, in particular, being physically separated from their families (Cunningham, 2013; Wells, 2015). Importantly, the association made between the nature of childhood and attributes such as immaturity and incompetence resulted in a perception of children as being deficient and inferior to adults (Corbett, 1985; Boyden, 1997). As a result, it was recognized that children required special protection and rights specifically designed for them because of their immaturity, lack of sound judgement and lack of experience in the ways of the world (Ncube, 1998). The consequence of this was that children's lives, including their mobilities and spatialities, came to be seen as requiring restriction by adults (Valentine, 2003). Liebel captures the process well:

> The protection of children can lead to limiting their freedom and space for decision-making. This can go as far as increasing children's helpless and need for protection despite all good intentions, as they are asked to settle into dependence and to rely on adults. Even if this limitation can be justified, it can be used by adults to implement their own interests and to make use of the power advantage or even to extend their scope of power. (Liebel, 2012: 45)

These constraints faced by children as a result of being 'attributed with certain qualities or disabilities' (Boyden, 1997: 191) had the corresponding effect of enhancing adult power, especially those of professionals, over children. Thus, this transformation made to protect children resulted in the extension of the control and power of certain groups of adults. These developments show that while we often talk about the innocence of childhood as though it is a natural condition of this phase of life, notions of 'weakness', 'innocence' and 'immaturity' were actively constructed and imposed as a requirement of the reconstructed conception of childhood taking place at the time, supported by institutions such as the school. In the process, children were made dependent on adults to such an extent that they were expected to rely on this group, professionals in the main, to speak on their behalf as they were now seen as passive and voiceless. They further became subject to the discipline administered by adults and were socialized to accept it as part of the experience of childhood (Corbett, 1985; Franklin, 1986). The resulting outcome, it has been argued, is that Western societies have nurtured young people into the conception of childhood that has prevailed since the early decades of the 20th century (Corbett, 1985).

From child saving to child rights: changes in lexicon but continuity in approaches

While philanthropists were critical to many of the reforms and discussions that took place from the 18th century onwards, by the end of the 19th century the issue of child saving had become recognized as coming under the umbrella of the state as it was felt that it was only through government intervention that *all* children could enjoy the special status of childhood which was now recognized in numerous Western European and North American countries (Cunningham, 2013; Wells, 2015). Key to the increasing role of the state was the recognition, by the early decades of the 20th century, that the work of philanthropists could not be universally applied, leading to patchy and uneven delivery of interventions. Added to that, it had become evident that the efforts of some philanthropists had led to many children, including some who were removed from their families for the purpose of being 'saved', to actually come to even more harm (Wells, 2015). Cunningham explains it thus:

> Children themselves, the evidence suggests, on balance did not feel themselves to be beneficiaries of the discourse of rights. In its name, some of them were removed from their families, incarcerated in institutions, and transported across oceans. Most who were rescued found it difficult to come to terms with institutionalized norms and practices which now shaped their lives. Children sent to institutions to be saved, many without having committed, any offence, saw it as a punishment. Fostered and emigrated children were often mistreated, and adjusted with difficulty to the communities and moral environment which it was hoped would be the saving of them. Their sense of personal identity, derived from their families, was systematically undermined by discouraging the maintenance of any links with their past lives. (Cunningham, 2013: 371; see also Wells, 2015)

It is also important to note that the motivation behind state intervention was not merely about ensuring the 'enjoyment' of the newly constructed childhood that was gradually being realized for diverse groups of children in different European and American contexts. Factors such as preserving race and nation were additionally central to the rationale for government intervention. For example, in France the process of tightening state intervention and ensuring that laws and policies introduced from the 1880s had an impact on a wider range of children can be associated with the defeat of the country in the Franco–Prussian War (July 1870 to January 1871). This defeat highlighted to the government the importance of perceiving state education as a 'national investment in a system which would make the French language universal and instil in the population a sense of pride in being French' (Cunningham, 2013: 368). In England and Wales, where the 1880s saw compulsory schooling introduced for those aged five to ten, the government's objective was underpinned by a desire to 'instil morality, and patriotism, and to train children in regular habits' (Cunningham, 2013: 368). Therefore, schools were charged with fostering a national identity and creating citizens who would adhere to the social order. State interests were also about state rivalry (Cunningham, 2013; see also Plumb, 1972). In the case of Britain by the end of the 19th century the country was at the height of the construction of its vast empire, which cut across Africa, the Middle East, Asia, the Pacific, the Caribbean and parts of North America. At this crucial time for Britain, then, children were seen as being 'of the nation' (Plumb, 1972). This made the construction of childhood and the attendant roles of children in society a priority in government policies and broader agendas.

All these developments resulted in the construction and use of the term rights in relation to children. This shift was significant as, according to Wells (2015: 28), by moving child welfare from 'the private to the public it changed the status of the child from a subject to a citizen, from a dependent to a semi-legal person'. While the term rights had been applied to children prior to the 19th century,[2] arguably the increasing role of the state in the welfare of children led to the increasing use of the language of children's rights being adopted in the framing of strategies and interventions, especially by the state, to protect children by the turn of the 20th century in diverse Western European and American contexts. While increasing state intervention facilitated the language of rights, the deployment of this terminology at this time was not all that dissimilar from the language of children's needs and welfare, which underscored the language of child saving led by philanthropists driven by religious, romantic or utilitarian motivations (Freeman, 2011; Cunningham, 2013; Wells, 2015). In this configuration of children's rights led by the state by the end of the 19th century the focus was on the right of children to be protected from the adult world in ways that were identified by primarily middle- and upper-class elites, mainly professionals and, increasingly, government agencies (Cunningham, 2013). Therefore, children were seen as passive and vulnerable even though at the time there were numerous instances of actions by children which contested the assumed passivity of childhood such as the aforementioned school strikes in England which persisted into the 20th century.

Conclusion

These historical developments laid the foundation for the image of childhood that has, today, become dominant or normative not only in Western European and North American imaginations, narratives or discourses, but also in public conceptualizations, legal frameworks and discourses in societies which followed different historical trajectories. The next chapter will explore the global diffusion of these ideas about childhood emerging from European Enlightenment. In particular, it will examine how the concept of rights evolved from being a subject of national discussion in European and American contexts to a discourse of an international nature which eventually resulted in the passage of the Convention on the Rights of the Child, the first binding international treaty on any subject as well as the first in the history of the UN to have been ratified by all but one country in the world.

2

From the National to the International: The Makings of the Global Discourse of Children's Rights

Introduction

While many of the developments around conceptualizations of childhood and constructions of children's rights were taking place around a similar time across societies in Western Europe and the Americas, they remained distinctly national discourses and movements in these regions. It was not until the end of the First World War that these disparate and distinct discourses and efforts about children's rights started to take a more international form, or, at least, a European regional form. This internationalization of this discourse has largely been attributed to Eglantyne Jebb, who is credited with being the founder of the Save the Children movement[1] and who after the First World War became concerned about the welfare of children in the countries that had lost the war, notably Austria and Germany, due to her belief that 'they could hardly be blamed for the war and therefore should not suffer as a consequence of defeat' (Cunningham, 2013: 371). In her attempt to achieve her objectives, Jebb is said to have established Save the Children in London in 1919 in order to send food to children affected by the blockade against Germany and Austria following the war.

Once the immediate crisis facing children (and indeed, adults in their families) in these countries had abated, Jebb started to realize that there existed a range of other difficult situations, again, mainly in Europe, from which children needed to be saved. This regional focus needs to be situated against a backdrop of the rise in internationalism in public discourses at the time which has been well outlined by Baughan:

41

The Save the Children Fund (S.C.F.) had been formed in 1919 to provide food for child victims of the post-war blockades in Austria and Germany. It claimed to be Britain's first 'truly international charity,' and by the mid-nineteen-twenties was at work in twenty-four countries throughout Europe and the Near East, and gave relief to children 'regardless of nationality, religion, and the political views of their parents.' The international focus of the S.C.F. mirrored a wider shift in the popular imagined geographies of inter-war Britain. Wartime travel, communication and news reports had increased public knowledge of places and peoples in Europe. This increased sense of connection was reinforced through new diplomatic bonds in the form of the League of Nations, which had been founded in 1919 and drew widespread support from the British public who hoped it might bring a 'lasting peace' in the wake of the First World War. (Baughan, 2013: 117)

Hence, due to Jebb's desire to address the emerging needs of children in the aftermath of the war a committee of British Save the Children representatives was established to start working on a declaration that could elicit commitment for action to support children by different countries and individuals. Subsequently, on 16 March 1922, Jebb produced a memorandum in which she called for the creation of a Code for Children which would 'not be a piece of legislation but rather a document defining the duties of adults towards children, which each country should recognize either by means of state intervention or by private action' (cited in Veerman, 1992: 155).

To further develop her ideas, she travelled to Geneva (Switzerland) to hold a meeting with the Secretary General of the Save the Children International Union, Etienne Clouzor. Together, they drafted the initial text of the declaration which was later further edited and developed by others within the organization (Veerman, 1992). By the time the Save Children International Union General Assembly was held on 23 February 1923 two drafts had been developed – one with five principles, the other with seven – and were presented to members in attendance. The recommendation to formulate a declaration was adopted and this led to one of the draft versions being developed further by the Editorial Committee who then resubmitted it to the Union for agreement. This was received on 17 May 1923 with Jebb offering a title for the document: the Declaration of Geneva. Finally, the declaration, the version consisting of five principles, was signed by all members of the Save the Children International Union at a ceremony in Geneva which took place on 28 February 1924, at which were present diplomats and representatives of various international organizations and churches. It was additionally presented to representatives of the local government authority in Geneva for signature (Veerman, 1992). In the months that followed other individual actors and governments in Europe signed the declaration, which had been translated into other languages. Examples were Sweden, Albania, Finland, France, the UK, Lithuania, and the Kingdom of the Servs, Croats and Slovaks. On 26 September 1924, the newly established League of Nations General Assembly accepted one of two resolutions which urged the member states of the League 'to be guided, when dealing with child welfare in their home countries, by the principles mentioned in the Declaration of Geneva and endorsed by the Assembly of the League of Nations' (Veerman, 1992: 156). This endorsement by the League was seen as critical to enhancing the status of the declaration on the global stage.

As a non-binding treaty which only encouraged governments to be guided by its principles, it was up to governments to decide how best to make use of the Declaration within their national boundaries. Ultimately, only a few governments ended up incorporating it into domestic law (Fottrell, 2000). As such, this Declaration has been referred to as aspirational (Veerman, 1992; Fortin, 2009). Nevertheless, it has come to symbolically represent the foundation of the international children's rights movement, which has now come to dominate discourses around child welfare and wellbeing. As Boyden (1997: 198–199) has argued, 'the declaration provided the blueprint for a universal idea, specifying a series of rights for children that were separate from and additional to those of adults'.

Although entitled the Declaration on the Rights of the Child, it is evident that the language used throughout the text was aligned with Western European and American 19th-century child-saving movements. These rights as stipulated in the Declaration were simply the inverted duties of adults (see Cunningham, 2013; Wells, 2015). Therefore, the language here was centred around the protection and provision of the rights of children which were in the hands of adults to bestow upon children almost as gifts in their power to give, or as acts of charity to offer to children who were not recognized as anything other than vulnerable and passive.

The geographical and racial limits of early children's rights discourses and norms

While the 1924 Declaration is seen as the beginning of a period which sought to universalize the concept of children's rights globally, it is important to note that this remained a very European and American (North and Latin America), specifically White, project despite the fact that a number of European countries had started to formalize their exploitation of territories which were largely inhabited by Black and Brown peoples of different shades in regions such as Africa, Asia, the Middle East and the Pacific in the decades before the adoption of the Declaration by individual governments or the League of Nations. In the process, elements of these child-saving, children's-rights discourses and policies were exported to these contexts. The most notable example of the reproduction of these discourses in contexts outside of Europe and the Americas can probably be located within, not state efforts, but in the work of European missionaries, many of whom had similar ideas and beliefs to philanthropists and reformers engaged in child-saving movements in their home countries. Through the institution of the school, in particular, missionaries of different denominations sought to concentrate their conversion and civilizing agendas of peoples they considered to be 'primitive' and 'backward' heathens on the young due to the belief that converting this generation would eventually lead to the religious transformation of these societies as a whole (Valentin and Meinert, 2009; Vallgårda et al, 2015). Therefore, schools provided missionaries with the opportunity to impart, in a systematic way, what they deemed to be 'proper' values to children, an effort that sought to counter the perceived negative influence of family and culture.

In relation to state efforts, evidence shows that colonial governments drew on some of the emerging understandings of childhood to frame new laws introduced in their colonies. For example, in the Gold Coast, a British colony which became known as Ghana upon independence in 1957, the Children and Young Persons Act of 1933 stated that 'it shall be conclusively presumed that no child under the age of 8 years can be guilty of any offence'. Using this definition of childhood, it asserts, in Article 52, that:

(1) A child shall not be ordered to be imprisoned or be sent to a penal servitude for any offence, it be committed to prison in default of payment of a fine, damages, or costs.
(2) A young person shall not be sent to penal servitude for any offence.
(3) A young person shall not be ordered to be imprisoned for an offence in default of payment of a fine, damages or costs, unless the court certifies that he is of so unruly a character that he cannot be detained in a remand home or that he is of so depraved a character that he is not a fit person to be so detained.

The understanding of childhood is further outlined in Article 53(1) when it states:

> Sentence of death shall not be pronounced or recorded against a person under the age of 18 years, but in lieu therefore the court shall sentence him to be detained during His Majesty's pleasure, and if, so sentenced, he shall notwithstanding anything on the other provisions of this Act, be liable to be detained in such place and under such conditions as the Secretary of State may direct.

This understanding of the age at which an individual could be seen as culpable of committing a crime was broadly similar to legal understandings taking place in England and Wales at this time. Specifically, the Children and Young Persons Act of England and Wales 1933 sets out in section 50 that 'it shall be conclusively presumed that no child under the age of ten years can be guilty of any offence' (UK Government, 1933). Thus, there is evidence that demonstrates the extent to which new ideas about childhood emerging in European contexts filtered into laws and policies in colonized territories to some degree.

However, while some of the new ideas about childhood that had been consolidated by the end of the 19th century in Europe were exported to colonized territories, it is important to note that these conversations about newly constructed notions of childhood and their attendant rights were selectively applied to children in these contexts (Nieuwenhuys, 2012; Balagopalan, 2014). Focusing specifically on debates around child labour, Nieuwenhuys makes the case that:

> Both justification for the civilized mission of the mother country and the smooth functioning of colonial administration required that overt competition over labour, even among the colonizers, be either kept strictly in check or be hidden under the veil of traditional, socialization, education, or corrective disciplining. To disguise child labour on their plantations, planters-cum-missionaries in Swaziland, for example changed the identity of their child labourers into school children by offering some form of free education in the hours of work (Simelane 1998). (Nieuwenhuys, 2012: 152).

This leads her to argue that child labour elimination in Europe and the US went hand-in-hand with new forms of child exploitation unfolding in colonial territories.

Therefore, these initial discussions, while framed as international, were very much centred on Western Europe and North American societies – specifically on the childhoods experienced by White children in these contexts. Further, efforts were made, by colonial authorities, to ensure that these discussions led by the League of Nations, or the International Labour Organization (ILO), did not prohibit their ability to continue to exploit, and benefit from, the labour of specifically Black and Brown children within colonial contexts. Not only were Western European and North American societies particularly centred in this new discourse of childhoods and children's rights, so also were White children in colonized/subjugated (or formerly colonized) territories, most notably those with settler populations in Southern Africa, Australasia and Latin America, for example. Therefore, although by the early 20th century these new ideas about childhood and children's rights had also entered these contexts, the way they were applied within these settler colonies or former colonies varied depending on race.

The racial element to the articulation of these notions is noted by Hepburn and Jackson (2022: 223), for instance, who, focusing on the interwar period, postulate in reference to British colonial Africa that 'colonists constructed white childhood as a time for education and protection and black childhood as a period of labour, as part of efforts to prepare children for their racialised and unequal future role'. As this position was at odds with broader discourses around children's rights and child work that had started to take place as part of the internationalist movement as well as humanitarian concerns about children, this led colonial governments such as Britain to attempt to influence international agencies, notably the ILO, to adopt more 'plural rather than universal labour norms and standards, in an attempt to protect their abilities to mobilise and exploit colonized children's labour' (Hepburn and Jackson, 2022: 225). These arguments had some traction with ILO staff who often adopted the recommendations of British colonial officials in subsequent policies and interventions about child labour. The key point to note is that this early period of the international discourse of children's rights was one which sought to exclude Black and Brown children in colonized or formerly colonized territories in Africa, the Caribbean, the Middle East, Asia-Pacific and Latin America. Instead, in this period this new image of childhood and children's rights was the preserve of White children either in the metropole or in countries where colonization had involved settlement by Europeans.

The route towards a more global discourse of children's rights

Following the end of the Second World War, the plight of children was, once again, observed as being especially dire, leading to a new momentum to develop new formulations of rights relating to this group. Key to this process was the role played by the International Union for Child Welfare, an affiliate of the Save the Children International Union. This organization started lobbying, in 1946, the members of the Economic and Social Council of the newly established UN, and its Temporary Social Commission, to confirm, with minor amendments, the 1924 Declaration, which had been adopted by its predecessor, the League of Nations. The Temporary Social Commission was receptive to this idea due to the recognition that 'the welfare of children, physically, mentally, and spiritually, must be the first concern of every nation, particularly having regard to the ravages of the two world wars' (cited in Veerman, 1992: 159). However, there was a feeling that the 1924 Declaration was now outdated, especially in view of the changes that had taken place in the fields of healthcare and child welfare since its adoption (Veerman, 1992). As a result, the Economic and Social Council agreed to adapt the 1924 Declaration and propose a revised version to the General Assembly. Two years later, on 19 April 1948, the commission initiated a discussion about the revised declaration. These discussions continued for a further 11 years before the Declaration was adopted unanimously by the UN General Assembly on 20 November 1959.

Extending the 1924 Declaration further, this new declaration consisted of ten principles instead of the five that had been outlined by its predecessor. While informed by the 1924 Declaration this principle was also different in significant ways. For instance, it removed the child's right to work, replacing it with children's entitlement to free and compulsory elementary education. Its significance has been noted by various commentors, including Fortin (2009), who claims that it led to a more serious consideration of children's rights. However, similar to the previous declaration this treaty was also limited in key respects. Children remained perceived as passive beings in need of protection and special consideration rather than as rights-bearing individuals (Wells, 2015). Further, despite the best efforts of a number of communist countries, in particular, Poland, which had been trying to push for a binding treaty, the decision was made that the 1959 Declaration, like its predecessor, would also be non-binding, which meant that 'states were merely required to take note of the principles contained therein on the basis that they were universally accepted as being applicable to children' (Fortin, 2009: 38; see also Veerman, 1992).

Although there had been little support for a binding treaty in the discussions that led to the adoption of the 1959 Declaration, by the 1970s this notion had started to gain wider support. This was largely due to the fact that by this time there was widespread concern about violations of children's rights and an increasing belief that these could only be addressed through a series of legal obligations (Fortin, 2009). In response to a request from the United Nations Children's Fund (UNICEF), the UN General Assembly agreed, in 1976, to declare 1979 the International Year of the Child. To commemorate that year governments were encouraged to make special contributions to improving the wellbeing of children in their contexts. As its contribution to the year, the Polish government, in 1978, submitted a draft for a new binding convention to the UN Commission on Human Rights. This initial document, which was very similar to the 1959 Declaration, was rejected. However, the revised submission, which 'provided the first indication of the emergence of children as rights-bearing individuals' (Cohen, 2006: 189, cited in Wells, 2015: 29), was accepted. This acceptance paved the way for the establishment of an Open-Ended Working Group on the Question of the Convention on the Rights of the Child, which was charged with reviewing and reformulating the text of the proposed Convention (Veerman, 1992, Harris-Short, 2001).

The open-ended nature of the working group, which consisted of 43 member states, has been celebrated for facilitating inclusion as this structure meant that all member states of the UN or states and non-state agencies that held observer status were entitled to participate in the proceedings underpinning the drafting of the Convention (Harris-Short, 2001). Such non-state agencies included non-governmental organizations (NGOs) in consultative status with the Economic and Social Council (ECOSOC). While a number of NGOs were involved in the process from the outset, it was not until after 1983 that their role in the process intensified and started to gain more momentum due to the fact that they became more organized – an achievement facilitated by the formation of an alliance of NGOs called the NGO Ad Hoc Group in the Drafting of the Convention on the Rights of the Child which consisted of 50 organizations, with Defence for Children as the hosting secretariat (Harris-Short, 2001). This was further strengthened, in 1985, when UNICEF, initially reluctant to join the drafting process due to its desire to avoid confrontation with UN member states as well as its framing of its work in terms of needs as opposed to rights (see Oestreich, 1998), became a member of the working group.

The involvement of UNICEF has been acknowledged as being critical to expanding the involvement of member states from the Global South in the working group and the subsequent near universal and rapid ratification of the Convention (see Alston, 1994). At the point the working group was established the UN consisted of 158 member states. However, only a small proportion of these governments took part in the discussions of the open-ended working group, especially in the early stages. Participation was dominated by states from Western Europe as well as Australia, New Zealand, Canada and the US. From the Global South only Argentina, Brazil, the Central African Empire, the Dominican Republic and India sent their delegates to all the sessions of the open-ended working group (Harris-Short, 2001). Most other Southern governments did not participate in the meetings of the working group. In relation to Africa, only three African states participated for at least five of the nine years that the working group took to draft the final proposal of the Convention (Mbise, 2017). This poor representation of countries from the South had implications, as Harris-Short (2001: 321) has posited: 'Even with extensive NGO participation, the disappointing level of participation by states from Africa, the Asia-Pacific, Latin America and the Middle East seriously undermined the possibility of securing a fully inclusive final text.'

After nine years of discussions and debates, all of which took place entirely in Geneva, the open-ended working group, which was chaired by Adam Lopatka, the former Director of the Institute of State and Law of the Polish Academy of Sciences, completed the first reading of the draft text of the Convention on 5 February 1988. This was followed by an in-depth technical review within the UN secretariat (to ensure that the text contained no contradictions and that it was worded in accordance with the terminology of international legislation). This review paved the way for the second reading of the text and its eventual approval. Following a few procedural and administrative steps which required the final text to be reviewed by both the Committee on Human Rights and ECOSOC, it was then presented for discussion by members of the General Assembly in the autumn of 1989, leading to its adoption by consensus on 20 November 1989 by the 158-member Assembly after only two minutes of procedural discussion (Veerman, 1992). Once open for signature in January 1990, 61 states signed the Convention on the first day (Fottrell, 2000). According to Mbise (2017), ten out of the first 20 countries to initially sign the Convention were from Africa. With regards to ratification while some delayed their ratification of the treaty, others made the decision to ratify it immediately, with Ghana being the first country to do so on 5 February 1990 and a number of other countries following suit in the following months, thus enabling the treaty to enter into force less than a year after its adoption by the UN General Assembly – on 2 September 1990 – a record in UN history.

Today, the Convention has been ratified by all states except the US. This universal ratification is unique in the history of the UN and has led to assertions of a consensus in governmental attitudes towards children's rights (Alston, 1994; Fottrell, 2000; Woll, 2000). According to Oestreich:

> The near-universal acceptance of the document (more than 180 states are parties to it) and the speed with which it was accepted (it had entered into force within a year of being offered for ratification) are unique among human rights documents and suggest an unusual level of international agreement. The fact that the content of the CRC is considered in many quarters to be particularly 'Western' makes it more interesting still. (Oestreich, 1998: 184)

In relation to the US, which has signed the Convention, but has still not ratified it, its position relating to the treaty has been attributed to a number of reasons. Central among these is the vocal opposition from conservative, often Christian, groups who fear that the Convention 'will undermine parents' authority over their children through its sweeping and unprecedented creation of autonomy rights for children [which] may, in the long run, threaten children's wellbeing' (Fortin, 2009: 45). The irony of the lack of ratification by the US cannot be overlooked given the fact that it played a pivotal role in ensuring the inclusion of civil and political rights in the text of the Convention despite opposition from the Eastern bloc, led by Poland, whose members were hoping for a treaty that would foreground the socioeconomic rights of children.

Once publicized, the Convention came to be recognized as a step-change in international law. Not only was it the first binding treaty on children's rights and the most rapidly ratified treaty in the history of the UN, but it was also the first piece of international law to recognize children as rights holders – subjects, not objects, of international law (Freeman, 1992; Veerman, 1992; Verhellen, 1994; Fottrell, 2000; Woll, 2000; Pupavac, 2001; Liebel, 2012; Wells, 2015). As Veerman (1992: 184) argues: 'it promotes children's welfare as an issue of justice rather than one of charity'. Thus, no longer were rights framed as the inverted duties that benevolent adults offer to powerless and passive children; instead, they were now framed as claims, entitlements that children could assert against adults – be they states, family members or professionals.

The recognition of children as subjects of international law was key to the inclusion of civil and political rights as well as socioeconomic rights in the contents of the Convention. Therefore, in this way it not only recognized children's right to protection as previous declarations had done, but it also granted them enabling rights, especially centred around the right to freedom of expression and association (Cantwell, 1989, cited in Boyden, 1997). As Veerman (1992: 184) puts it, 'it is the first international instrument that explicitly states that children have a right to "have a say" in processes affecting their lives'. In this way, then, the Convention is seen to recognize the agency of children. This innovation to international law has led to arguments that the Convention moves beyond the paternalistic framings of previous declarations (see Twum-Danso Imoh, 2023). It is these aspects of the Convention that led to a frisson of excitement, at least in policy and practitioner circles, in the immediate aftermath of its adoption by the UN General Assembly (Freeman, 2000). These innovations within the Convention can be credited with bestowing it with a status that other treaties have not received both in the periods that both preceded and followed.

In the 35 years since the Convention was adopted its impact has been wide-reaching in numerous respects – certainly at the level of law and policy (see Twum-Danso Imoh, 2014). As Stahl (2007: 805) argues, 'the CRC has influenced the world, both in how societies regard children and in how they react to children as people'. This is supported by Kilkelly and Lundy (2006: 335), who assert that '[t]he coverage and scope of the UNCRC in recognizing the rights of children and young people, and setting out how they are to be both promoted and protected is unrivalled in terms of their comprehensive nature, international and national standing, and relevance' (see also Myers, 2001).

The UN children's agency, UNICEF, which played a key role in the last few years of the drafting process, continued to play a significant role in promoting the Convention and encouraging others to adhere to its standards in the years following its adoption. Oestreich (1998: 187) effectively captures the centrality of the Convention to UNICEF's operations when he states: 'By the mid-1990s, the CRC had become a sort of unofficial constitution of

UNICEF, with almost every facet of its operations directed toward the Convention's implementation, at least on the rhetorical level. UNICEF operations are now routinely justified, and progress measured, with reference to the goals of the CRC' (see also Myers, 2001).

Other international organizations have similarly drawn on the provisions of the Convention to inform their strategies and programmes. This support for the Convention can not only be seen at the level of the international community, but also in national contexts. For instance, as ratification requires government to ensure that their national laws are in line with the Convention's standards, many governments have reviewed their child-focused laws and amended them accordingly (see Twum-Danso Imoh, 2019). Hence, in the period following the adoption of the Convention, many governments reviewed, amended and introduced new laws focusing on children's rights and welfare. Additionally, many also reviewed and modified their Constitution to bring it in line with the Convention's standards. A good example is that of the government of post-Apartheid South Africa, which ratified the Convention in 1995 soon after its first free elections in April 1994 following decades of racial segregation and the exclusion of Black Africans from meaningful political (and, indeed, economic and social) life under the Apartheid system (Richter and Dawes, 2008).

In contexts in Africa, for instance, the Convention has resulted in the idea of children's rights filtering down into the language and discourses of communities, even those that can be characterized as illiterate, poor and marginalized (Abebe and Tefera, 2014; Twum-Danso Imoh, 2019; Mbise, 2017). For example, Tatek Abebe and Tamirat Tefera (2014) demonstrate the extent to which the discourse of children's rights has filtered into local community contexts in Ethiopia – to the extent that it is now discussed by local governments, schools and even community-based organizations such as burial and credit associations. While the visibility of children's rights principles in local community discourses has been noted, this does not necessarily indicate, as the authors show, that they have been automatically accepted. Instead, for many these rights are contested, rejected or dismissed as a 'passing fad'. My own work (Twum-Danso Imoh, 2019) has shown how, within the context of Ghana, many actors within local communities, including those who are illiterate, have not only started to define childhood using the chronological age of 18, but have also started to confer upon those under this age the status of dependency and vulnerability which aligns with global discourses around childhood and children's rights. Furthermore, local actors – either as individuals or as collectives, including children and young people themselves – have called for action that would facilitate the Convention's standards within their contexts (Myers, 2001; Shepler, 2005; Mniki and Rosa, 2007; Grugel and Peruzzotti, 2012; Twum-Danso Imoh, 2019). The important point to note about the impact of the Convention on public discourses and policies is that the understanding of childhood depicted in such discourses in diverse contexts is now very much intertwined with the Convention's own understandings, which, in turn, are an outcome of the evolution of the modern conception of childhood that emerged in Western Europe and the Americas from the 17th century onwards.

However, at the same time these rights for children articulated in the Convention, which have been praised for the consensus they are seen to represent, have struggled to be effectively implemented in diverse contexts both in the Global North and the Global South (Burman, 1994, 1996; Boyden, 1997; Pupavac, 2001; Liebel, 2012, 2020; Reynaert et al, 2012, 2015; Hanson and Niewenhuys, 2013; Twum-Danso Imoh and Ansell, 2014; Abebe and Ofosu-Kusi, 2016; Twum-Danso Imoh, 2019, 2023). Grugel, for instance, argues:

> Thanks in part to their work the CRC has contributed to a sea-change in how children are perceived in international development. But it is less clear that either the CRC or the new campaigns it has given birth to have genuinely or extensively transformed the lived realities of children, especially poor children in the developing world, to the extent that the drafters of the CRC hoped. (Grugel, 2013: 22; see also Jupp, 1999)

Therefore, while there have been some changes in children's lives in many contexts, especially in relation to survival and development rights in the decades since the adoption of the Convention, there remain persistent questions about the extent to which these changes have been genuinely transformative for diverse groups of children around the world (see also Grugel, 2013). While this limited impact can be attributed to external factors such as the cultural and socioeconomic context in which it is being implemented, it is also important to take account of inherent factors within the make-up of the Convention and broader children's rights discourses. For example, the conceptualization of children's rights in the Convention represents an order that, over the years, has acquired a status as the hegemonic order, leading to a situation whereby it has come to be seen as the only possible way to address demands in the public sphere converting all political and moral issues into this narrow understanding. This hegemonic status conceals numerous pluralities and conflicts in approaches to realizing children's welfare and interests. While dominant global norms around children's rights can be understood as an attempt to establish a global order or norms and political values, it is also important to note that, in practice, the deployment of these norms has been characterized by a lack of order at different levels (see Sandin, 2014; Holzscheiter et al, 2019). Thus, far from establishing a new global order that would improve the wellbeing of children who are now recognized as rights holders, the Convention (and indeed, other child-focused global policies that have followed in its wake) has created or reinforced a global disorder centred around exclusion as it relates to children's lives and, hence, their status and wellbeing (Wells, 2015). These norms have further become a cornerstone in systems of governance that follow other logics and trajectories which do not all seek to advance the rights and inclusion of children and young people as individual rights holders (Sandin, 2014; Holzscheiter et al, 2019).

Moreover, while the Convention is widely seen to symbolize a step-change in children's rights discourses, it remains, in many ways, very similar to the previous declarations which were critiqued for their paternalism (Twum-Danso Imoh, 2023). For instance, in the process of identifying, defining and articulating the rights of children, neither the 1924 Declaration, 1959 Declaration nor the Convention attempted to include the views or perspectives of children themselves (Freeman, 1992, 2000; Boyden, 1997; Liebel, 2012). This has led to a situation whereby the rights of children articulated in all these treaties are rights of children as they have been imagined or envisioned by adults, primarily Western-based professionals working within international organizations. Related to this, although the Convention is unique in its recognition of children as holders of civil and political rights as reflected in Articles 12, 13 and 14, these are limited to children 'having a say', especially on issues affecting them as opposed to issues affecting their communities or societies more generally. Beyond this, these provisions do not recognize the right of children to independent decision-making or self-determination which would include, for example, children having the right to vote (see Pupavac, 2001; Wall, 2011; Liebel, 2012; Josefsson and Wall, 2020).

Thus, although often praised as a transformative advocacy tool (Cantwell, 2011), which has played a pivotal role in changing the status of children in international law and global social policy, the Convention, in some major respects, remains as limited in its vision of childhood and children as the 1924 and 1959 Declarations. This has implications as such limitations lead to a situation whereby: first, adults' interests drive the conceptualization and reconceptualization of children's rights which compounds the dependence of children on adults, especially those who are professionals while, at the same time, expanding the power of these adults over their lives; and second, the space for children to exercise autonomy and decision-making has continued to become increasingly restricted and constrained (Pupavac, 2001; Liebel, 2012; Twum-Danso Imoh, 2023). These limitations that can be seen as persistently underlying different iterations of the articulation of children's rights in global treaties have arguably stagnated the progression of children's rights and, consequently, have limited the extent to which these conceptualizations and principles of rights can have a transformational impact on the position and status of children in diverse parts of the world.

As a result, in recent years calls for rethinking the concept of children's rights have been increasingly vocalized. As the eminent, now retired, human rights scholar, Michael Freeman (1992, 2000), repeatedly argued in the years following the adoption of the Convention, this widely lauded and celebrated treaty was not supposed to represent 'the last word' on children's rights. As he asserts:

> There is a tendency to assume that we have a Convention, we have reached the finishing line. But laurels wither and medals tarnish. The Convention must be seen as a real achievement but also as a spur to further action. We need to strengthen both the substance of the Convention and its implementation mechanisms. There are new rights to be detailed, new features of existing rights to be tested and examined, and new child groups to be emphasized. We must not assume that a Convention formulated in the last third of the 20th century will fit the needs of children of the new millennium. There is a need for revision, reform, and innovation. The Convention was not formulated by children, nor did they have any real input into it. How different a convention in which the child's voice is heard would look is a matter of some controversy. There is, though, not a little irony in having a Convention which emphasizes participatory rights (in Article 12) whilst foreclosing the participation of children in the formulation of the rights to be encoded. The next Convention cannot afford to ignore the voice of children. Nor can it assume that all children are the same. (Freeman, 2000: 382; see also Liebel, 2012)

Thus, the Convention should not be seen as the final step in the formulation and conceptualization of the notion of children's rights. Instead, it should be approached as yet another incremental step in the evolution of rights thinking relating to childhood, which was set in motion, at least globally, by the 1924 Declaration on the Rights of the Child, and significantly advanced by the Convention on the Rights of the Child. As we approach the centenary of the 1924 Declaration on the Rights of the Child and the 35th anniversary of the Convention on the Rights of the Child, there is no better time to consider and articulate what these 'next words' on children's rights will consist of, or look like (see also Hanson, 2022).

Conclusion

This chapter has traced the global construction of the concept of children's rights, highlighting the shift it made from a national discourse in much of Western Europe and the Americas, centred around certain groups of children, notably those who were racialized as White, to an international discourse, which by the end of the 20th century sought to apply to all children regardless of context. While the chapter demonstrates the impact of the Convention and its influence on a whole host of policies and discourses about child welfare in diverse contexts, its transformative impact on the status of children and their inferiority in relation to adults, ultimately, remains limited.

3

Global Children's Rights Discourses: Imperialistic, Irrelevant and Inapplicable to Southern Contexts?

Introduction

The association between dominant children's rights discourses and developments which took place in Western Europe and North America from the 18th century onwards has been at the forefront of debates about children's rights certainly in the past 100 years. This linkage has provided the foundation for much discussion about the children's rights movement and its attendant global policies and laws such as the Convention on the Rights of the Child. In particular, the Western European and North American origins of dominant children's rights discourses have resulted in the proliferation of publications that have sought to show that the conceptualizations of childhoods, child development, child protection and children's entitlements that are currently being diffused through a range of international policies and legal frameworks as well as programmatic interventions to countries around the world are based on the upheavals of Western European and North American societies from the 17th century onwards. As a result, it is claimed, they are at odds with the understanding of childhood and child development in contexts which have, historically, had different ideas about the nature of childhood, the roles of children and the very essence of what it means to be human (see Burman, 1994, 1996, 1999; Boyden, 1997; Aitken, 2001; Pupavac, 2001; Burr, 2002; de Waal, 2002; Ansell, 2010; Cregan and Cuthbert, 2014; Wells, 2015).

That these policies and discourses have had an impact is evident by the fact that they are now increasingly used to frame discourses around child wellbeing, welfare and interests in a range of countries whose historical trajectories are not necessarily similar to those of Western Europe and North America (Burman, 1996, 1999; Boyden, 1997; Aitken, 2001; Harris-Short,

2001; Pupavac, 2001; Burr, 2002; de Waal, 2002; Balagopalan, 2014; Liebel, 2020). This has been pointed out by other scholars; Burr, in reference to Boyden (1990), makes the following point: 'What Boyden (1990) has called the global model of childhood, dominated by modern western understanding of children, has set in motion an international agenda that makes it problematic for children to work or to show a level of independence that is now deemed inappropriate in the West' (Burr, 2002: 53; see also Burman, 1999).

The resulting outcome of this exportation is that this model of childhood developed amidst the upheavals of Western European and North American societies has become seen as normative, or the gold standard, by which all societies are judged (see Burman, 1996; Boyden, 1997; Pupavac, 2001). Therefore, in this way a vision of deficit childhoods is created whereby the childhoods and child development models of other societies are stigmatized and seen as problematic (Boyden, 1997; Burman, 1999; Aitken, 2001; Pupavac, 2001; Holt and Holloway, 2006; Ansell, 2010, 2016). Such arguments have led to claims that dominant children's rights principles are a form of cultural imperialism which result in the dismissal, marginalization and devaluation of the local peculiarities and conditions relating to constructions of childhood and children's lived experiences as well as Indigenous worldviews (see Burman, 1994, 1996, 1999; Boyden, 1997; Burr, 2002, 2006; Liebel, 2020). This chapter seeks to subject the idea of children's rights as imperialist, irrelevant and inapplicable to non-Western or Southern contexts to scrutiny in the contemporary period. It will do this by exploring the extent to which the concept is intertwined with developments in Western Europe and North America and then proceed to contrast it with other understandings of childhood and personhood in other contexts, especially in sub-Saharan Africa.

Problematizing dominant children's rights principles: two examples of the Eurocentric nature of the discourse

Central to outlining the dissonance between dominant discourses of children's rights and the worldviews and practices of other societies is the concept of individuality, which can be traced back to the new vision of a human being which underpinned discourses of human rights that emerged from the 18th century onwards in Western European and North American societies. Key to this new understanding of what it meant to be human was the centrality of the isolated and autonomous human being who had rights he[1] could claim from the state (see Howard, 1992). This was a crucial component of the new understanding of being human that emerged in these societies as they evolved from what was seen as their 'primitive' pasts into a new modernity that had been consolidated by the end of the 19th century (Twum-Danso Imoh, 2020). As human rights traditions formed the premise for the articulation of children's rights, the individuality at the core of the human rights tradition became central to the conceptualization and articulation of children's rights (although the centrality of autonomy was significantly modified) (see Twum-Danso Imoh, 2020). The primacy attached to the concept of individuality within human and children's rights discourses is reflected in many of the related discourses and policies that have developed in the past 100 years as part of what Burr (2006: 17) calls an 'overemphasis on the individualistic conceptions of rights in its development of human rights procedures'. With specific regards to the Convention on the Rights of the Child, Burr, in an earlier publication, claims:

> The CRC is grounded in a modern Western of the self. It is 'I' who have 'rights,' it is the 'individual' child who needs protection and support. It is this modern western sense of self that is referred to and made universally applicable in the internationalized discourses on children's rights. (Burr, 2002: 51)

This critique of the Convention is borne out throughout its contents, but also in its preamble. For instance, paragraph 7 of its Preamble stipulates: 'Considering that the child should be fully prepared to live an individual life in society and brought up in the spirit of the ideals proclaimed in the Charter of the United Nations, and in particular in the spirit of peace, dignity, tolerance, freedom, equality, and solidarity.' This focus on the individual within dominant rights discourses such as the Convention is seen as problematic as it is recognized to be incompatible with the cultures and values of communitarian communities in, primarily, Africa, Asia, the Middle East and the Pacific (Harris-Short, 2001; Kaime, 2010; Liebel, 2020; Twum-Danso Imoh, 2020). Specifically, the problem that has been framed foregrounds the extent to which the concept of individualism clashes with the notion of collectivism that is embedded in understandings of culture in the South, resulting in challenges to the implementation of global human and children's rights principles. Kaime puts it well when he states:

> [T]he initial formulation between rights and culture has been one of opposition. Recognition of rights was seen to entail the denial, rejection or overriding of culture; and conversely, recognizing culture was seen to prohibit the pursuit of individual rights. The binary opposition between these two paradigms has been played out to great effect by a fundamental tension between on the one hand, the desire to establish universal rights, and on the other hand, the awareness and

respect for cultural difference. (Kaime, 2010: 638; see also Twum-Danso Imoh, 2020)

This argument is not without validity, as is evidenced by an analysis of the understanding of personhood and childhood which emerges in the worldviews of societies that have hitherto been labelled as 'non-Western' or Southern. In the case of sub-Saharan Africa, for example, despite the variation in the political and social organization of the different societies and states that existed in the region prior to the formal colonization of much of the continent in the 19th century by European countries, the organizing principle underpinning many societies historically was centred around interdependence between individuals (see Twum-Danso Imoh, 2022). This understanding of relationality was so critical that it formed the basis of concepts and values that informed the structures of these societies historically. The most obvious or well-known example, perhaps, is the notion of *Ubuntu*, which is a Bantu philosophical and religious concept that recognizes that the humanity of individuals is achieved through their social interaction with others, including those of different generations. This led to a situation whereby notions of mutual aid, obligation and support were foregrounded in social relationships (Gathogo, 2008).

The principles or values underpinning this worldview were expected to be evident in how individuals related to each other. Specifically, within this context there was an understanding that individuals not only had duties towards each other, but also possessed rights they were entitled to claim from one another. Cobbah (1987: 321), writing of the Akan of West Africa, explained it thus: 'the right of one kinship member is the duty of the other and the duty of the other kinship member is the right of another'. These expected behaviours from individuals as a result of communitarian principles do not only relate to *intra*generational relations. They also shape, and inform, *inter*generational relations. In effect, what these principles mean is that adults and children depend on each other in order to achieve their wellbeing and personal objectives as well as broader household or family needs. Returning to the concept of *Ubuntu*, Abebe and Biswas draw a linkage between the interdependencies between parents and children in contexts in Africa to the very understanding of personhood:

Ubuntu suggests that – like every member of the family and community – children develop personhood through social interactions, which means that they must 'prize communal and harmonious relationships with others' (Metz 2016, 324). This emphasis on the community over the individual does not reject the individual but acknowledges that the two are co-creators, interdependent, and mutually sustaining (see Chilisa 2020). This implies that adults also realize their personhood through relationships with children, making room for a co-generational understanding of education for sustainable futures. (Abebe and Biswas, 2021: 123)

These principles are not simply descriptions of social relations in African societies of the past; they continue to remain evident in social relations in many contemporary societies across the continent (Abebe, 2007, 2013; Coe, 2012; Kassa, 2017; Twum-Danso Imoh, 2022, forthcoming 2024b). This understanding of personhood has resulted in a perception that childhood is a phase of life in which children are recognized as competent and capable and, thus, are able to undertake responsibilities which are increased incrementally as they become more mature and competent – as demonstrated through the tasks they undertake. The work of German anthropologist, Enid Schildkrout (1978), in northern Nigeria is instructive here. Her work in urban Kano, in particular, led her to conclude that as children undertake responsibilities from an early age, many of which adults rely on so they can undertake other tasks or adhere to religious or cultural practices (especially in the case of women), growing up, then, was not a case of children transitioning from being *unproductive* members of society to becoming *productive* members because as children, they were already productive members of society (see also Twum-Danso Imoh, forthcoming 2024b). Thus, within this context, while individuality may be recognized, it was the collective and, in particular, the interdependence and the mutual obligations between kinfolk or community members more generally which were prioritized. This is further supported by Abebe who, writing about childhood in southern Ethiopia, states that:

> The desire to sustain family solidarity and interdependent lives often overshadows children's individual needs and interests. These children's lives represent the antithesis of the hegemonic model premised on the idea that children should have a safe and happy existence and childhood is seen as a work-free and care receiving phase of the life course. I argue that this is not so because of the inability of rural Ethiopians to acknowledge children's individuality but on account of a hegemonic ideal from a once localised Western construction of childhood being exported to the rest of the world against momentum. (Abebe, 2013: 72)

He goes on to add that although the rights language has become commonplace and appears clear at the level of the international community, it is not meaningful for working children in the contexts in which he researches where collective duties are prioritized over the rights of the individual. In fact, in relation to southern Ethiopia he argues that an individualistic reading of children's lives results in adverse outcomes for working children as it results in isolating children from their family and community (Abebe, 2013).

In addition to the concept of individualism another key concept that illuminates the dissonance between global children's rights principles and understandings of childhoods in other contexts surrounds the focus on biological age. As a concept that evolved from historical developments in Western Europe and North America, one of the key features of the construction of children's rights that came to prevail by the mid-20th century was the definition of childhood which now encompassed all individuals under the age of 18. Like the concept of individualism, the idea of a chronological age to delineate the age of majority emerged within the political upheavals of Western European and North American societies during the course of the 18th and 19th centuries. The establishment of the specific age of 18 as the age of majority had occurred in most Western European and North American countries by the early decades of the 20th century (de Waal, 2002; Wyness, 2006). The use of the age of 18 to mark the boundary between childhood and adulthood was facilitated by the institution of the school, as explained by de Waal (2002: 14), who notes that: 'Eighteen years is the outcome of a convergence between a reducing age of majority and an increasing school leaving age in Western societies.' Added to this was the belief that had emerged in Western Europe and North America by this time that by the age of 18 individuals are 'socially and morally responsible enough to vote, pay income tax and be sexually active' (Wyness, 2006: 25).

This understanding of childhood and its termination subsequently came to frame legal and policy frameworks at both the global and national level (see Clark-Kazak, 2009). For example, Article 1 of the Convention establishes the definition of childhood which provides the basis for all its other articles: 'For the purposes of the present Convention, a child means every human being below the age of eighteen years unless under the law applicable to the child, majority is attained earlier' (United Nations, 1989). While this definition has been critiqued for its limitations (see, for example, Grover, 2004), in its application various actors have interpreted it to mean that all those under the age of 18 are children and thus, entitled to the rights stipulated within this treaty (see Twum-Danso Imoh, 2019). Beyond the global, this understanding of the ending of childhood has also been assumed in regional laws such as the African Charter on the Rights and Welfare of the Child, which, although drafted to take into consideration the virtues of the African cultural heritage, historical background and the values of African civilization (framed using singular as opposed to plural nouns), adopted a more stringent definition of childhood than the Convention which is set out in Article 2. 'For the purposes of this Charter, a child means every human being below the age of 18 years.'

Diverse national contexts also illuminate the existence of this understanding of childhood, especially in the decades following state ratification of the Convention – a process which requires governments to ensure that their legislative framework corresponds with its standards. As a result, a review of child-focused laws introduced into the legislative frameworks of numerous countries since 1989 reveals a consensus in understandings of the stage at which an individual transitions from childhood to adulthood, with most countries setting their general age of majority at 18 (see Twum-Danso Imoh, 2019). However, it is worth noting that some of these amendments in national law have been motivated by the desire of some governments in so-called 'developing' or Southern countries to meet conditions set for the receipt of development assistance (see Clark-Kazak, 2009).

With the adoption of the age of 18 in not only global social policies and international laws such as the Convention, but also in the domestic laws and policy framework of a wide range of countries, which have historically made different assumptions what it means to be both a child and an adult, the age of 18 years has now become an arbitrary cut-off point for childhood in the laws and policies of both so-called Western and non-Western societies (see Twum-Danso Imoh, 2019). Furthermore, because of the dominant discourses, those who fall under the age of 18 in diverse parts of the world are now categorized as being in a special and precarious phase of life which needs extra protection, development and care if complete and responsible adulthood is to be achieved. Therefore, not only is an individual under the age of 18 now recognized as a child, but this recognition also comes with the understanding that they require special treatment above and beyond those adults – now also defined as those over the age of 18 – need.

However, the use of chronological age, most notably the age of 18, as the demarcation between childhood and adulthood is not a process that is universally understood. Within contexts in Africa the ending of childhood historically had little to do with achieving a particular chronological age, and more to do with the physical capacity to perform acts reserved for adults depending on gender. This contrast has been borne out by a considerable number of academic studies that have shown how the attainment of adulthood was historically based on milestones other than chronological age (Schildkrout, 1978; Nsamenang, 1992; Ncube, 1998; Cheney, 2007; Clark-Kazak, 2009; Ansell, 2010). For boys, key markers to determine their transition to adulthood in many societies across the region were economic independence, the ability to look after oneself and others, and having their own house or land. For both boys and girls key to this transition process was the acquisition of a dependent. While for boys this was achieved by marriage, for girls, it was attained upon motherhood, which would normally take place soon after sexual maturation (Schildkrout, 1978; de Waal, 2002; Nsamenang, 2002). The emphasis placed on marriage and motherhood in determining the recognition of adult status meant that 'an unmarried childless person is never accorded full adult status and marriage alone just confers proto-adult status on a person' (Nsamenang, 1992: 84).

For a person to achieve adult status, then, they need to be 'married with children' (Nsamenang, 1992: 84–85). Therefore, without achieving these landmarks, a person was seen as somewhat lacking, or incomplete within their community (Twum-Danso, 2008).

These depictions remain evident in numerous contexts in the region. Mozambican anthropologist, Alcinda Honwana (2012, 2014) developed the concept of 'waithood' to describe the situation of young people who are recognized as adults by law, but yet have not attained the markers required in the contexts in which they live their everyday lives to become fully recognized by their communities as adults. Honwana (2014: 28) explains it thus: 'After they [the majority of African youth] leave school with few skills, they are unable to obtain work and become independent – to build, buy or rent a house for themselves, get married, establish families, and gain social recognition as adults.' The persistence of cultural markers to determine the ending of childhood is also supported by Tafere and Chuta (2020) who, in relation to Ethiopia, assert that motherhood remains a key indicator for the attainment of womanhood, and hence, full adult status, within some communities in this context. Therefore, in contexts where markers other than chronological age prevail in determining who is an adult or a child, a child of 14 can, even today, be recognized as an adult as they have achieved the social markers set for the attainment of adulthood while a man of 40 may be denied this very recognition by his community because he has failed to achieve this requirement (de Waal, 2002; Nsamenang, 2002; Twum-Danso, 2008; Honwana, 2012, 2014; Twum-Danso Imoh, 2019).

The persistence of these markers indicates that understandings of childhoods which are at odds with dominant discourses of children's rights remain evident in communities in countries across the continent, leading to a situation whereby international laws and global social policies are at odds with fundamental understandings of not just childhood, but also with constructions of personhood and social relations in these contexts. This results in the limited implementation of not only international laws such as the Convention on the Rights of the Child, but also a range of domestic laws that have been inspired by global discourses in the last century. A notable example is that of Nigeria where the government, which ratified the Convention in 1991, introduced a Children's Rights Bill in October 2002 as part of its attempt to ensure that national legislation corresponded with the Convention's standards. However, the Bill was overwhelmingly rejected by the House of Representatives (the Nigerian federal legislative lower chamber) at its second reading primarily because a significant number of the representatives objected to the establishment of 18 as the minimum age for marriage as they felt it was incompatible with religious and cultural values in the north of the country, in particular, where many women are sent into marriage before the age of 16 (IRIN, 2002; see Twum-Danso, 2009; Twum-Danso Imoh, 2019).[2] Such resistance has been noted in other countries (see, for example, Harris-Short, 2003). Therefore, much of the empirical evidence that exists demonstrates that the use of the chronological age of 18, or indeed of any age, to mark the boundary between childhood and adulthood is still not a norm for certain sections of the population in diverse countries on the continent, leading to the lived realities of communities clashing with dominant rights discourses. These arguments about the individualism underpinning rights discourses and the use of biological age to define childhood are among those that can be drawn upon to counter the idea of a consensus in international law and policy on children's rights as suggested by the rapid and almost universal ratification of the Convention.

A further consideration when critiquing the extent to which the Convention represents a global consensus is the politics that underpinned the ratification process. De Waal (2002), for example, has raised the possibility that some African governments may have ratified the Convention in the expectation that doing so will enable them to receive more aid from Western European and North American governments (see also Clark-Kazak, 2009; Mbise, 2017). The politics of the ratification process is further underscored by the fact that although the African Charter on the Rights and Welfare of the Child was adopted by the Organization of African Unity[3] less than a year after that of the Convention on 11 July 1990, it did not come into force until 29 November 1999 – over nine years after its adoption. This delayed path to enforcement in the case of the Charter was a result of African governments taking a longer time to ratify this treaty compared to the Convention. In fact, even today there remain five countries that have not ratified the Charter, but have ratified the Convention (Morocco, Sahrawi Republic, Somalia, South Sudan and Tunisia). The politics of the differential ratification process is further reflected upon by Mbise (2017: 1237), who puts forward two possible explanations for the approach African governments adopted to the ratification of the Convention compared to the ratification of their own regional charter. The first relates to the psychological legacy of colonialism and coloniality which has resulted in Africans reproducing the notion of Western superiority and African inferiority in their own decision-making processes and actions. The resulting outcome of this legacy is that knowledge that emerges in the west or the Global North has come to be seen by both African leaders and many within the populations they govern as sources of 'authorized truths', leading to a greater inclination among African governments to ratify the Convention which had been predominately drafted by Northern governments. The second relates to the nature and status of the first country that ratified each of these treaties and the position it holds in the eyes of other countries on the continent. As Mbise puts it:

Being the first African colony south of the Sahara to declare sovereignty from colonial rule in 1957, Ghana was hailed as the trailblazer for what president Kwame Nkrumah[4] called the decade of independence in Africa … and even sowed the seeds of the civil rights movement in America. This political legacy may have influenced African countries to rally behind it in the ratification of the Convention triggering a bandwagon effect for the rest of the continent. However, we do not see the same trendsetter in the adoption of the African charter. As the first adopter to ratify the Charter (in 1992), the state of Seychelles did not have the same effect on subsequent adoption. It took much longer for most major states on the continent to follow through, with Nigeria, Egypt, South Africa, and Kenya only ratifying the Charter after 2000. This stunting effect has continued from the policy to implementation. Indeed, many child welfare personnel on the continent are unaware of the Charter and this has significantly limited its utilisation. (Mbise, 2017: 1238)

Therefore, for Mbise, Ghana's position in the political imagination of other African countries as the first sub-Saharan African country in the continent to gain independence from European colonial rule provided an impetus for other countries in the region to also seek to quickly follow in its footsteps in ratifying the Convention once it had done so. By contrast, the fact that Seychelles, a country which appears not to hold the same status as Ghana in the imagination of other African governments, is, according to Mbise, a contributory factor to the distinct lack of momentum in ratifying the Charter.

Critiquing the disproportionate focus on dissonance between Southern childhoods and global children's rights norms

Narratives or arguments about dissonance between dominant children's rights discourses and the realities of the lives of children and their families in contexts in the South are not the only narratives that can be identified on the continent. This is due to the fact that at the same time as notions of human and children's rights were evolving in European and North American contexts, transformations were also taking place in so-called 'non-Western contexts' – not least because of interactions – voluntarily or involuntarily – with Western European and North American societies. These evolutions, which have spread unevenly across contexts, provide the backdrop for the emergence of exceptions to a narrative that has, hitherto, centred around the imposition of a 'Western' concept of children's rights on diverse parts of the world as a form of cultural imperialism.

Notably, there are emerging groups in countries in the South who define human rights or children's rights in light of dominant global discourses, and use the indicators set by global rights norms to measure the wellbeing and welfare of children (and indeed, other groups) in their own contexts (see Archibald and Richards, 2002; Merry, 2006; Kaime, 2011; Atiemo, 2012; Twum-Danso Imoh, 2019). For example, Shepler (2005, 2012), in her work on childhoods in post-conflict Sierra Leone, demonstrates how both adults and children in local communities use the Western construction of childhood and the children's rights discourse strategically, particularly to facilitate the reintegration of former child combatants, many of whom have committed horrible atrocities on their fellow community members, back into these same communities. This is supported by Archibald and Richards (2002: 351) who, in their study on Sierra Leone, found that 'young people are making claims in terms of human rights – that becoming an adult is an inevitable aspect of common humanity, and that whether or not young people make a successful transition to adulthood should not have to depend on the whim of patrons'. They add that young people use the language of rights when commenting on 'injustices leading to social exclusion and problems over the transition to adulthood' (Archibald and Richards, 2002: 351–352). Based on their findings they suggest that the local rights discourse has been reshaped both by the weakening of local hierarchies as well as a widening of the space for the increase in individualism. Both of these developments, they argue, are as a result of changes brought about by the decade-long war and the post-war recovery process (Archibald and Richards, 2002). In turn, Cheney (2007: 44) demonstrates that the concept of children's rights has permeated Ugandan society to such an extent that 'even children – often more than their parents and guardians – emphasize attaining their rights as essential to full citizenship' (see also Twum-Danso Imoh, 2019). These narratives are not unique to Africa. Similar attitudes have been noted in Latin America. Writing of Chile, Argentina and Ecuador, Grugel and Peruzzotti (2012) note that the introduction of children's rights discourses in discussions of children's welfare transformed how civil society organizations started to think and act in the years after 1989. Liebel (2020) provides further evidence of this in relation to Australia where he highlights the case of Indigenous activists who are committed to ensuring the realization of the best interest principle as articulated within dominant children's rights frameworks for children within their communities (see also Harris-Short, 2001).

These attitudes and actions that exist complicate narratives about global and dominant children's rights discourses and their progress (or lack thereof) in different contexts. The reality is, in fact, more nuanced. While for many children in these societies there is a significant gap between their lived experiences and the childhood envisioned in dominant global human rights discourses, for others, their experience may be more mixed – consisting of both dissonance and synergies (see Twum-Danso Imoh, 2019). Specifically, the experiences of these children show that narratives about the inapplicability of children's rights in relation to contexts in the South do not provide a sufficiently holistic portrayal of the plurality of childhoods in these societies. Furthermore, they do not demonstrate the varying ways these diverse constructions of childhood respectively interact with global rights discourses and their attendant policies. By contrast, there are emerging other studies that illustrate that in addition to the challenges that children's rights and human rights traditions more generally face, there are sections within a given population who see, or wish to see, the applicability of these principles and provisions in their own contexts (see Twum-Danso Imoh, 2019, 2020). What this, in effect, means is that within a given context, understandings, perceptions and the meaning of childhood may differ, notably as a result of variables such as class, geographical location, family type, education and socioeconomic background as well as the uneven impact of the legacy of colonialism and globalization (Hecht, 1998; Hollos, 2002; Rizzini and Barker, 2002; Naftali, 2014; Twum-Danso Imoh, 2016). This, in turn, has implications for attitudes, perspectives and lived realities of children's rights or human rights more generally in a given locale.

The importance of this intra-societal diversity in the Global South makes it difficult to assert claims about the inapplicability of children's rights within a whole country or even a given community. Certainly, while these rights may be inapplicable for some, it cannot be overlooked that for others – albeit a minority in some contexts – these rights as stipulated in international law are seen as applicable or, at the very least, desirable (Twum-Danso Imoh, 2019). As Naftali puts it in relation to China:

> From a pragmatic point of view, however, the fact that the child rights discourse 'claims to be universal but is really the product of a specific cultural and historical origin' (Kennedy, 2004:18) may be irrelevant. Just as the western origins of the child rights tradition may cause some people in non-Western countries to regard it with suspicion, for others these specific origins make it all the more attractive. (Naftali, 2014: 11)

Naftali's point about how the 'Western' origins of dominant children's rights principles have become appealing to some sections of Chinese societies illuminates a perspective that requires some discussion. Notably, it leads us to pose questions about the extent to which 'the West' or the state of being 'Western', which needs to be understood as a construction in and of itself, has been not only displaced from its spatial and geographical boundaries, but has also been dislodged from its association with countries that had been settler colonies of European countries (for example, Australia, New Zealand). Instead, it is now being reconstructed or reproduced in contexts which have, hitherto, been considered as 'non-Western' (due to their geographical location or the distinct absence of significant European settler populations) after centuries of interactions between these countries and so-called 'Western' countries which have primarily taken the form of trade, including that based on humans, colonial rule, missionary engagement and the establishment of formal education systems. The resulting outcome is that within these contexts there exist sections of the population for whom what it means to be 'Western' or 'non-Western' is no longer clearly distinguishable (see Atiemo, 2012; Twum-Danso Imoh, 2016).[5] This clearly has implications for attitudes towards childhood, child-rearing, child welfare and children's rights.

Factors driving intra-societal diversity in intersections between children's lived realities and dominant children's rights discourses in sub-Saharan Africa

Numerous factors underpin this intra-societal diversity in understandings of childhood in Southern contexts. In relation to sub-Saharan Africa, while much of this can be attributed to the enormous social changes that the continent has experienced, some of it was already evident in the structure and organization of pre-colonial African societies. Hence, a variability of experiences and attitudes is not a new development in the region due to processes of social change because culture, in any context, cannot be regarded as monolithic and uniformly interpreted by *all* members of a group at any given moment in time. Consequently, it cannot have the same impact on all members of a group (Korbin, 2002). For instance, An-Na'im and Hammond (2002: 35) posit that the extent to which a particular culture provides value and meaning to the lives of the people who participate in it 'may vary among the members of the culture and may itself be the subject of different interpretations'. Further, as a conscious construction, culture can be manipulated by dominant forces in society who possess considerable power within the community. As Liebel puts it:

> Affirmations about culture made on behalf of entire minority groups neglect the interests and power structures within that group that should be examined and criticized to the same extent as similar claims in society at large. Indigenous and minority communities, as well as society in general, are made up of privileged members who have the powers to represent and even define the group, and members who are silenced or lack power. The process of categorizing individuals and making assumptions about their needs and preferences based on minority status limits them and excludes the possibilities they might have preferred. (Liebel, 2020: 141)

Thus, it is possible that in a given society, a large proportion of the population may not have been included in the prevailing construction of that culture, and may, in fact, not subscribe to it or may reluctantly adhere to it due the fear of being ostracized or sanctioned. This argument's significance can be seen in several ways. For instance, if we recognize that culture is a construct as opposed to something that is a given in a society, then it can be argued that culture is not a homogeneous entity that serves the interests of all members of a particular community at any given moment and that there are, in fact, always some members of a group who deviate, or wish to deviate, from prevailing norms (Renteln, 2004; Liebel, 2020). The implication of this for the discourse of children's rights is that within a community there will be different perspectives on child-rearing which will have a knock-on effect on different children's experiences of their rights within a given community (see Twum-Danso Imoh, 2012b, 2016, 2019; Liebel, 2020).

Beyond this variability between culture and its different interactions with community members depending on their socioeconomic positioning in the context in which they live, the fluidity of culture is a factor that needs to be taken into account as this has implications for changing attitudes and practices towards childhood conceptualization and child wellbeing over time. Sub-Saharan Africa presents a good example as it demonstrates the importance of considering colonialism and capitalism in understanding the ways culture intersects with the lived realities of diverse groups of children and their families. Of particular significance are developments relating to the colonization of territories in the region in the years after the Berlin Conference in 1884/1885, and the activities of missionaries, which preceded the formal colonization of much of the continent and sought to spread, through evangelization, their particular denomination of Christian teachings among Indigenes (see Merry, 1992; Stephens, 1995; Valentin and Meinert, 2009; Vallgårda et al, 2015). With regards to the majority of sub-Saharan African countries, colonization led to efforts to inculcate changes in behaviours by a powerful state machinery which was charged with civilizing Indigenous populations through the introduction of a range of laws and policies. These included those that directly affected children, such as education, marriage, family life, hygiene and social welfare (Alber et al, 2010; Spronk, 2014; Aderinto, 2015; Twum-Danso Imoh, 2016, 2020). In fact, it has been argued that children were particular targets of the colonial administration which sought to 'remake African childhoods in a way that would both support and justify the social and economic priorities of the colonial project' (Diptee and Klein, 2010: 3; see also McNee, 2004). While a number of policies had little effect on local populations, it must be acknowledged that some have managed to seep through into society. In fact, they have been imbibed by certain sectors of the population who work hard to preserve these values while scorning more local beliefs or whose outlook incorporates both local and Westernized values (see Twum-Danso, 2008; Twum-Danso Imoh, 2016, 2020). This fluidity in outlook and behaviours is what leads Howard (1986: 23) to claim that 'people are quite adept at being cultural accommodationists; they are able implicitly to choose which aspects of a "new" culture they wish to adopt and which aspects of the "old" they wish to retain'. Among these diverse social groups that exist in a given society, transformations in local behaviours and practices were observed during this period, many of which affected conceptualizations of childhood and experiences of child-rearing practices (Alber et al, 2010; Aderinto, 2015).

For example, a key element of the historical transformations stimulated by the colonial state in all territories was the introduction of cash into economies that had previously used other forms of currency (Little, 1953; Rwezaura, 1994; Allman, 1997; Alber et al, 2010). While the initial use of the new money was limited, colonial governments in territories across the continent found ways to create a demand for this new currency by, for example, imposing a range of taxes on individuals and households, the forced sale of livestock, and the enforced cultivation of cash crops (Rwezaura, 1994). The resulting outcome for many colonized territories on the continent was the emergence of the concepts, and the reality, of individualized wealth (Alber et al, 2010) and private property (Merry, 2006) as well as the realization that this new currency could become a substitute for customary obligation (Little, 1953; Rwezaura, 1994). The increasing reliance on cash led to a dependency on the market to meet the needs of the household. This resulted in the migration of economically active men from rural areas to urban centres in search of wage employment to be able to meet various needs and demands which now required cash as a form of payment (Little, 1953; Rwezaura, 1994; Merry, 2006). In the process, social relations were affected in a number of societies. For instance, by moving to urban areas and engaging in a form of wage labour, young men were able to pay for marriage-related costs themselves instead of relying on their elders. This offered them more autonomy in the choice of marriage partners and positioned them to challenge the authority of their elders, thereby enabling them to make key decisions about their lives. This transformation emerges in Grier's (2006: 70) account of child labour in colonial Zimbabwe when she argues that young men and adolescent boys' experiences of living away from home and earning wages ended 'the monopoly senior males hitherto exercised over the homestead's resources and the male transition to senior status' (see also Rich, 2010). In particular, young men were able to use their wages to pay for their own bride wealth which enabled them to have more control over the time and the manner in which they transitioned from junior to senior status in their society.

As individual men increasingly assumed sole responsibility for paying the required bride price, which was key to the initiation of marriage in many societies, they assumed sole responsibility for, and rights over, not just their wife, but also any children produced as a consequence of that union. In particular, the costs of raising those children, which increasingly came to consist of school fees (Rwezaura, 1994; Allman, 1997; Allman and Tashjian, 2000), became the responsibility of biological fathers to bear as opposed to the wider kinship group. The implication of these developments in some societies was that children born within such a marriage began to be seen as the sole responsibility of their biological father, which, it has been argued, was critical to forging and strengthening closer bonds within the nuclear family unit (Kaye, 1962).

Another example that highlights the factors driving social change in African societies is the introduction of formal education, which was initially largely provided by missionary groups as a principal component of their strategy for converting and civilizing groups they saw as 'primitive heathens'. Schools offered missionaries the opportunity to impart, in a systematic way, what they considered to be 'proper' values to children as part of an attempt to counter the perceived negative influence of family and culture. Boarding schools, in particular, provided an effective environment to ensure the transmission and consolidation of the ideas and values of missionaries while reducing engagement with the familial grouping of the child. The impact of this was that children attending these schools were taught to perceive their culture and families as inferior, ultimately leading in some communities to tensions and conflicts between generations (Okonjo, 1970; Smythe, 1997).

In relation to individualism, literacy acquired in schools allowed the private acquisition of knowledge through books (Howard, 1992). What this meant was that no longer did children and young people have to rely on the knowledge of their elders for their own learning and development. The spread of school-based education and its reliance on books meant that they were now able to gain knowledge independently, which may also have led to the development of worldviews that contrasted with those of previous generations (see Twum-Danso Imoh, 2020). This contributed to the breakdown of group cohesion in diverse contexts (Howard, 1986; Windborne, 2006). In some cases, the development of this knowledge gained from books led young people to challenge traditional power relations which no longer corresponded with their desires, wishes and personal goals. Added to that, progressing through this form of education gradually led to a further disconnection between individuals and their community. Smythe (1997) puts it well when she claims that those boys who were able to access schooling among the Fipa of Tanzania were, as adults, more likely than those who had not been educated to move away from their hometowns in search of work as well as strive to ensure that their children were also educated within schools. Therefore, a successful school career resulted in an individual, especially those from rural areas, moving further and further away from their natal community in pursuit of the highly desired salaried jobs which often came with a pension and sometimes accommodation. Related to this, it is important to note that the jobs that individuals were able to access following a successful school career were distinct from those occupations previously characterized as key to the domestic economy of their natal communities. No longer did the education provided seek to develop skills that were critical to the domestic economy of each community – farming, fishing, weaving and other crafts. Instead, the institution of the school resulted in new occupational opportunities that often required individuals, especially those from rural areas, to move away from their hometown (see also Rich, 2010). Thus, colonialization and the widespread evangelization of missionary groups were critical drivers of many of the social and cultural changes witnessed among certain sectors of populations in countries across sub-Saharan Africa in recent decades.

These two examples represent well some of the factors that have driven Africa's own social transformations over the last few hundred years and, thus, help to reinforce the argument that in the same way European and North American societies encountered upheavals in their societies, which resulted in new ways of being, so also have African societies. Such changes in sub-Saharan Africa are among those that have contributed to a situation whereby new ideas about childhood, child development and child welfare coexist with understandings that have been passed down for generations. What this means is that while dominant discourses of children's rights may be very much at odds with the realities of some children's lives on the continent, for others, this discourse of children's rights, underpinned by a particular image of childhood, may not at all be alien to the worldview of their families and communities or their lived realities of growing up.

Interestingly, despite the fact that many societies in the South have been experiencing enormous changes, not least as a result of their encounters with Western Europe and North America, studies of Southern societies have tended to sacralize culture in their analyses of these contexts. This results in a failure to sufficiently consider the fluidity of culture and the impact of social change within a given locale. As Harris-Short notes:

> The 'freezing of 'traditional' cultures in pre-colonial history ignores the effects of decades of colonial rule, the breakdown of traditional communal structures in the wake of economic transformations, and the 'corrupting' influence of 'Western values' on the ideological aspirations of the members of the group. It also denies these various cultures the capacity to change, develop and evolve. (Harris-Short, 2001: 211–312)

This sacralization of culture has been especially evident in accounts seeking to explain African societies. Hountondji (1996), for instance, outlines how effectively this has been done in relation to the continent:

Different anthropologists at various times have always either affirmed the supremacy of the West, presenting it as possessing the only mature civilization while other societies are at best at the early stages of a process which the West has already completed (Levy-Bruhl and the classical evolutionists), or conversely, in a gesture of repentance which is still motivated by the same comparative problematic, they have tried to show that European civilization is not unique but that there are others, equally valid. But of course, these other civilizations are now in contact with Europe and as a result of colonization have been subjected to an involuntary process of Westernization; pluralist anthropologists refuse to consider their present condition, but prefer to try and reconstruct their pre-colonial existence. Moreover, when they investigate this pre-colonial past, they refuse to see the evolution, revolutions and discontinuities that may have affected it, and the precarious balance which has made these civilizations temporarily what they are today. (Hountondji, 1996: 163)

In relation to the field of childhood studies, Sarada Balagopalan critiques the social constructionist or multiple childhoods paradigm put forward, most notably by Allison James and Alan Prout (1997). Specifically, she claims that this paradigm allows for 'a certain essentialist, non-modern understandings of these cultures to prevail' (Balagopalan, 2002: 21). In a later publication, Balagopalan expands on her critique of the multiple childhoods concept promoted by the social construction of childhood:

While multiple childhoods had conceptually aided in avoiding a pathological reading of children's lives in the non-west, it had inadvertently placed their cultural worlds as largely outside of history, the state, and the market. Delinking these lives from the larger workings of power had simultaneously parochialized them, inadvertently setting up a 'separate but equal' comparative register for understanding children's lives in the non-west. (Balagopalan, 2014: 12)

Her critique extends to the various localized studies that have been produced as a result of this paradigm as they contain such descriptive details about the lives of children in the South leading to the production of 'a cultural specificity that simultaneously rendered them more isolated and anachronistic' (Balagopalan, 2014: 13). It is this lack of situating Indigenous childhoods within a broader context shaped by history, globalization and market forces that leads Balagopalan to claim that what she refers to as the 'culturalist paradigm' presents children's lives in the Global North compared to the Global South as separate but equal. This, she argues, is problematic as it suggests that the childhoods of children in non-Western societies are to be respected but not desired.

Conclusion

As part of its objective of subjecting the notion of children's rights as imperialistic and a Western imposition to scrutiny, this chapter has demonstrated that while arguments about cultural imperialism are valid in relation to the way dominant children's rights discourses and policies intersect with the lives of some groups of children and their families, their experiences of rights are not the only story or narrative that exists in a given locale at any moment in time. Instead, added to these narratives that illuminate the dissonance between dominant discourses of children's rights and other worldviews and lived realities, there can also be identified attitudes and lived experiences that demonstrate other perceptions and experiences of dominant children's rights principles, some of which align with these very principles to varying degrees. This variation in conceptualizations and experiences can be attributed to the specific positioning of an individual, not only in relation to contemporary processes of social change, but also with regards to structures established or driven by colonial governmental and non-governmental forces.

4

Historical Approaches to Child Welfare in Ghana

Introduction

Ghana presents an interesting case study to explore the variability that exists in a given society in relation to the intersections, or interactions, between dominant children's rights norms and the lived realities of children and their families. In order to understand the plurality that this variability produces it is first important to take a long historical view to child welfare and the emergence of children's rights as a framework to guide policy interventions and public debates. Such an exercise helps to situate narratives about the plurality of childhoods within a broader historical, political, economic and cultural context. Thus, the next two chapters seek to provide the contextual background needed to explain the road upon which the country now known as Ghana travelled to reach the point whereby dominant children's rights language and thinking entered the lexicon used nationally to discuss children's welfare, wellbeing and interests in this context.

This chapter, in particular, aims to track, from a historical perspective, strategies and approaches adopted to ensure the welfare and development of children's rights from the pre-colonial to the post-colonial period, with the view to trying to identify the point at which the concept of children's rights started being deployed to discuss issues of child welfare. While the structure of the chapter is set out chronologically, it is important to understand that I do not view the adoption of the approaches discussed in this chapter as a linear process, especially in relation to those discussed in the section I refer to as the 'pre-colonial' era as these were not only prevalent during that period, but continue to serve as key strategies to secure child welfare for many families and communities, even today. Further, policies and approaches discussed during the colonial period continued to have an impact in the post-colonial period through the continued use of laws and policies established in the colonial period in the decades that followed the country's achievement of independence from Britain, including in the present day.

Pre-colonial strategies to ensure the survival, welfare and education of children

Strategies to ensure children's education, welfare and protection were an inherent part of the social and political organization of all societies in the country now known as Ghana in the period before colonization or before their first documented encounters with foreign actors. Historically, such arrangements were embedded within communities and involved numerous families belonging to a kinship group or clan. This approach was based on the belief that children belonged to the entire lineage, not to their biological parents (see Goody, 1973, 1982; Oppong, 1973; Azu, 1974; Isiugo-Abanihe, 1985). As Verhoef (2005: 370) claims, writing more broadly about sub-Saharan Africa: 'Motherhood might be central to the female identity throughout sub-Saharan Africa, but rarely is it assumed that the birth mother alone can raise competent children. Instead, the "motherhood" concept allows for various "relatives" to participate in different aspects of nurturing, socializing, and educating children.' The implication of this understanding of relatedness and parenting is that while a man and woman may have a child together, many other members of the kinship group will be involved, and in fact, should be, in the rearing of the child, especially after they have been weaned (Oppong, 1973; Nsamenang, 1992; Nukunya, 2003).

This communal responsibility was largely carried out through kinship fostering – a process in which children were passed on to people other than their own parents (but still within the same kinship group) for training services or companionship without losing parental rights (Ardayfio-Schandorf and Amissah, 1996). This system of fosterage enabled such children to gain access to resources and eased the burden of care on parents who could not cope with the childcare responsibility. It also strengthened, or reaffirmed, family ties or political relationships and enabled children to learn a trade (see Goody, 1982). Its importance in society can be seen by the fact that it was not an ad hoc practice but institutionalized in many societies within the area now known as Ghana. In some cases, biological parents had little authority over their children due to the expectation that children will be fostered out to members of kin from an early age. Depending on the lineage pattern of the family and the gender of the child, maternal or paternal uncles, aunts and grandparents could claim a child from their sibling or child and biological parents would not be able to refuse (Goody, 1973, 1982; Oppong, 1973; Schildkrout, 1973; Azu, 1974; Isiugo-Abanihe, 1985; Nsamenang, 1992; Kuyini et al, 2009). Oppong (1973), for instance, presents evidence in her study of children in Dagbon, northern Ghana, which illustrates the key role socializing agents other than biological parents played in a child's life. In particular, she demonstrates how members of kin had claims upon the children produced by their biological or classificatory brother or sister, a claim, which, if exercised, was almost impossible for biological parents to refuse. She adds that:

> In the extreme case a father's sibling may come and take a child to train as he wishes, or a mother's brother may come to claim a son on the pain of death, or again grandparents may curse their children with death, disease, or hell for not giving them some grandchildren to rear and serve them. (Oppong,1973: 44; see also Kuyini et al, 2009)

Among the Gonja of northern Ghana, it was an obligation of parents to send their children either to the mother's brother or the father's sister depending on their gender. The exception to the rule was the eldest son who was not required to leave his father's house (see Goody, 1973). It was difficult to refuse such requests as doing so could endanger the life of the child. Therefore, within these contexts distinctions were historically made between those who conceived and bore the child (biological parent) and those who reared the child (social parent) (Goody, 1982; Isiugo-Abanihe, 1985; Nsamenang, 1992). This understanding of what constitutes relatedness and 'proper' parenthood provides an insight into the institutionalization, at least historically, of the practice of one form of child fosterage, kinship fosterage, within Ghanaian society, in particular. As a result of the institutionalized nature of the practice, fosterage not only occurred during times of crisis, but also as part of everyday child-rearing and training arrangements within families during times of stability.

Central to the function of kinship fosterage were the arrangements put in place for not only the rearing of children, but also their training. Learning, in this period, was embedded within the community, and it was believed that for children to learn effectively in this environment, numerous actors were required to take responsibility for their training and education, from a young age and for long periods of time, sometimes until they transitioned to adulthood. As White (1996) puts it, since learning occurred in a community setting, the child was able to have several teachers at any given stage of development (see also Okonjo, 1970; Urch, 1974; Zoller Booth, 2004). As a process that was community-based, the education provided at this time was intrinsically linked to the lifestyle, daily routine and priorities of a given community and its domestic economy. Further, this form of education sought to preserve traditional norms and patterns of life and thereby ensured continuity within a community from one generation to the next (see Zoller Booth, 2004; Ugboajah, 2008). These arrangements were put in place due to the importance placed on both parenthood and the training of children. Therefore, it was imperative for members of the extended family to participate in the rearing of the children within their kinship grouping in order for them to grow up disciplined and well trained (see Nukunya, 2003).

As a result, fosterage among kin was a key function in the learning process as it enabled children to gain access to resources, receive a good education or learn a trade such as cultivation techniques, animal husbandry, fishing, metal work, sculpture and weaving (see Goody, 1982). This education was not merely skill-based; it also sought to instil discipline in children and ensure they imbibed teachings about good behaviour, politeness and coping skills as well as behaviours which were seen as important attributes in the development of a 'good' character within their community (Azu, 1974; Renne, 2003; Riisoen et al, 2004; Alber et al, 2010; Twum-Danso Imoh, 2012a). In terms of character development and behaviour, kinship fosterage was seen to facilitate the development of these attributes as biological parents were not perceived as the best people to look after their children and, as a result, should not keep all of them. Among the Ga-Dangme ethnic group of the Greater Accra region there was a belief that parents pampered their children and did not exercise that 'little bit of hardness, if not harshness, that the *Gas* [*Ga-Dangme*] believe to be an essential ingredient of the socialization process' (Azu, 1974: 45).

In making these arrangements about child-rearing and caring the language of rights was absent in the same way it was missing from the framing of child welfare and children's interests in much of Europe and the Americas prior to the 20th century. As Kwaw (2015) states, the notion of children as holders of rights that are distinct from their parents did not exist in this period as children were seen as part of a network of relationships in a community that centred around mutual rights and reciprocal obligations (see also Manful and Manful, 2014). Further, within this framing, children were regarded as properties of their lineage (Frimpong-Manso, 2014).

This issue of lineage raises an important point that requires underscoring; notably, it highlights the prominence of collectivist principles within these communities which foregrounded interdependence, mutual support, collective responsibility and reciprocal obligations (see Twum-Danso Imoh, 2020, 2022; Chapter 3, this volume). Underpinning this focus was the construction of personhood underscored by the understanding that humans are communal and social by nature as well as weak and, hence, cannot fully fend for themselves or live or function effectively in isolation from others (Gyekye, 1996, 2013). Instead, the belief historically in this context was that in order for an individual to survive and to fulfil their own personal objectives in life they need others (see also Cobbah, 1987). This positioning of the individual within the context of the group led to a situation whereby the rights and wellbeing of the kinship group tended to be prioritized over those of the individual. This does not mean that within these contexts individuality and the worth of the individual were not recognized (see Asante, 2009; Gyekye, 2013; Oyowe, 2014; Twum-Danso Imoh, 2022); but it does illustrate the extent to which the interests of the community or collective were held above those of the individual.

While this emphasis on collectivity was recognized as supporting the wellbeing of communities and their members, it did have adverse implications for some individuals, especially if subsuming the needs of individuals within those of the collective would better serve the interests of the community (see Twum-Danso Imoh, 2020). Windborne (2006: 160), for instance, writing of Ghana, refers to Zechenter (1997), who argues that sacrifices are 'consistently made by the least powerful for the benefit of the most powerful members of the group'. To elucidate this point, it is worth noting two practices. The first, child pawning, also known as debt bondage or pledging, which, although prohibited in the Gold Coast in 1874 along with slavery, continued to be identified in parts of the country well into the 20th century (Coe, 2012). The occurrence of the practice of child pawning among the matrilineal Akan of Ghana occurred within a context in which the household head was seen as holding legal responsibility for his sister's children, including being responsible for any debts they incurred or crimes they committed (Grier, 1992). The flip side of this responsibility was that he also possessed the legal right to pawn these dependents for whom he was legally responsible. This pawning involved the transfer of an individual, in most cases a child (often a girl), from his or her natal home to that of a third party to be held as collateral or security for loans owed by the household head and remain there until the debt was fully repaid (Coe, 2012). Although in most cases the period of bondage was temporary, the household head did reserve the right to sell the pawn outright if he so wished (Grier, 1992). The labour of these bonded children, which included trading, farming and panning for gold, served as interest paid on loans and was used to pay off the debt owed (Grier, 1992; Coe, 2012; Cammaert, 2015). Added to profiting off the fruits of her labour, the creditor also had the right to have sexual intercourse with the pawn without compromising the terms of the debt (Grier, 1992). Any child born as an outcome of such an act was seen as belonging to the debtor – that is, the household head who had pawned the child, not the creditor.

The second practice, *trokosi*, is a form of ritual servitude which, although outlawed, is still practised among the Ewe ethnic group which is, historically, associated with the Volta and Oti regions of the country. Although there are various entry routes for, invariably, a girl to become a *trokosi*, which means 'slave of the gods', one of the primary reasons is due to the belief that as an individual within a family had committed a transgression against a god, such as lying, theft, adultery, murder or rape, it is required for one person within that kinship grouping to bear the brunt of the punishment. The rationale behind this is explained by Bilyeu (1999: 471): 'Ghanaians believe the practice stems from a philosophy that sees justice and punishment as communal; an individual with no connection to a crime may be punished to spare others. Similarly, when one person's offence goes unpunished, vengeance may be wreaked upon the entire community.' Those individuals who are put forward as the 'sacrificial lamb' to compensate the gods for perceived infractions have invariably been virgin girls who are usually aged between six and eight years old (Bilyeu, 1999; Ameh, 2004; Greene, 2009; Asomah, 2015). Unlike pawning this arrangement had a much longer-term duration (Bilyeu, 1999; Asomah, 2015). While for some the period of their bondage comes to an end by the time they turn 15, for others it continues for the rest of their lives. In fact, even life-long servitude is not always sufficient to appease the gods:

> Occasionally, the family must offer another female virgin if the *Trokosi* dies while at the shrine. If the *Trokosi* is not replaced, it is alleged that the refusal will lead to a recurrence of calamities in the family of the wrongdoer. It can go on for generations. Different girls pay for the same offense, from generation to generation. Today, there are some women bound to shrines who represent the fifth successive generation to pay for a [single] crime. (Bilyeu, 1999: 472; see also Asomah, 2015)

It is noteworthy that in the early years when this practice was initiated, cattle were seen as the satisfactory sacrifice for the gods for an incurred infraction. However, the eventual decision to use a young girl to pay the penance for the transgression of her family member came about as a result of the demands of the priests who insisted that only a virgin could appease the gods for the crime committed as well as because of an economic rationale on the part of families as girls were seen as a cheaper form of compensation than cattle (Bilyeu, 1999). During their time of servitude *trokosis* are expected to cook and clean for the priests as well as work on their farms, with any profits going to the priests. Although the girls live with the priests, it is their families who are expected to continue providing for them and eventually pay for their funeral. Priests are not obligated to provide for the girls or any children they may bear during their period of servitude. While becoming a *trokosi* means that a girl is now married to the gods, in reality this signifies that they are recognized as the wives of the priests who are seen as representatives of the gods. As a wife, then, girls are subjected to sexual intercourse by priests, who, as the human form of the gods, act on their behalf, especially after the girl's menarche.

What emerges in this section is that Indigenous communities in the area now known as Ghana had clear strategies for ensuring the survival, development training and welfare of children embedded within their organizational structures. It is important to note that these strategies are not assigned to the past. They continue to persist among families and communities and demonstrate the extent to which, despite the social changes that have affected the country, these have not led to the wholesale replacement of child-rearing practices that have existed for generations with new norms and practices. Further, this analysis has shown that, as a result of the emphasis placed on the interests of the group above those of the individual, some strategies developed were not designed to ensure the welfare and wellbeing of children, especially due to the fact that preserving the wellbeing of the group tended to override the welfare of the individual. Therefore, some approaches to the survival of the group resulted in adverse outcomes for certain sections of the population within a given community, notably women and children.

The interventions of colonial actors on child welfare issues

The involvement of foreign actors in children's welfare, protection and education can arguably be traced back to European missionaries of different denominations who arrived in the area now known as Ghana in the 15th century with the objective to both civilize and convert what they perceived as the 'primitive', 'backward', 'heathen' 'savages' they found across the land. While missionaries had been present in the area from the 15th century it was the 19th century which saw an intensification of missionary engagement in this locale:

> Socially, the Gold Coast experienced a flurry of missionary activity in the 19th century. The Basel Mission gained foothold in Akropong from the 1830s, where they laid a firm foundation for the Presbyterian Church. The Wesleyan Mission sent out Rev. Joseph Dunwell in 1835 in response to an appeal from a Cape Coast Scripture Society. He was succeeded in 1836 by Thomas Birch Freeman. The Bremen (North German) Missionary Society opened a station at Peki (1847) and at Ho (1857). In 1880, the Catholics returned to resume evangelical work in the Gold Coast. Besides planting the Christian faith these Christian missions were the first to introduce western-style education. (Addo-Fenning, 2013: 40)

Using the institution of the school in particular, missionary groups focused their efforts on transmitting so-called 'civilized knowledge', recognized as being critical to the achievement of religious and moral conversion, on those perceived as children as they were seen as being conduits into their communities (see Chapter 3, this volume). Thus, converting this group, it was believed, would lead to the eventual religious transformation of society as a whole (Koonar, 2014). As missionaries managed schools as well as churches, going to school meant converting to Christianity for many as school children were required to be baptized in the Christian denomination to which the school they attended belonged. As a result, missionary engagement within a community led to widespread conversions in predominately southern and central parts of the country largely due to the increasing popularity of the institution of the school.

Other than the provision of schooling, which had the objective of enabling new converts to be able to read the Bible, missionaries were also involved in other welfare projects relating to infant and maternal welfare and caring for vulnerable groups of children and others. In relation to children, Frimpong-Manso summarizes the role these groups played:

> Informal, missionary activity in caring for abandoned, orphaned and infirm children was of particular importance especially in instances where cultural inhibitions forbade certain categories of children from being raised in the traditional family or the urban centres where the traditional foster care was non-existent. The Presbyterian and Methodist churches, for instance, established schools for disabled children (Anson-Yevu, 1988). Infant welfare centres operated by Missionaries also helped to reduce infant mortality, from 360/1000 live births in 1915 to 95/1000 live births by 1931. (Frimpong-Manso, 2014: 412; see also Allman, 1994)

A notable example of early missionary activity within the formally declared colony of the Gold Coast was evident shortly after its then Governor, George Cumine Strahan (1874–1876), abolished slavery and slave dealing through two pieces of legislation: the Slave Dealing Abolition Ordinance of 1874; and the Emancipation of Slaves Ordinance, which declared all slaves free on 5 November 1874. While these laws had little impact on the lived experiences and practices of many Indigenes, some missionary groups played a central role in assisting and protecting freed slaves. As Lawani writes about Basel missionaries:

> Accounts of the Basel Mission indicate that in most areas, slaves left their masters upon hearing of the emancipation proclamation. The Basel missionaries on several occasions manumitted slaves and also helped emancipated slaves to resettle by way of training. Indeed, mission stations, particularly in Kukurantumi and Anyinam became places of refuge for runaway slaves. (Lawani, 2016: 44)

While missionaries continued to play a significant role in welfare activities, the role of government became more apparent in the early 20th century following the formal colonization of the region. Numerous European countries established their power and control over the land that the Portuguese, upon their arrival in 1471, named Costa da Mina ('Coast of the Mine'); however, it was the British who translated it into English as 'the Gold Coast' when they established formal colonial structures in this area upon their arrival due to the copious supplies of gold found in this locale. Britain's initial interactions with this area in the 19th century were centred on trade in palm oil, cotton, rubber and gum copal. This represented a shift in trading focus that was partly driven by the abolishment of the transatlantic slave trade in the British Empire in 1807 (Addo-Fenning, 2013). Gugler and Flanagan explain it thus:

> After the abolition of that inhuman enterprise, European commercial involvement in West Africa expanded rather than diminished. Industrial growth in Europe created rising demand for oils and fats; palm oil and later palm kernels and groundnuts became the staple exports of West Africa. Palm products and groundnuts could be produced efficiently and on a small scale by households possessing little capital, employing family labor, and using traditional tools. An economic transformation in major parts of the coastal hinterland set in that took them from subsistence to cash crop production by independent agriculturalists. (Gugler and Flanagan, 1978: 98)

These efforts by both traders and the colonial authorities to explore alternative ways of exploiting the sub-region's resources, in turn, resulted in the growth of commercial agriculture, leading Indigenous groups in the Gold Coast, including children, to migrate to other parts of the territory in search for more land to cultivate for profit. This led to changing the economic roles of both women and children in Indigenous societies (Gugler and Flanagan, 1978; Allman, 1994; Addo-Fenning, 2013; Sackey and Johannesen, 2015).

While formal colonialization by the British, which was built around the concept of indirect rule through native administration, did not take place until the late 19th century – 1874 – some elements of a formal colonial structure were established by the British in the early decades of the 19th century; a notable example is the Gold Coast police force founded in 1831 (Boateng and Darko, 2016). This initial attempt to formalize the control and subjugation of this area and its peoples by the British was initially focused on the coastal areas of the Gold Coast, but over time, it encroached further inland, eventually encompassing a greater land area by the end of the 19th century. Konadu and Campbell outline the geography of what constituted the Gold Coast by the turn of the 20th century:

> The physical geography of the colony that later became Ghana was formed by 1901, after the Yaa Asantewaa War[1] of 1900. The victorious British sought to consolidate their martial dominance of the region by incorporating the Northern Territories and the Asante heartland

into protectorates that became part of the Gold Coast Colony proper. (Konadu and Campbell, 2016: 207)

Given the emphasis in colonial policy on the extraction of resources in its colonies in Africa, British colonial government expenditure on social welfare and education was limited due to the determination to keep expenditure low in all its colonies (Frimpong-Manso, 2014). Thus, policies that the government could not fund were not encouraged or pursued. The few they did introduce were adapted from policies developed in Britain (Laird, 2002; McCrystal and Manful, 2011; Frimpong-Manso, 2014). The focus of many of these policies was centred around juvenile delinquency due to a strong emphasis placed on maintaining social control and order within the colony at a time of rapid social change, especially urbanization, rather than the provision of child protection or the realization of children's rights, a concept which was starting to be framed as international primarily by policy makers in the metropole by the second decade of the 20th century (McCrystal and Manful, 2011; Kwaw, 2015). A notable example of the government's focus on juvenile delinquency is the 1928 Children (Care and Reformation) Ordinance, which gave the juvenile courts the authority to sentence juvenile delinquents, orphans and neglected children who were under the age of 15 to a reformatory, many of which were centred in urban areas (Frimpong-Manso, 2014; Kwaw, 2015).

This limited approach to social welfare improved somewhat in the 1940s with the passage of the Colonial Development and Welfare Act in 1940, which provided funding for welfare services in British colonies (see Laird, 2002). This resulted in sectors such as health, education and welfare receiving more systematic attention from the colonial government. Also, in the Gold Coast Ordinance 19 was passed in 1940 to prohibit the employment of children under the age of 12 in any occupation, except where the employment was with the child's family. However, as Kwaw (2015: 84) asserts, this was a tokenistic piece of legislation devised 'to create the illusion that the practice of forced child labour was abolished'. In reality, he argues, the authorities did not seek to interfere with the practice and, therefore, it continued unabated. In 1943 the government in the Gold Coast appointed a Secretary for Social Services who established the foundation for the Department of Social Welfare and Housing, which was established in 1946 drawing on the structures that underpinned social welfare services in Britain – probation, care for children and those with disabilities (Laird, 2002; Frimpong-Manso, 2014). This new institution, which was later renamed the Department of Social Welfare in 1950, was charged with managing both reformatory and industrial schools for juvenile delinquents. Another institution set up at this time was the first children's home in the country, the Osu Children's Home, established in 1949 by the Child Care Society for the purpose of providing a home for orphans and abandoned children (Frimpong-Manso, 2014).

Although many of the policies were introduced in the early 20th century, some early initiatives were introduced by the government at the end of the 19th century as part of broader attempts to abolish slavery and regulate wage labour. For instance, in 1877 the Master and Servants Ordinance was passed, which although concerned with a wide range of salaried workers, its scope also included what was then the largest area of employment, carriers, many of whom were children and were instrumental in the transportation of goods throughout the Gold Coast. Following this, in 1892 the government introduced the Gold Coast Criminal Code which strengthened provisions against slavery and pawning (Kwaw, 2015). Archival research undertaken for Study 5 sheds light on the direct and active role government officials played in decisions about the care of children who had been freed from slavery in the years following the adoption of the 1892 Criminal Code. This can be seen, for instance, in a communication between the District Commissioner of Saltpond to the Acting Commissioner of the Central Province. In the initial message from the District Commissioner, he provides an account of the welfare of children whom the authorities had housed with a resident in the locality in order for the Commissioner to decide about what action the government should take to ensure their continued safety:

> Sir
>
> I have the honour to inform you that I was at Mankessim on the 7th instant when I visited Mr Taylor at his house and saw the three slave children at present with him. The names of the three children are Ambah, a girl about 16 years, Mkua Awunya, a girl about seven years, and Kwamin Sembon, a boy about 16 years. The girl Ambah has a child about two weeks old. Mr Taylor is the father of this child. All three children say they are quite happy and well treated and wish to remain with Mr Taylor; they do not know their parents' names or where they came from, but the boy says he came from Hinterland, he does not know where hinterland is, but he used to hear people say it. My own belief is that the children are perfectly happy and well treated; I saw them quite alone and told them not to be afraid but to tell me the truth.
>
> I have the honour to be, Sir,
> Your obedient Servant
> From District Commissioner, Saltpond to Acting Commissioner,
> Central Province (Ghana National Archives, Cape Coast, 21 June 1909).

In response to this letter the Acting Commissioner of the Central Province indicates that he is assured that the children's welfare is being taken care of and, as a result, is satisfied that they should continue to stay with the resident with whom they had been placed:

Sir

With reference to your letter No. S.P. 11/09 of June 21st, 1909, it appears therefrom that all these children are of an age when they can judge for themselves and are hardly young enough to be bound down to anyone. As long you are sure that these girls and boy quite understand that they are at liberty to go away any time they wish, and that Taylor cannot call on them for any money or to return anything he may have given them I think the matter may rest as it is.

Please see that Taylor produces them regularly.

I have the honor to be,

Sir,

Your obedient servant
H.C.W. Grimshaw
(From Acting Provincial Commissioner, Cape Coast Castle
to District Commissioner, Saltpond, Ghana National Archive,
Cape Coast, 25 June 1909)

This communication is noteworthy for several reasons. First, it illuminates the extent to which, beyond drafting laws and initiatives, local colonial authorities sought to directly intervene in child welfare cases, making specific arrangements to care for particular groups of children and continue monitoring their wellbeing once arrangements had been finalized. Second, it demonstrates that colonial officials operating in the Gold Coast at the turn of the 20th century had an understanding that individuals aged 16 years of age were considered children. However, what they understood about the treatment of children or what was expected of children in terms of behaviour and treatment (beyond not being enslaved) is questionable as neither official raises a concern about the fact that the children's guardian, Mr Taylor, had fathered a child with one of the children placed in his care by the Provincial Commissioner. Thus, this raises a question about how child welfare was understood and conceptualized by authorities in the colonies at this time.

Beyond district commissioners, other sections of the colonial government played a central role in providing welfare services, including medical staff. For example, Allman outlines the initiatives undertaken by doctors to engage with communities in the Gold Coast as part of a strategy of ensuring the welfare of infants:

Like many of the earliest broad-based efforts to make 'proper' mothers out of existing mothers in colonial Africa, those initiated in Kumasi were put forth in the name of public health, in this case by Kumasi's Sanitation Office in 1925. It was in that year that the first Health Week was organized by Dr Selwyn-Clarke who was then the Senior Sanitary Officer in Kumasi. Activities included neighborhood clean-ups, the inspection of pupils' personal hygiene, exhibits and an essay contest. But the biggest event, by far, was the Baby Show. Selwyn-Clarke had hoped that two hundred babies would be entered, but 'as many as five hundred were brought to the Baby Show.' In the following year, Selwyn-Clarke decided to refuse admission to babies whose names had not been entered in the Register of Births. The result was a nearly threefold increase in the number of births registered between September and October 1926. By 1929, the Baby Show had been transformed completely into a mechanism of social regulation, if not social control, as women were encouraged and then rewarded for entering the world of colonial motherhood. The Baby Show was open only to children who had regularly attended the newly opened Welfare Centre and whose births had been registered. In the judging of the baby contestants, extra points were given to children who had received vaccinations. (Allman, 1994: 29–30)

Additionally, Boy Scouts, Girl Guides, the Salvation Army and the Red Cross, with some of these actors providing support on a voluntary basis (see Ashford, 2019), all contributed to the provision of welfare services impacting children.

It is important to note that while these initiatives were established by governments, missionaries and other actors, local chiefs, in some instances, provided financial and other support due to the value they attached to them. This emerged in archival research I undertook in Ghana (Study 5). An example highlighting this is evident in a letter sent by a traditional leader in the Central Province (now known as the Central Region) which included a small donation as part of a contribution to the running of a clinic that had been established in his local area:

My good friend,
As I am interested in the welfare of infants in this country, I beg to enclose herewith the sum of £2-2/- in postal orders as a gift from my Stool towards the work of the Clinic in Cape Coast.

I will take an early opportunity to visit the Clinic and will let you know beforehand the date and hour.

I am Your good friend.
Signed Amanfi III, Omanhene Odumakuma Asebu
(From Odumakuma Fie, Amantsindu, Asebu State to the Medical Officer of Health in charge of the Clinic, Ghana National Archives, Cape Coast, 3 May 1933)

What this shows is that as colonization transformed Gold Coast society, bringing in new values and ideas, Indigenous leaders and rulers, who had come to buy into some of these new ideas and their attendant structures, sought to explore how they and their communities could lend further support to strengthening these initiatives being introduced by a range of colonial actors – governmental or non-governmental. Therefore, initiatives established by colonial authorities, especially in the areas of formal education and healthcare, gained the support of some traditional leaders who provided monies, often collected from their subjects, to support colonial projects in their local areas.

These initiatives notwithstanding, it has to be noted that some policy positions resulted in the worsening of the status of children in this context during this period. British colonial rule, driven largely by an economic agenda, which was centred around exploiting the resources of the continent, led to the introduction of policies that transformed the economic position of women and children. It did this, in particular, by encouraging forced labour in the cash crop economy. With specific regards to children Kwaw (2015: 73) asserts that: 'Colonialism brought about a shift in the ideology of childhood in the Gold Coast. It introduced an insidious exploitative factor that had hitherto not existed, into the treatment of children.' Van Hear (1982: 500) supports this by demonstrating how the establishment of the cash economy by colonial authorities resulted in an increase in children's involvement in cocoa farming, the main cash crop in what was then known as the Gold Coast. Specifically, he highlights how the expansion of cocoa production (from 536 tons in 1900 to 176,000 tons in 1920) resulted in more children taking on the role of porters, most of whom carried the heavy loads given to them to transport on their heads. Despite some concerns raised, by medical staff in particular, about the adverse effects of carrying loads on the head for children's physical development, the colonial government remained reluctant to act for many years (Van Hear, 1982). Therefore, while internationally, movements were being made by international organizations and governments to define parameters around the nature and scope of child work and limit the involvement of children in it, in colonized territories such as the Gold Coast colonial administrators continued to support and actively encourage forms of work among children that had started being considered to be child labour in the metropole. In fact, the evidence shows that as a result of the utility of children to this industry, colonial authorities in the Gold Coast took a rather negative view of international discourses at the time seeking to eliminate child labour:

> Several of the conventions passed at the League of Nations International Labour Conference in 1921 concerned the employment of children; for agricultural work, a minimum age of 14 was set except for work outside school hours, while work was not to interfere with schooling. But the

opinion of the colonial administration was that the implementation of this and other conventions was impracticable, and the response was a prevaricating 'steps will be taken ... as local conditions may decide'. (Van Hear, 1982: 501; see also Chapter 2, this volume)

This position changed somewhat in the 1930s and the colonial government was forced to act due to the increased demand for labour and the implications this had for child welfare (Van Hear, 1982).

In the case of missionaries, research has shown that although they were key to the export of new understandings of childhood, this was limited to only certain elements of the conceptualization of childhood that had started to emerge in European and American societies – specifically that which related to school-based education, although even that was in its most basic sense – being able to read and write, as literacy was required to engage with biblical teachings. Their attitude to applying other components of the emerging conceptualization of childhood from Western Europe and North America to colonized territories was much more ambiguous, especially when it came to the issue of children's work and labour. This emerges in Koonar's study of Basel missionaries in the Gold Coast in which she effectively underscores the extent to which this group actively promoted, and made good use of, children's work for their own purposes:

> In colonial Ghana, the arena in which the Basel Mission had the most direct and sustained access to African children was the mission school. Freed adult laborers often left the mission station, making it difficult for the Basel Mission to secure the consistent paid labor of adults. Children, on the other hand, were constantly present at mission schools, where they were engaged in various kinds of domestic and agricultural labor. During the second half of the nineteenth century, the Basel Mission established stations and schools in various parts of the interior in an effort to establish the Protestant religion. The Mission's quarterly and annual reports offer insight into the missionaries' approach to the education and Christianization of African children as well as the ways in which they attempted to control their labor. (Koonar, 2014: 79)

This narrative around the Basel missionaries drawing on children's work was further supported by a participant in Study 5, which explored the impact of British colonial rule on understandings of childhood in the Gold Coast. This participant, who had attended a boarding school run by Basel missionaries in the Eastern region of the country, shared his experience as follows:

> 'At [name of school] we were taught that hard work is what we should be doing. The devil will find work for idle hands you know. ...

They drummed hard work into us. Hard work. By age 13/14 you are repairing one-one-quarter mile road on an empty stomach. ... The students woke up at 5.30 in the morning on Saturdays and you'll be repairing the road, one-one-quarter mile, all the galleys that the rainwater had created, you filled with stones and controlled the waterway into the valley. You had your breakfast at maybe nine o'clock and you worked until one o'clock. I mean that's the training we had, hard work and it was like a military camp. Your seniors had control over you, I mean they gave the orders. We were weeding the field, cleaning the compound and whatever, washing our clothes. At that time, we didn't have water on the hill, so we walked three miles from [name of location] to [name of location] to fetch water. Those who were strong carried two buckets of water up the hill. We walked three miles [there], three miles [back], six miles, and then you climbed the hill one-one-quarter miles. I mean that toughened us. There is nothing that, after going through that school, there is nothing that you can't do. And the work ethic was really hammered into you.' (Participant 11; male; year of birth: 1938; region of origin: Eastern; interviewed 29 June 2018, Accra, Study 5)

This statement demonstrates that not only did the work this participant engaged in as a child of 13/14 centre around relatively light chores such as cleaning, weeding, fetching water and washing clothes, but they went much further to include repairing part of a road that led to the school. This provides further support to Nieuwenhuys' (2012) argument that the institution of the school was, in effect, a disguise behind which 'planters-cum-missionaries' could gain access to the labour of children (see also Koonar, 2014; Chapter 2, this volume).

While the interests of missionary actors and colonial government authorities did not always align, the evidence shows that on the issue of children's labour there was some consensus on the need to ensure its continuation in colonized territories in sub-Saharan Africa such as the Gold Coast. In particular, archival documents analysed for Study 5 clearly show the extent to which views on child labour often differed between colonial officials in colonized territories and officials based in London, with some trying to make a case for how children were understood differently in the contexts in which they governed. Thus, they sought to advocate for the need to respect these cultures. This can be seen from the responses submitted to a questionnaire sent on behalf of the Secretary of State in London by the Colonial Secretary's Office at Victoriaborg, Accra, to the Commissioner of the Central Province dated 10 August 1931. The questionnaire asked the colonial government to consider the question of whether legislation should be enacted to fix the minimum age for admission of children to industrial employment. Out of the six questions posed on the questionnaire the last was phrased as follows: '[A]re there any industrial undertakings in the Central Province in which the employment of children should, in your opinion, be prohibited?' Upon receipt of this questionnaire from Accra, the Acting Commissioner of the Central Province sent out the questionnaire to the various district officers in his province and received the following responses to the last question:

> With suitable safeguards, there is no reason in my opinion why children under 14 should not be employed. If satisfactory employment could be found, children over 12 would benefit by being put to some work; at least until the educational facilities of the Colony are sufficient to absorb them. It is recognized on all sides that at 14 the average child in this country has entered the adolescent stage. (From District Commissioner's Office, Cape Coast, to the Acting Commissioner, Central Province, Ghana National Archives, Cape Coast, 24 August 1931)

> I see no reason why they should not be employed in certain occupations such as farming, petty trading, and diamond sorting. (From District Commissioner's Office Akroso to the Acting Commissioner, Central Province, Cape Coast, 25 August 1931)

> There are no industrial undertakings in this District in which the employment of children should, in my opinion, be prohibited. (From District Commissioner, Saltpond to the Acting Commissioner, Central Province, Cape Coast, 19 August 1931)

While one respondent sees no problem with the notion of child employment, the other two offer more qualified responses, specifying either the type of work or the level of work. This demonstrates that not only did views on child work vary between authorities in colonized territories and the metropole, but also between local colonial actors. However, in this example, at least, all concede that children of a certain age should be able to engage in some kind of industrial-related work.

To sum up this section, then, while the colonial period saw the introduction of strategies that sought to support new ideas about the welfare of children, these were not framed in the language of rights even at a time when such a language had started being deployed to discuss issues of justice as they related to children at a more global level. Instead, such language remained framed very much in welfarist terms. However, similar to pre-colonial societies, the needs and interest of the colonial state were prioritized over the needs of individuals, leading to a situation whereby children suffered adverse outcomes as a result of decisions and actions by the Gold Coast colonial government whose main objective was not only economic, but also self-preservation as they sought to ensure the protection of themselves and other colonial actors (missionaries, health workers, business people) in what they perceived as a 'hostile environment' (Boyden, 1997: 205).

Post-independence child-focused policies

The role of government continued in efforts to address issues of child welfare following the achievement of independence on 6 March 1957. For instance, in 1960 the government passed the Criminal Offences Act. Part I of the Act lays down all the essential principles within which every court of law in the country is expected to operate (see Section 5 of the Act). Sections 71, 91 and 92 of this law criminalized the abandonment or exposure of a child to danger as well as the abduction of a child. Further, this Act gave the state responsibility for the Osu Children's Home, which led to greater recognition being placed on residential homes as suitable alternative care provisions for children in the country (Frimpong-Manso, 2014).

Not surprisingly, one of the first key pieces of legislation that directly affected children which was introduced in the immediate years following independence by the government of Kwame Nkrumah, the country's first post-independence leader, related to formal education due to the fact that 'the government viewed education and industrialization as the tool by which accelerated development could be achieved, and so it adopted a two-pronged approach to development' (Kwaw, 2015: 88). Specifically, the Education Act of 1961 made primary education, or basic education, both compulsory and free for all:

> Section 2 (1): Every child who has attained the school-going age (six-years) as determined by the Minister shall attend a course of instruction as laid down by the Minister in a school recognized for the purpose by the Minister.

> Section 2 (2): No fee, other than the payment for the provision of essential books or stationery or materials required by pupils for use in practical work, shall be charged in respect of tuition at a public primary, middle or special school.

With this Act the country's post-independence government went a step further than colonial governments who had, for the majority of the period, been reluctant to expand schooling beyond the most basic levels except for a small group of talented children and continued to charge fees. Historian,

Claire Robertson, outlines some of the steps undertaken by post-colonial governments in this area and their impact:

> At first, formal education expanded quite slowly, affecting mostly males. But in the twentieth century, especially after Ghana's independence from Britain in 1957, the Ghanaian government gave top priority to the provision of formal education for everyone; in 1961 the Nkrumah government made middle school free and compulsory. There were two chief results of this for people in Accra. First, by 1970 girls were equally represented with boys in formal education at the entry level, an unprecedented achievement in a town where the sex ratio in primary schools was 100:33 in 1938 and 100:78 in 1960. Second, the Ghana government increased its allocation of resources to formal education; in 1960 it absorbed 14.5 percent of expenditure while in 1975 the government funded 20.3 percent, a level that then fell off to 16.1 percent in 1978. In devoting so much of its resources (which were steadily dwindling as Ghana moved toward bankruptcy) to education, Ghana typified many less developed countries in showing an undiminished faith in the worth of formal education for development. (Robertson, 1984: 639–640)

This expansion of legislation pertaining to schooling occurred within a context in which many people had, by this time, started to define education as primarily formal education and had come to value it as the route to success for both individuals and the country. The First Republic of Ghana also saw the introduction of a range of other laws all seeking to safeguard the country's children: the Adoption Act 1962 (Act 104), introduced to regulate procedures relating to the adoption of children; the Registration of Births and Deaths Act 1965 (Act 301), which made birth registration compulsory; and the Children's Maintenance Act 1965 (Act 297) to set regulations relating to paternity and maintenance issues.

Following the fall of the first republic in 1966 through a *coup d'état*, successive governments, often short-lived due to a period of instability in relation to the political leadership of the country, which ranged from 1966 to 1981, continued to introduce policies centred around child welfare. The Maintenance of Children Decree (1977), which was passed to replace the Children's Maintenance Act (1965), made both parents legally liable for the maintenance of their child(ren). Further, the Labour Decree Act of 1967 stipulated that until the age of 15 children may only be employed within their own families, undertaking light work of a domestic or agricultural nature. This Act is an indication of the extent to which in the post-colonial period Ghana sought to align itself with international laws relating to child labour, arguably going a step further than colonial authorities who, for the bulk of the colonial period, sought to facilitate, or not explicitly prohibit, child employment in various industries.

In these provisions aimed at ensuring children's welfare in this period, the language of rights was not used to frame interventions relating to child welfare and wellbeing. While the 1957 Constitution, adopted in the months following the declaration of independence, made some provision for human rights, most notably around freedom of religion, racial discrimination and protection against compulsory acquisition of private property without compensation, it did not touch upon the concept of children's rights at all (Dadzie, 2009; Kwaw, 2015). Similarly, the 1960 Constitution was not responsive to the notion of children's rights even though it was passed shortly after the 1959 Declaration on the Rights of the Child was adopted by the UN General Assembly. It was not until the Second Republic's Constitution (1969) when the language of rights was first used in relation to children. Article 13 (Chapter 4) of this Constitution stipulates that parliament should enact laws that will ensure 'the right of women and children to such special care and assistance as are necessary for the maintenance of their health, safety, development and well-being' (Government of Ghana, 1969). Regardless of its use of the language of children's rights, as Kwaw states:

> The ideological underpinning of the government's approach to children continued to be welfarist. It emphasized the place of children within the family, and adopted a paternalistic stance that called attention to the vulnerability of children and their dependence on their parents. Children's rights were viewed as indistinguishable from family rights, and the rights of children was minimized within the context of family rights. (Kwaw, 2015: 88)

Bearing in mind the focus of successive post-independence governments centred around development of the country's human resources, the approach taken to child wellbeing and welfare very much adopted a protectionist perspective, which is even evident in the way the concept of children's rights was first deployed in this context. Therefore, while a range of laws and policies were introduced during this period, some of which were framed in the emerging language of children's rights, this was limited and was underpinned by more child protectionist and developmental concerns given the linkage made between formal education of children and the consequences for national development.

Conclusion

This historical review of child welfare strategies in the country now known as Ghana has highlighted the extent to which diverse actors in charge of child welfare in this context devised a range of strategies to protect children's welfare or facilitate their development. However, at the same time it has shown that at various stages of the country's history, the search for securing the welfare of the group or the state resulted in poorer or adverse welfare outcomes for, primarily, children. This, at least, in relation to the evidence that pertains to the colonial state, resulted in an ambivalent approach to understandings of both childhood and child welfare.

5

From Marginal to Central: Tracing the Deployment of Children's Rights Language in Laws and Action in Ghana

Introduction

While the language of children's rights officially emerged in the Ghanaian legal and policy lexicon in the 1969 Constitution, it is the period following 1979 that has come to be associated with the systematic deployment and expansion of not only the language of rights, but a culture of rights, at least within legal and policy discourses, in the country. Therefore, this chapter explores the systematic emergence of dominant children's rights discourses in not only legal and policy discourses in Ghana, but also in broader public discourses. Given that the initial development of this framework coincided with a military take-over of the country that ushered in essentially 13 years of authoritarianism, with its attendant strategies of brutality and intimidation, this chapter additionally devotes attention to the factors that resulted in the development of a so-called culture of children's rights, at least in relation to the policy and legal frameworks of the country, at a time of political repression and suppression.

The emergence of the systematic use of the language of children's rights in policy and legal discourses in Ghana

Although the wording of children's rights was first used in the 1969 Constitution, the language was more fully developed in the legal and policy lexicon of Ghana from 1979, the same year that the International Year of the Child was marked globally. The first step in this construction of children's rights was the 1979 Constitution, which came into force on 24 September

1979, and attempted to ostensibly change the ideological underpinnings of state laws towards a more child-rights focused approach. As part of this commitment the Constitution made numerous provisions relating to human rights. With regards to children's rights, provisions are made within Article 32(3) instructing parliament to enact such laws as are necessary to ensure and safeguard the rights of children to care, assistance, maintenance and protection (Government of Ghana, 1979). A review of this Constitution demonstrates the extent to which it was influenced by broader and more global debates about children's rights, especially those underpinning the 1959 Declaration on the Rights of the Child, specifically: the principle of non-discrimination emerges in the text, most directly articulated in provisions a) and b); children's interests are seen as being paramount; the right of children to be entitled to special protection due to their special needs is recognized; and 'natural' or biological parents are charged with the responsibility of providing and caring for their children unless they surrender their rights.

The Constitution also sets out instructions for the passage of a new act of parliament which specifically centred around the establishment of the Ghana National Commission on Children in August 1979 as an autonomous institution reporting directly to the office of the president. With this status the institution was charged with the responsibility of promoting the welfare of children through the coordination of the activities of relevant government agencies and reviewing laws and policies relating to children in order to advise government (see Tengey, 1998; Kwaw, 2015). Despite the burgeoning focus on the rights of the child in the constitution, the approach of the Commission was welfarist due to the fact that it largely coordinated and integrated existing fragmented child-focused welfare services and policies which were all, up to that point, centred around education, protection, welfare and safeguarding (Kwaw, 2015).

Following the establishment of the Commission the government of the time embarked on a series of initiatives centred around both educational reforms and preparing the country for its ratification of the Convention on the Rights of the Child. In relation to education, the government launched a series of reforms in 1987, which produced the Free Compulsory and Universal Basic Education policy, which came into force in 1996, and aimed to provide good quality basic education for all children of school-going age in Ghana by the year 2005 through improving the quality of teaching and learning, strengthening access to education, expanding infrastructure, and addressing teacher behaviours. To ensure that children enrolled and completed basic education, at the very least, the government further introduced the capitation grant through which the government absorbed school fees that were previously paid by parents and caregivers. Additionally, the government, through the Ghana Education Service, initiated, in 1987, a programme known as the Science, Technology and Mathematics Education clinic for girls which provided scientific talks, activities, career guidance sessions and video programmes as well as facilitated interactions between girls and established women scientists. The objectives of the programme were centred on increasing and sustaining the participation of girls in science, technology and mathematics (Amua-Sekyi, 1998).

In relation to engagement with the drafting process of the Convention on the Rights of the Child, the government's initial response was to produce, in 1985 and 1986, a study on the state of Ghanaian children, led by the Ghana National Commission on Children. The completed report was the first attempt to obtain comprehensive data on the status of the country's children. Following the First Reading of the Convention in 1988 the government began to pay greater attention to the drafting process, which resulted in the Ghana National Commission on Children embarking on efforts to publicize the Convention to obtain public support, and to familiarize District Assemblies with the contents of the treaty before actual ratification took place (see also Windborne, 2006). Specific activities undertaken at this time included: visits by the Commission to individual Regional Houses of Chiefs to explain the contents of the treaty; research by the Ghana Institute of Journalism on the issue of child labour, which was followed by a public dissemination workshop; the organization of a national seminar on child abuse in order to raise the awareness of the general public on particular aspects of the Convention; and the participation of representatives of District Assemblies in a programme at State House, the seat of government, to look through articles of the draft Convention (Tengey, 1998).

Once the country ratified the Convention in February 1990 the Commission became the focal point for advocacy on, and work related to, the Convention. In this role, soon after ratification the Commission set up, and coordinated, on behalf of government, a multi-sectoral taskforce, which adopted a National Plan of Action (NPA or CRC), also known as the Child Cannot Wait. This taskforce undertook an assessment of the situation of children in Ghana and set the framework for the implementation of the goals of the World Declaration and Plan of Action adopted at the 1990 World Summit on Children. According to Ghana's end decade report submitted to the Committee on the Rights of the Child, the NPA, which was finalized in 1992, was integrated into national planning processes such as the Human Development Strategy and Vision 2020 – the National Development Policy Framework, prepared by the National Development Planning Commission, to which all District Assemblies submit their development plans. It was further recognized as having a significant impact on numerous organizations and institutions in Ghana, serving as a guide and focus for work concerning children, as well as outlining programmes and policies to be undertaken. In the case of the Ghana National Commission on Children, the NPA is said to have given it a new direction, moving it forward from ad hoc events to a long-term programming process (Tengey, 1998).

After ratification, the role of the Commission continued through sensitization and training activities aimed at civil servants, professionals, caregivers, lawyers, journalists, police and prison officers and children themselves. As part of its dissemination efforts, the Commission printed the Convention in daily newspapers and summarized it in leaflets by collaborating with the Ghana Bureau of Languages to translate it into four widely spoken local languages: Twi, Ga, Ewe and Hausa. Annual days of nationwide celebration such as the country's Independence Day (6 March) and National Children's Day (31 August) further offered the opportunity for government to promote awareness of the Convention and the issue of children's rights more generally.

Two years after its ratification of the Convention, the country returned to democracy, in 1992, through the return of multi-party elections and the introduction of a constitution which emphasized decentralization as part of an expressed desire to bring the government closer to the people and facilitate greater political participation (Oquaye, 1995; Crawford, 2009). In comparison to the previous constitutions – 1957, 1960, 1969 and 1979 – the 1992 Constitution provided the greatest articulation of human rights governance in the country's political history. Most notably, Chapter 5 sets out a comprehensive list of provisions on human rights, fundamental freedoms and administrative justice (Oquaye, 1995; Dadzie, 2009; McCrystal and Manful, 2011). In order to ensure that the provisions of the Constitution were enacted, including those relating to children, the Commission on Human Rights and Administrative Justice was established in 1993 by an Act of Parliament as a national institution with a network of offices in all regions of the country and charged with the responsibility 'to investigate complaints of human rights violations by both state agencies and private bodies' (Dadzie, 2009: 116). Alongside this the National Commission for Civic Education was also established in the same year by an Act of Parliament for the purpose of providing public education on human rights and responsibilities as well as to encourage the public to work to protect the Constitution against any abuses (see Dadzie, 2009; Zuure and Taylor, 2018).

As a result of the advocacy work of the Ghana National Commission on Children, the 1992 constitution, a product of the return to democracy, included specific provisions relating to children's rights. Specifically, it makes provisions, in Article 28 (Chapter 5), that:

(1) Parliament shall enact such laws as are necessary to ensure that-
(a) every child has the right to the same measure of special care, assistance and maintenance as is necessary for its development from its natural parents, except where those parents have effectively surrendered

their rights and responsibilities in respect of the child in accordance with law; (b) every child, whether or not born in wedlock, shall be entitled to reasonable provision out of the estate of its parents; (c) parents undertake their natural right and obligation of care, maintenance and upbringing of their children in co-operation with such institutions as Parliament may, by law, prescribe in such manner that in all cases the interest of the children are paramount; (d) children and young persons receive special protection against exposure to physical and moral hazards; and (e) the protection and advancement of the family as the unit of society are safeguarded in promotion of the interest of children.

(2) Every child has the right to be protected from engaging in work that constitutes a threat to his health, education, or development.

(3) A child shall not be subjected to torture or other cruel, inhuman, or degrading treatment or punishment.

(4) No child shall be deprived by any other person of medical treatment, education or any other social or economic benefit by reason only of religious or other beliefs.

(5) For the purposes of this article, 'child' means a person below the age of eighteen years. (Government of Ghana, 1992)

While Article 28 provides detailed provisions on children's rights, other articles in the Constitution also have implications for children's wellbeing such as Article 25 (Chapter 5) which pertains to the education of individuals in the country, including children, and Article 39 (Chapter 6), which makes provisions abolishing traditional practices which are seen as harmful to the health and wellbeing of an individual such as female genital cutting. The inclusion of this latter provision can be traced back to 1989 when the president at the time, Jerry John Rawlings, issued a declaration against such traditional practices (US State Department, 2001). In developing these provisions consideration was not only given to the common law of the country, including previous constitutions, but also to numerous international treaties such as the UN Convention of the Rights of the Child, the UN Standard Minimum Rules for the Administration of Juvenile Justice, and the International Labour Organization's Conventions 138 and 182 (McCrystal and Manful, 2011; Zuure and Taylor, 2018).

Building on the provisions of the Constitution, in 1995, the government, through the Ghana National Commission on Children, initiated a comprehensive law reform process to ensure full compatibility between national laws and the Convention. After a three-year drafting process the Ghana National Commission on Children successfully presented a bill entitled 'The Children's Act 1997' to parliament on 17 January 1998. Alongside its adoption was the passage of the Legislative Instrument for the Children's Act (LI 1705). While the development of this law was informed by the Convention on the Rights of the Child as well as the UN Standard Minimum Rules for the Administration of Juvenile Justice (see McCrystal and Manful, 2011), it is said to have also been influenced by British child protection legislation, most notably the 1989 Children Act, including its concept of parental rights and responsibilities, the emphasis on investigations by social workers and the use of supervision and care orders to protect children from abuse and neglect (Laird, 2002).

The Children's Act 1998, which is now the major legislation protecting children in Ghana, came into force in January 1998 and was intended to domesticate the Convention into the laws of the country. The Act, in and of itself, is widely seen as being a good comprehensive piece of legislation as it seeks to reform, and consolidate, the laws relating to children in the country (see Twum-Danso, 2011). Four principles underline the Act:

1. the need to support the family as the key welfare stakeholder for children;
2. the concept of the state as a parent when a child needs to be removed from his/her natural parents;
3. the recognition of traditional systems of conflict resolution and reconciliation within the community; and
4. the need to increase the responsibility of the child with age (McCrystal and Manful, 2011).

Part I of the Act provides the definition for a child, setting 18 as the age at which childhood ends, in line with the Convention on the Rights of the Child although at odds with Indigenous understandings of childhood, which can still be identified among some families and communities in contemporary Ghana. However, while its provisions cover the protection of all children below the age of 18 in all aspects of their life, the Act also makes provisions for those over that threshold due to the recognition that some young people still require parental support due to ill-health or continuing education (Zuure and Taylor, 2018). This part of the Act further outlines the basic rights of children, which are all in accordance with the principles underlining the Convention. These include the right to grow up with their biological parents, unless it is not in the best interests of the child, the duties and responsibilities of parents towards a child, the right to parental property, the right to education and wellbeing (that is, immunization, adequate diet, clothing, shelter, medical attention), the right to social activity, the right to be able to express an opinion and participate in decisions affecting their wellbeing and the right to protection from exploitative labour and torture. This section also defines what is meant by a child 'in need of care and protection', which covers children who are orphans, neglected or ill-treated, destitute, under the care of parents or guardians who are unfit to take care of the child or who is wandering and has no home and no visible means of subsistence. Any contravention of this part of the Children's Act is liable to a fine of not more than five million cedis, which is 500 Ghana cedis[1] or a term of imprisonment not beyond one year or both.

Part II captures the principle of the best interest of the child in line with the Convention on the Rights of the Child by making provisions relating to children's right to protection from: abuse, neglect, and sexual contact with adults; the worst forms of child labour; stigma and discrimination; and customary practices which degrade and humiliate them. It further sought to protect groups seen as particularly vulnerable such as street children as well as those in conflict with the law. Additionally, it outlines measures for the establishment, and operation, of Child Panels and Family Tribunals. Part III focuses on provisions relating to parentage, custody, access and maintenance while Part IV regulates adoption and fosterage. Part V provides some guidelines concerning child labour and apprenticeships. The final section makes provisions for the institutionalized care of children and sets guidelines for day-care centres, as well as outlines miscellaneous provisions relating to issue areas such as birth registration.

In analysing the Act several key features stand out. First, it brought together and harmonized laws previously scattered throughout the statutes, thus making them, in principle, more accessible, easier to promote and easier to enforce (see Twum-Danso, 2011). Second, the legislation allowed for children aged 15 years and above to undertake apprenticeships (in various sectors, including the informal) whereby their employers have an obligation to provide a safe and healthy work environment along with the requisite training and tools. Third, the Act also amended existing legislation to reflect the best interests of the child, particularly in relation to the principles of non-discrimination, increasing responsibility with age, and the balance between the child, family and state. Finally, it introduced provisions on foster care, which means that for the first time the age-old practice of kinship fosterage was subject to regulation.

One of the key innovations of the Children's Act was the establishment of child panels in an acknowledgement of the need for a more communal and traditional approach to complement the formal judicial system. In particular, the Child Panel provision of the Act addresses the establishment of a quasi-judicial body that is charged with mediating minor civil and criminal matters at the community level. As the only legal structure at the community level charged with the socio-legal protection of children, it was seen to have the potential to absorb not only the civil issues pertaining to the non-maintenance of children, child labour, parental neglect or maltreatment, truancy/failure to send a child to school, but also minor crimes committed by children such as petty theft. By dealing with minor offences committed by children, Child Panels, in principle, offer the opportunity to assure justice is meted out to the child without recourse to the main justice system, which tends to be expensive and time-consuming. Further, these panels were seen as a culturally responsive way of addressing minor criminal or civilian transgressions in a context whereby the attitude that problems must be resolved within the community in such a way that all parties can continue living side by side is a key foundation on which the society is built. Further, as the deliberations of the Child Panel and its settings are informal, it was seen as being less intimidating for children and, thus, more child-friendly. Finally, its approach is supposed to be participatory, not only because it allows children to participate in proceedings, but also because it asks the interested parties, including children, if they have any proposal for the settlement of the matter under discussion.

In ensuring the implementation of the Act, District Assemblies, which, as part of the decentralized system established under the 1992 Constitution, are given the responsibility for protecting the welfare of children, as well as promoting their rights. Hence, District Assemblies take on a range of roles relating to the implementation of the Children's Act. They establish family tribunals within their district and are responsible for setting up child panels to advocate for children's rights and tackle the abuses meted out against children. With regards to custodial power, District Assemblies can take up the custody of children whose parents have neglected them or who, for some reason, are exposed to risk of abuse from guardians. Moreover, they address issues relating to children's right to property inheritance, the elimination of child labour and the monitoring of schools and day-care institutions in their district. In order to achieve their goals, District Assemblies work closely with the Department of Social Welfare, which was until recently part of the Ministry of Manpower Development and Employment, to address issues of child protection in each district. In essence, the District Assembly is expected to make the necessary by-laws while the Department of Social Welfare seeks to ensure their implementation, especially as they relate to the following programme areas: justice administration, child rights promotion and protection, and community care.

In addition to the passage of the Children's Act, the Criminal Offences Act 1960 was amended and strengthened – also in 1998. This amendment saw the age of sexual responsibility increased from 14 to 16 years. Alongside this was the inclusion of provisions which sought to protect children under the age of 16 from prostitution and prohibited their presence in brothels. Provisions relating to statutory rape, widely referred to as defilement in Ghana, were tightened as this now attracted a penalty of a minimum prison sentence of seven years and a maximum of 25 years without an option of a fine. In turn, the penalty for rape was also increased to a minimum of five years in imprisonment and a maximum of 25 years, again, without the option of a fine. A new offence of indecent assault was further introduced in this legislation. The Criminal Code additionally criminalizes the abandonment or exposure of a child to danger, the abduction of a child and a range of other sexual offences, including forced marriage and incest. Added to this, it abolishes customary or ritual servitude, thereby banning practices such as *trokosi*.

Beyond legislation a range of policies were also introduced during this period, notably those relating to Adolescent Reproductive Health and School Health. Key institutions were established to support the implementation of laws and policies. The Domestic Violence and Victims Support Unit of the Ghana Police Service (formerly known as the Women and Juvenile Unit), which was initially set up in Accra in November 1998 in an attempt to make the criminal justice system more responsive to what were considered as the special needs of children and women who experience violence. Other relevant services introduced include the Shelter for Abused Children and the Shelter for Trafficked Children, among others. In recognition of the challenges facing girls in relation to formal education, a Girls' Education Unit of the Ghana Education Service was established in 1995 to advocate for policy and special programmes for achieving the participation of girls in formal education.

The 2000 elections were the first to be held since 1979 that resulted in a change in government as it ushered in the New Patriotic Party, led by John A. Kuffour. Shortly after assuming power, this newly elected government established, in February 2001, the Ministry for Women and Children's Affairs (now known as the Ministry of Gender, Children and Social Protection) with a mission to '[c]hampion the cause of all women and children, through the promotion of gender equality and the survival, development, protection, and participation of children, to achieve equal status, equal opportunities and equal rights for women, men, and children in the development of Ghana' (Ghana National Commission on Children, 2005).

Consequently, the Ministry assumed responsibility for coordinating, monitoring and reviewing the formulation of gender and child responsive policies, as well as overseeing their implementation within the relevant sector ministries. As a result, it took over two interrelated organizations, the National Council on Women and Development and the Ghana National Commission on Children. With regards to the latter Commission, its incorporation into the Ministry in 2006 through an Act of Parliament changed its status from an independent policy-making body to a department under the Ministry responsible for implementation. As a result, as a department within the Ministry, it is responsible for undertaking research, coordinating children's rights implementation, and monitoring the operations of other child-focused agencies. Further, as a department of the Ministry, the Commission which later became known as the Department of Children, coordinated the National Multi-Sectoral Committee and all Inter-Agency Committees on children's rights and protection (UN and Government of Ghana, 2004). In

2013 the Department of Social Welfare, which was previously part of the Ministry of Manpower, Youth and Employment, was incorporated into the Ministry of Gender, Children and Child Protection as part of an attempt to ensure better coordination on issues affecting both women and children.

Having established a sector ministry focusing on women and children, the new New Patriotic Party government further proceeded to pass a series of laws that had an impact on children and their families: the Juvenile Justice Act (2003), the Domestic Violence Act (2007), the Persons with Disability Act (2006), the Education Act (2008) and the Human Trafficking Act (2005). This latter piece of legislation was introduced due to the need to have a law that centred on victims of the phenomenon as opposed to the perpetrators who were already covered by the provisions in the 1998 Criminal Offences Code. As part of this Act a Human Trafficking secretariat and management board was established at the Ministry of Gender, Children and Social Protection along with an Anti-Trafficking Unit set up as part of the Ghana Police Service. These laws and initiatives were supplemented by the introduction of a number of policies, including the Gender and Children's Policy (2002); the Early Childhood Care and Development Policy (2004), which has recently been revised; the NPA on Child Labour and the Worst Forms of Child Labour (2009–2015); the NPA on Orphans and Vulnerable Children (2010–2015); the National Domestic Violence Policy and Plan of Action (2009–2019); and the NPA for the Elimination of the Worst Forms of Child Labour in Ghana (2009–2015).

The context of children's rights emergence in Ghana

A critical point to note about the turn to the systematic use, and application, of the concept and language of children's rights by successive governments in Ghana is that its initial foundations took place against the backdrop of authoritarianism. In the same year that the Ghana National Commission was established, Flight Lieutenant Jerry John Rawlings, a junior officer, 32 years of age, was successful in a *coup d'état* which overthrew, on 4 June 1979, the government of General Fred Akuffo in a bid to tackle what he perceived as rampant corruption. This resulted in the establishment of the Armed Forces Revolutionary Council (AFRC), primarily composed of junior officers, with Rawlings as Chairman. Although four months later Rawlings handed power to the elected government of Hilla Limann of the People's National Party on 24 September 1979, leading to the establishment of the Third Republic of Ghana, two years later, on 31 December 1981, he overthrew, in another *coup d'état*, Limann's civilian government due to his perception that it was weak and, therefore, incapable of addressing the economic crisis the country was facing at the time (Buah, 1998). The constitution was once again suspended and a military government, the Provisional National

Defence Council (PNDC), was established as the official government of the country, with Rawlings placing himself, again, in the position of Chairman, overseeing a two-tier administration consisting of: a Council, which was the supreme body, comprising members of the military and four civilians appointed by Rawlings in his role as chair; and a second tier composed of civilian secretaries of state – again appointed by Rawlings (Buah, 1998).

The ascension of Rawlings, a Marxist who later became a capitalist, to power this second time came amidst the context of economic decline and harsh socioeconomic realities facing the majority of the population. Indeed, this was one of the reasons he initiated the coup against the civilian government of Limann. Due to the oil crises of the 1970s (1973 and 1979) which resulted in oil price hikes, a consequence of embargoes set by the Organization of Arab Petroleum Exporting Countries, Ghana's economy suffered stagnation and decline in the 1970s and 1980s. 1983, in particular, became seen as a turning point in Ghana's economic history and has been referred to as the 'nadir' of the country's economic fortunes by Brydon and Legge (1996: 10) due to the fact that in that year the economic situation of the country was simply dire, characterized by drought, bush fires, food shortages and the influx of over one million Ghanaian nationals who had been expelled from Nigeria following an executive order issued by its then president, Shehu Shagari, in early 1983.

Amidst this context of economic decline, the military government of the PNDC, headed, by Rawlings, embarked on an economic recovery programme which it recognized as critical due to its focus on the socioeconomic rights of its subjects. As Oquaye states:

> From the point of view of the regime, the promotion of socioeconomic rights was advanced through the economic recovery program. The economic recovery program included rural development (including water, electrification, health, and roads), higher producer prices paid to cocoa farmers, a primary health care program, and educational reforms (including junior and senior secondary school programs). In addition, the Intestate Succession Law (PNDCL 11) protected the rights of widows whose husbands died intestate. Under this law, widows were granted specific portions and rights in the property of deceased husbands and could not be ejected from their matrimonial homes by the family of the deceased. Furthermore, the Head of Family (Accountability) Law (PNDCL 114) changed an unfortunate aspect of Ghana's customary law by which the head of a family was not readily accountable to other members of the family and could deprive them of their property rights. (Oquaye, 1995: 562)

The emphasis on socioeconomic rights by the PNDC regime was also noted by one of my key informants in Study 6, who sought to highlight Rawlings' self-perception as a revolutionary and progressive leader whose stated ambition, in initiating the coup in 1981, was to facilitate the advancement of Ghanaian society and its peoples:

> 'We had the so-called revolution at first in 1979 and then Rawlings came again in 1981 and I think Rawlings' idea was to completely revolutionize Ghana socially, economically and so on, you know, but there was a fair understanding that, er, you needed to solve the bread and butter issues before you can actually get people to socially change so it was a grand idea of transforming society and Rawlings had, er, projected himself as a progressive alright, er; this was a 33-year old person who was a junior officer which was, er, out of line with our previous understanding of who coup military leaders were – almost all of them were generals or colonels or people very high up in the military hierarchy, and definitely much older than he was at that time and I think his children probably were very very young. He hadn't ... he may not have even finished having children that time. So here you are with someone who was conducting a revolution, someone who was relatively young, and someone who had put up the persona of a very progressive leader who wanted to change things in the country.' (KI2, 1 December 2022, Study 6)

To effectively achieve its objectives, the regime accepted foreign funding as it realized that this would be essential in helping it to implement its own economic recovery programme (Buah, 1998). To this end, loans and aid were accepted from the World Bank, the International Monetary Fund and the UN Development Programme as well as other agencies. With this assistance the government set up key services such as the extension of electricity and water supply as well as educational reform programmes. However, these foreign loans, granted as part of a Structural Adjustment Programme, were conditional based on a number of demands, including the withdrawal of government subsidies on goods and services, the reduction in the number of employees in the public service and a massive devaluation of the national currency, the cedi. The extensive liberalization and adjustment in the 1980s produced some growth in services and mining but did little to produce and sustain growth in agriculture and manufacturing (Government of Ghana, 2003). This stagnation of growth and incomes continued into the 1990s when the economy was characterized by high rates of inflation, high interest rates, the continuous depreciation of the cedi, dwindling foreign reserves, excessive public debt overhang and stagnant economic growth. This resulted in a high cost of living and hardship which affected many people, leading to: increased immigration to urban areas by individuals in search of work, including children; and increased pressure on families, especially women, who could no longer afford medical care and other basic necessities for the children and elderly relatives in their care.

While socioeconomic rights were foregrounded in PNDC government policy, much less regard was paid to the civil and political rights of its citizens. Oquaye explains it thus:

> In launching the revolution, Rawlings emphasized socioeconomic rights while ignoring political and human rights. To Rawlings, 'democracy is not realized by having a machinery for registering voters and getting them to vote every four years but also by there being a machinery for identifying the needs of those voters in between the election periods and monitoring the realization of these needs.' Emphasizing the importance of economic rights, Rawlings said: 'we do not see a democracy with hollow political content but one rooted in our economic realities.' PNDC Law 42[2] gave the regime unfettered, limitless, and absolutely discretionary powers in determining and disposing of the rights of Ghanaians. All legislative, executive, administrative and judicial powers were vested in the PNDC. (Oquaye, 1995: 561–562)

This disregard for civil and political rights led to a regime which was characterized by torture and human rights violations which 'not only traumatized society as a whole, but also engendered an atmosphere of fear, insecurity, recrimination, and suspicion that marred the transition' (Oquaye, 1995: 56). This is further supported by Emiljanowicz (2021), in a recent article for *The Conversation* in the aftermath of the death of Rawlings in November 2020 in which he stated: 'The reconciliation commission archive records show that human rights abuses were remarkably high during the first four years of Rawlings' ruling from 1979 to 1982. And over 67% of all human rights violations that occurred in Ghana in the review period happened under his government.'

Torture was employed as part of the regime's control mechanism, including the deployment of methods such as solitary confinement, detention incommunicado, detention in very dark or brightly lit cells, the application of lit cigarettes to male organs, mock executions, denial of medical facilities and the withdrawal of essential drugs. Assault and battery, stripping, and denial of legal representation were all used to brutalize and instil fear in the population. Citizens who were seen as opponents of the PNDC were found murdered on beaches and in rubbish dumps. Some were raped and assaulted by soldiers and members of the militia while others vanished after speaking derogatorily about the Chairman, Rawlings (Oquaye, 1995). Key targets of the government's attention were especially those in positions of power, including three high court judges and a retired army major who were abducted, tortured and murdered on the night of 30 June 1982. Freedom of expression of the media was curtailed by a new law passed by the government, the Newspaper Licensing Law (PNDCL211). This resulted in the arrest and detention of journalists as well as attacks and arson on media companies. Other freedoms were also restricted, including religious freedom, which saw churches vandalized, priests killed and the arrest of members of church congregations for speaking against the regime (Oquaye, 1995). Further, student demonstrations were brutally crushed. Civil society organizations that opposed the regime were persecuted and new organizations were founded which had the approval and support of the government. A good example is the establishment of the 31st December Women's Movement, a voluntary organization with support from the government. As a government-approved entity its activities were sponsored by the state (Buah, 1998). This organization, which was led by Rawlings' wife, Nana Konadu Agyemang Rawlings, purportedly promoted the cause of disadvantaged women with the supposed objective of improving their standard of living, facilitating their involvement in national affairs and building their capacity to enact their rights as women. Despite this expressed purpose, in reality the benefits of this organization were mainly felt by those who supported Rawlings and his government.

The return to democratic rule in 1992, marked by the passage of the Constitution, was not necessarily the end of the authoritarianism that underpinned the Rawlings government, which had remade its image through the formation of a new civilian party fit for the country's new democratic status – the National Democratic Congress (NDC). In the years following the return to democracy the police and municipal security forces continued to use excessive force, and the powers of the independent media remained curtailed, as was the political system which was circumscribed by a parliament monopolized by the ruling party and a judiciary that was timid as a result of bearing the brunt of the PNDC's violence during the period of dictatorship (see Buah, 1998). While elections were held in 1992 and 1996, both of these, which returned Rawlings and his NDC party to power each time, were seen as tainted by corruption (Oquaye, 1995, 2000). The significance of this is that while the language of human and children's rights, and the efforts to turn these norms into reality, intensified and became deployed through the introduction of a range of laws and institutions, there were limits to genuine government action in realizing these rights at this time. This was due to the fact that despite the return to democracy, a culture of human rights remained limited and constrained in the country.

Given this context the question then becomes how did a government of this hue come to play such a leading role, not only in the systematic establishment of human rights laws in Ghana, but also specifically in the development of comprehensive children's rights legislation and policy? In effect, how did such a government come to be the one to lead the way for Ghana to become the first country in the world to ratify the first binding treaty on children's rights – the Convention on the Rights of the Child – in February 1990? This political context in Ghana is critical to consider as many of the developments that occurred in relation to children's rights can be directly attributed to Rawlings, who led a military junta that terrorized the country and later became a democratically elected president on two successive occasions as a result of elections that have been recognized as controversial. The consideration of the role of Rawlings as an individual specifically is a key factor as, given the authoritarian nature of the government at the time, the decision to ratify the Convention was not a process which was subject to discussion either at the political level involving members of a parliament, for example (as there was no parliament), or at the public level through consultations with the country's citizenry. As the head of the military junta in 1990, the year when Ghana ratified the Convention, the decision to ratify the treaty was made by Rawlings himself, possibly following advice from close members of his coterie. Thus, considering the political structures of the country at the time is essential when discussing the decision-making process that led to the government ratifying the Convention:

'Right until 1992 when Rawlings, the new party was formed [National Democratic Congress], and we went back to democracy it was, er, a military government; and military governments in Ghana by definition are based on decisions made by the Head of State perhaps with his inner circle. We didn't have, er, we were not operating as a democracy at that time in the sense that an idea comes up and is thrown to the public and they are given some period, you know, where people will debate it, they will discuss it, they will research it, they will write about it, and then we build a national consensus and we say this; and it wasn't just the Convention, it was everything else. If they wanted to make a policy, it is not thrown [out] to the public; the PNDC, they will meet, a couple of people will make the decision and the next day it comes out as a decree; obviously there was no parliament and so we did not have the benefit of our representatives there discussing and debating for us; so where Ghana wasn't a democracy and we were not in a state where people were consulted for everything then we can say that decisions were made by the Council and even by the Council it could be that, er, it's just the Head of State; maybe overnight somebody hinted an idea to him, he perhaps consults one or two people on there and then he goes. Now, what we know is that Rawlings was such a dominant figure ... so you know if you have such a leader of a government and he had made a coup and he was the leader of the coup and all those people on the Council were there by reason of his generosity or by his invitation, then I can see him as the single most dominant figure, and then if he wanted [something] he gets it. ... You do an objective assessment. We had no reason to be the first country to ratify it [the Convention on the Rights of the Child [laugh], you know, but we ratified it.' (K12, 1 December 2022, Study 6)

Therefore, within this context of authoritarian rule new laws and policies, or indeed, any governmental proposal, emerged without broader discussions, resulting in a situation whereby decisions about the introduction of new laws or ratification of international treaties could be done very quickly, possibly without the implications being fully thought through and considered, by Rawlings as a result of a whim or following a discussion with his advisers. This decision-making process, which was tightly centred around Rawlings and those closest to him, including his wife, needs to also be factored in when considering early initiatives such as the establishment of the Ghana National Commission on Children on 29 August 1979 through an Act of Parliament, the Ghana National Commission on Children Act – 1979, just over two months after he assumed power through a coup on 4 June 1979 and the passage of the 1979 Constitution, which was passed on 24 September 1979. While that was the day he handed power to the civilian government of Hilla Limann, the fact that the constitution passed into law on that date indicates the role he and his AFRC administration played in drafting it in the period between their assumption of control of the country via a coup in early June 1979 and the transition to civilian rule on 24 September of that same year. What this indicates is the direct leadership and personal involvement of Rawlings, the individual, in the decisions around the numerous policies and initiatives developed between 1979 and 1992 around children's rights and welfare, including the decision to ratify the Convention on the Rights of the Child soon after its adoption by the UN General Assembly.

Let us now return to the question posed earlier: how did a government of this hue come to play such a leading role, not only in the systematic establishment of human rights laws in Ghana, but also specifically in the development of comprehensive children's rights legislation and policy? Several reasons can be proffered. The first relates to the involvement of Rawlings' wife, Nana Konadu Agyeman Rawlings, who was put forward as a consideration by key informants in Study 6:

'I can also conjecture that the 31st December Women's Movement, led by the First Lady at the time, might have played a key role. The movement was keen on children's issues and had crèche and nursery facilities throughout the country. This focus on children's development, I believe, might have influenced the early ratification of the CRC by Ghana.' (KI3, 1 February 2023, Study 6)

'In terms of the government's side, JJ Rawlings did a lot of work trying to improve children's rights in the country, ably supported by the wife, Nana Konadu Agyemang Rawlings, who set up the 31st December Movement and her friend [name of friend], who was then the executive director of [name of government agency]. And so, we had a lot of funding from government to support our work which had never happened before.' (KI1, 11 November 2023, Study 6)

Therefore, being married to a woman who was a former student leader, had political interests of her own and was a committed advocate of women's rights may have had an impact on some of the decisions made by Rawlings' government in relation to children. While the direct evidence of her role in the development of initiatives that pertained to children's rights is hard to identify, what is known is that she did play an active role in government law and policy development from the outset of the establishment of the PNDC regime. A good example is the 1985 Intestate Succession Act, which strengthened the inheritance position of married women following the death of their husband and which is acknowledged as being developed as result of her influence. Further, her interest in supporting the rights of marginalized women resulted in her organization taking steps that enhanced children's welfare, such as the establishment of preschools across the country and other child development initiatives.

The second factor to consider relates to external actors and the influence they may have placed on Rawlings' government as a condition for which the loans the government needed for its flagship economic recovery programme became attached. This is a point that Mbise has elaborated on in relation to sub-Saharan Africa more generally:

One coercive strategy used by dominant countries is to link financial aid to the adoption of a policy that is supported by the powerful country. Organizations such as the IMF and World Bank can impose conditionalities on their lending. As most developing countries are recipients of official development assistance (ODA) of various kinds, control mechanisms become important in explaining policy diffusion in these countries more than in the advanced economies. African countries in particular are no stranger to being coerced into adopting policies that are favoured by the developed countries and impressed upon them through the intermediaries of the International financial institutions. (Mbise, 2017: 1236)

This financial support provided by such international agencies leads to a situation whereby they hold a significant amount of power over governments, especially those in low and middle income which puts them in a position to pressurize such governments to adopt international policies that they support (Mbise, 2017). The long-term support of these international agencies for the successive governments led by Rawlings before, and after, the introduction of constitutional rule in 1992 (AFRC, PNDC and National Democratic Congress [NDC]) is an important consideration when trying to understand the factors that led a military government to embark on the return to democracy and a process of law reform that strengthened both human rights and children's rights, at least on paper. In particular, it is critical to consider the role of these agencies due to the influence they held over the government through the aid and support they provided for the government's economic recovery projects both at a time when the Convention on the Rights of the Child was being drafted and in the period after. This has been noted by Laird (2002), who attributes the introduction of children's rights framing in Ghana at this time to the influence of the United Nations Children's Fund (UNICEF) and other multilateral donor agencies due to the substantial funding they provided for child welfare programmes which exceeded any resources the government itself could provide for any of its programmes. Further support for this point is provided by Windborne (2006), who claims that it was pressure from such agencies that not only led to the return to constitutional rule, but also resulted in Ghana becoming the first country to ratify the Convention on the Rights of the Child in February 1990.

Beyond external pressure, there is a need to acknowledge that Rawlings played an active role in his relations with the international community as he sought to curry favour with Western governments and international agencies as part of his strategy for obtaining support for his socioeconomic recovery programme. Thus, Rawlings' desire to be seen positively by the international community in the 1980s after initially turning his back on this group in the early days of his revolution is a critical point to consider:

> '[When Rawlings came to power] he made an enemy of the United States and made an enemy of European countries because there was an anti-Western rhetoric and, er, he actually, the way he organized the political and economic system was based on Cuba's political system and he thought Ghana could be something like Libya in the sense of what the state was doing and if he wanted to think like Castro or like Ghaddafi, then, in essence you can't be on the side of the West because already these two people were supposed to be arch enemies of the West. So, by going that way he was easily rejected by the West and so the initial ideas of getting some support to rebuild the economy flattened out; nobody was interested. And then he had to, er, restate his position. He had to court these same people that he had continuously insulted, you know, er, when he came in; and the courting started with Ghana having its own version of the structural adjustment programme;

as I said they called it the Economic Recovery Programme ... it was the first step to show the West that, at least, we are serious about reforming our economy and so he started to get a few countries on the side of the country, but maybe he needed to move a few steps further to show that, er, I am actually trying to show that I am not a bad boy of African, of Ghanaian, politics. I am somebody who can be trusted and be sat down and had discussions with and so maybe quickly ratifying this [the Convention] was a form of pacification, you know. So, yes, the politics and so on was an important thing but maybe to show them look, I am ready, if I am asking for loans, help me; if I am asking for aid, help me, because I am progressive and look, you, you, have this Convention and I have quickly ratified it. I am not going to be a barrier; all to court them, to make them feel great.' (KI2, 1 December 2022, Study 6)

Thus, there is a need to acknowledge the agency of Rawlings in his interactions with Western governments and development agencies as he went out of his way to court the support and goodwill of these actors so he could obtain the necessary funds for his socioeconomic agenda, which he firmly believed would lead to the advancement of Ghanaian society. This illuminates de Waal's (2002) argument pertaining to the politics of ratification. Specifically, this example shows how, in the hope of changing his image within the international community, especially among Western governments, which would facilitate the acquisition of further financial support from developmental partners, Rawlings may have seen the Convention as well as other international laws and policies as a way to promote himself as the kind of political leader in Africa that was worth the support of Western nations and international aid organizations (a so-called 'good boy' of African politics). That his strategy was successful is evidenced by the level of financial support he was able to leverage from foreign governments and international organizations as indicated in an interview with a key informant in a recent study:

'At the time when the 31st December Movement was enjoying power, both the National Commission on Women and Development (today the Department of Gender) and the Ghana National Commission on Children (today being the Department of Children) enjoyed a lot funding for our work. There were times when we had to even return money that had been given us for work back to government chest and back to the donors which never happens in these days. So, some of us would always want to go back to the past.' (KI1, 11 November 2023, Study 6)

That government agencies such as the Ghana National Commission on Children, often marginalized in favour of expenditure on infrastructure and education, had received so much funding for their activities that they had some left over to return to the Treasury gives us an insight into the relationship that Rawlings and his government of the time had managed to develop with international development partners.

Fourth and related, it has to be acknowledged that the decision to return the country to constitutional rule and hence, democracy, which was initiated in the late 1980s as a result of not only an increased clamour for democracy from sections of the population, but also as a result of external pressure, notably from international agencies and foreign governments, was a pivotal factor. This change in approach to governance has been explained by numerous commentators. Emiljanowicz (2021), for instance, argues that 'military coups are relatively easy to stage. But sustaining them can prove difficult because they soon run out of political legitimacy, especially in the context of economic crisis'. These are the circumstances that led the PNDC government, in 1988, to establish a programme to return the country to constitutional rule, starting with the introduction of a new type of local government with different levels – district, municipal and metropolitan. As part of the return to democracy the organization of a national referendum focused on the development of a new constitution which 'the framers of the 1992 constitution of Ghana, although operating under the heels of a brutal military dictatorship, managed to include elaborate human rights provisions in the Constitution' (Kludze, 2008: 683). Given its development under the rule of a military government, it is important to bear in mind that the Constitution and its attendant initiatives were not developed by a constitutional assembly, but by a consultative assembly, which means that the body lacked the required political mandate as its membership was not democratically elected, but instead, selected by Rawlings and members of his administration. As a result of the development of a constitution against the backdrop of state violence and repression, some elements of society such as the Ghana Bar Association refused to participate in the process in order not to give it the legitimacy it both required and desired (Kludze, 2008).

A final factor to consider when thinking about the factors driving the Rawling government to ratify the Convention, a decision made before the official return to democracy, relates to the reforms Rawlings was making in the education sector after he came to power and how that may have additionally informed his approach to children's rights more generally. Prior to his seizure of power, the education system in Ghana consisted of ten years of primary education followed by a five-year secondary education, two years of sixth form and three years of university. Rawlings' reforms transformed the system leading to six years of primary education, three years of junior secondary, three years of senior secondary education and four years of university. In making these changes the resulting outcome was that on the completion of basic education, individuals were now more likely than not to be 'children' as was becoming understood in law and policy in Ghana at this time. The importance of these changes and their implications were outlined by one of my key informants in Study 6:

'It [ratifying the Convention] also could have been that "Ok if I am reforming education and I am hoping to get maximum returns or maximum benefits out of the information that I am putting forward then one way is to ensure that I don't just change the education system but that I also ensure that our children are given as much protection and attention as possible and right in the nick of time this document [the Convention] has come up and so let me quickly do this and kill many birds, er, with one stone". ... And we should note that in his reform we were going to reduce children's age from the previous situation [era prior to Rawlings' rule] to much lower ages so, for instance, during those elementary school days by the time somebody finished ten years of elementary school they would be on average about 16/17 some were even older than 18 years – before Rawlings, before he reformed the system – I think the average age was like 16 years by the time you go through primary school and you finished middle school you would be around 16 years, but definitely there were some who were much older and a few who were, er, younger than the 16 years and so now he was shifting attention to much lower ages. So, for instance, the JSS [students], they were like 12/13/14 thereabouts you know or 15 or 16 and then they would go on to secondary school. And so, most of the people in the JSS cohort were people who were children in every respect and so, again, [the thinking was] perhaps ok, we ratify the Convention to show that we take what we are doing very very seriously and at the same time we protect children, we want them to focus attention on their education rather than all the other things.' (KI2, 1 December 2022, Study 6)

Ironically, then, it seems that the speed at which Ghana ratified the Convention on 5 February 1990, just over two months after its adoption by the UN General Assembly on 20 November 1989, and its subsequent introduction of a range of policies and laws can be attributed to the lack of democratic rule in the country at the time. As one of my key informants in Study 6 reflected:

'I mean, er, in present-day Ghana, with the kind of democracy we are practising, if the Convention was a new thing that has to be tabled now there would be a lot of fights, I mean verbal fights, and all kinds of debates, innuendoes, and even demonstrations ... because any little thing now, we, we, debate and argue and fight exhaustively over it before [laugh] the government gets its way, you know.' (KI2, 1 December 2022, Study 6)

Therefore, the factors driving the ratification of the Convention have to be firmly centred around Rawlings as an individual who was influenced in his decisions by a small group of people surrounding him as well as the demands of foreign governments and international agencies such as the World Bank, a group he realized he needed to court in order achieve his own development agenda in the country which, in turn, he believed would result in societal transformation.

Civil society action in the post-ratification period

As stated elsewhere, civil society action has been notable in the advancement of dominant discourses of human and children's rights in diverse parts of the world (see Merry, 2006; Grugel and Peruzzotti, 2012). In the context of Ghana, civil society activism and its impact was evident in the 1980s, especially in the area of women's rights. However, due to attacks and suppression by the PNDC government, many, especially those that were openly opposed to Rawlings, were persecuted. As a result, it is widely acknowledged that the period following the return to democracy significantly facilitated the development and expansion of programmes led by civil society organizations, especially in relation to human rights: 'Civil society organizations and some non-governmental organizations, using the language of human rights, have been pushing for legislation to abolish or modify certain customary practices perceived to be oppressive and harmful' (Atiemo, 2012: 76).

In particular, the period after 2000 is seen to have ushered in a period of rejuvenation for civil society organizations (Adomako-Ampofo, 2005). One area relating to children's rights that has been impacted by civil society, especially non-governmental organization action, is the practice of *trokosi*, which can be predominately found in the Volta and Oti regions of Ghana, discussed in the previous chapter. While this practice, which continues today, has now been outlawed through the legislative framework of Ghana, the work of non-governmental organizations has been notable in reducing the practice. In particular, the anti-*trokosi* campaign was initiated by International Needs Ghana, a member of a global Christian organization with branches in diverse parts of the world. Its work on the elimination of *trokosi* can be traced back to a report it published on the subject in 1990, which brought the phenomenon under greater scrutiny, leading to a national discussion on the phenomenon and a recognition, for the first time, that it constituted a form of slavery. Its decision to associate *trokosi* with the term slavery was especially significant. In leading the campaign International Needs Ghana collaborated with a range of national and international agencies such as the Commission on Human Rights and Administrative Justice, the Ghana National Commission on Children, the Ghana Law Reform Commission, Anti-Slavery International and the UN Population Fund. Their efforts were instrumental in ensuring that the Criminal Code Amendment Act in 1998, which criminalized all forms of customary or ritual servitude, included provisions outlawing the *trokosi* system explicitly. In terms of the impact it had, through negotiations led by International Needs Ghana, their campaign resulted in the first-ever mass release of 40 *trokosi* which took place in July 1996. By December 2001, a total of 2,800 (59 per cent) of the known 4,714 *trokosis* at the time had been released (Ameh, 2004). Added to this their campaign also resulted in some fetish priests agreeing to encourage families to offer a goat, instead of a girl, as their sacrifice to the shrine (Bilyeu, 1999).

Realizing change? The impact of children's rights laws, policies and initiatives on children's lived experiences

Growing respect for children's rights versus persisting challenges

Given the context in which the language and attendant laws and policies relating to children's rights became embedded in Ghana the questions now become: to what extent have these various efforts led to transformation in the country? To what extent have they resulted in change, not only in terms of laws and policies, but also in relation to practices and the realities of the lives of children and their families? From data gathered over the years it can be argued that the various efforts initiated by government and civil society have resulted in a mixed bag in terms of children's rights outcomes as envisaged by globally inspired national policy frameworks in the country. In particular, as a result of over 40 years of systematic discussion of children's rights drawing on dominant global discourses, there have emerged sections of Ghanaian society who are aware of the rights of children as articulated in the Constitution, Children's Act and the Convention on the Rights of the Child[3] and draw on them to regulate their own lives and social relations, including those that relate to their children (Twum-Danso Imoh, 2019). However, at the same time there remain those who may, or may not, be aware of these notions that have entered their context and, consequently, adopt oppositional behaviours. For some commentators, these different responses to dominant children's rights have resulted in the creation of two sections of society:

> 'I think, er, we should think of the general public in two terms. Those who are technically competent to think of rights from the basis of all the codified rights that we have, for instance, the Convention on the Rights of the Child, er, Ghana's Constitution – the part on children's rights and then the landmark, er, you know Act, 1998 Children's

Act, and so for those people, we can probably look at rights as the entitlements they have to promote their welfare and their development and so on ... and then we may have to think of the people, let's say, the illiterate, no disrespect to them here, but these people who probably have heard that there is something called children's rights and people are using it in ways that sometimes er, er pisses, I beg your pardon, pisses them off [laugh], you know.' (K12, 1 December 2022, Study 6)

'There are no uniformed understandings of childhoods and child wellbeing amongst the public in Ghana. Anecdotally, one can talk about the literate and urban population on one hand and the less literate, rural and the conservative on the other. While the former may have read and therefore have more appreciation [of children's rights laws and principles], it may be a bit different with the latter.' (KI3, 1 February 2023, Study 6)

In both these statements the emphasis is placed on a literate versus illiterate divide which informs not necessarily the awareness of dominant rights discourses, but reactions and attitudes towards them. This increased recognition of children's rights among sections of the population in recent years has had an impact on greater scrutiny being paid to certain practices that had adversely impacted children for generations:

'We've been forced to look at issues such as child betrothals, dowries, early marriages and so on in the North and in other parts of the country. We've been forced to look at education, not just in terms of providing the infrastructure which we are not able to do very well, but in terms of schooling you know as something children have to undertake on a daily basis so that they can, er ... we've been forced to look at [the] teacher–child relationship and how the presumption that I am a teacher, an adult, and I have unlimited powers in the classroom and I can do whatever I want to do at any time, we've been forced to look at that; things like sexual abuse of children, you know, we looked at this; these are things that 30 years ago, 40 years ago, er, even 25 years ago happened on a regular basis. Some of them were not even questioned; some people even tried to make some of them as [part of] our culture and so on, you know. But saying all of this does not mean that these things are not happening in the country, you know, erm, there [are] still serious cases of sexual exploitation of children, there [are] still big cases of child labour, there is, er, er, there is still excessive abuse of children in the classroom and so on, but then one would have to reflect on what would have been the case if these policies and their attendant institutions and organizations, some of which have been facilitated by the government, hadn't been there.

Maybe we would be out of, completely out of step with the rest of the world in these things; so yes, I think we haven't reached there, but I think we have enhanced the protection that children can get, and this is manifested in all kinds of things that children, for instance, do.' (K12, 1 December 2022, Study 6)

'The dynamics have changed. Initially, children's issues were not brought out in the open, but now with social media and you know other modern things [modern technology] it's becoming more and more pronounced. For instance, issues of rape, defilement, and abuse of children which were initially kept behind, you know, [closed] doors, are no longer kept behind [closed] doors because a neighbour will see and record and it is all over the, the social media and we do follow ups and there are a lot of arrests, er, so this is something that would not have been possible, er, about ten years or even five years ago and I see that as a positive thing. The negative is that sometimes, er, the media, the way we portray children's issues in the media is sometimes unpalatable, for instance, a child has been defiled and you listen to the radio stations, the way the incident is reported it's as if it is the fault of the child to be defiled. This issue we have talked about severally, but it is still ongoing and sometimes you see children's pictures being splashed all over social media.' (KI1, 11 November 2022, Study 6)

Therefore, while these practices persist, the recognition and openness to children's rights discourses has created a situation whereby politicians and members of the public are now required, or forced, in the words of KI1, to problematize some of these practices and reflect on the linkage between such practices and 'Ghanaian culture'. This particular argument about the linkage between some of the practices and the culture underpinning the lives of some groups within the country demonstrates the extent to which culture is not only a construction, but also it shows the extent to which not all individuals within a given context buy into that culture, or at least, particular aspects of that culture.

Despite these changes relating to awareness that can be attributed to the emergence of a children's rights culture in the country, the progress of dominant children's rights discourses remains limited. In contemporary Ghana, many children remain out of school or unable to attend school on a regular basis. Statistics from the 2021 Population and Housing Census showed that a total of 1,215,546 children of school-going age (4–17 years) in Ghana were not attending school; of that figure 942,427 had never enrolled in school. Of the 16 regions that make up the country, the Savannah region, one of five located in the north, had the highest percentage of children who had never attended school (43.2 per cent) (Ghana Statistical Service,

2022). Sexual abuse, including those of an incestual nature, remains prevalent (Markwei and Tetteh, 2022). While such cases are under-reported, the Ghana Police Service estimated an increase in defilement cases from 730 cases in 2017 to 1,270 cases in 2019 (Markwei and Tetteh, 2022). Added to this, Quarshie's 2021 study, which centred around sexual violence victimization and associated factors among school-going teenagers in urban conurbations in Ghana, found that of 1,692 children and young people aged between 13 and 19 years in formal education in the Greater Accra Region of Ghana who participated in this study, 10.4 per cent of boys and 24.3 per cent of girls reported sexual violence victimization during the previous 12 months (Quarshie, 2021). In relation to physical punishment this continues to be recognized as being widely prevalent and accepted in many households in Ghana regardless of social class or geographical location (Kyei-Gyamfi, 2011; Twum-Danso Imoh, 2013; Ministry of Gender, Children and Social Protection, 2018; Dako-Gyeke, 2019). Its prevalence is further borne out by Multiple Indicator Cluster Surveys[4] produced by the Government of Ghana with support from UNICEF between 1995 and 2018 whenever the question of child discipline was asked as part of the survey. The latest published survey undertaken in 2017/2018 shows that 94 per cent of children aged between one and 14 experienced some form of physical correction, with 17 per cent experiencing severe forms of physical punishment while 76 per cent reported experiencing less severe forms of physical punishment.[5]

Understanding the reasons behind the limited impact of dominant children's rights

Various factors can be pointed to in order to explain challenges in turning dominant children's rights discourses into reality in Ghana. These obstacles can be grouped into three categories: lack of resources; lack of awareness of both the state and the public which results in lack of political will; and a rejection of the dominant concept of children's rights and what it stands for.

First, with regards to the lack of resources, the Department of Social Welfare, which is charged with implementing the 1998 Children's Act, has, in the years since its introduction, lacked the capacity to do so due to a severe lack of both financial and human resources (Twum-Danso, 2011). Conditions of service in the department have consistently remained poor and this, in turn, has demoralized the already disillusioned staff and resulted in persistent high turnover rates over the decades. This has caused a severe shortage of personnel to handle the workload of the department, which has increased tremendously since the passage of the Children's Act in 1998. Many social welfare district offices are only able to employ one social worker, which limits the department's ability to fulfil its mandate. As a result, instead of being able to investigate or follow-up cases and monitor violations of children's rights, district social workers are reduced to their desks and forced to wait for cases to be brought to them (see Twum-Danso, 2011). This is problematic in a context where state intervention in family affairs is still not welcomed and, thus, families rarely take the initiative to report cases of abuse to social workers (Gagnon, 2005). This barrier emerged in interviews with a key informant working in law enforcement on a project about physical punishment (Study 2):

> 'There is a barrier, a kind of information wall around the homes. You will not get that information [about excessive physical punishment] from the homes. The school is a public space so you can get that information. But in the home, parents believe that it is their child. So, if it is not tragic you will not hear about it. If you are not aware that an offence has been committed, you cannot record it. The wall is because of culture and economics. The perpetrator is often the breadwinner so he has the right to do anything, and the mother cannot say anything.' (KI4, Interview, 19 August 2009, Accra, Study 2)

From this comment what emerges is the significant power that the private sphere continues to have within this context which results in difficulties and, perhaps, a hesitation by governments to intervene in family affairs. As the breadwinner of the household, the head of the family, often a man, is seen to hold the final authority over his dependents, resulting in children continuing to be seen as the property of, not simply their parents, as Frimpong-Manso (2014) claims in relation to pre-colonial families in this context, but specifically of their fathers or male caregivers whose power over them is not problematized or challenged (see discussion in Chapter 4, this volume).

Second, the issue of the paucity of resources allocated to initiatives and government departments can be attributed to a lack of awareness among those who make decisions about the allocation of resources at both national and district levels. For instance, while District Assemblies are charged with the implementation of the Act, the evidence indicated that a limited proportion of the District Assembly Common Fund, which is allocated to District Assemblies by central government for the development of their districts, is used for the protection of children, with most resources being allocated to capital projects such as building roads (UN and Government of Ghana, 2004). The resulting impact is the inability of social workers to have access to vehicles so they can investigate cases. This can largely be attributed to the low prioritization placed on the Children's Act by District Assemblies, which results in low levels of awareness among local and national level politicians. In an interview with an Accra Metropolitan Assemblyman representing a central district of the city for Study 1, he admitted that he had not read the Children's Act and, thus, did not know what it contained (Ga Mashie Community Leader 3, Interview, 8 March 2006, Accra, Study 1). As a result of this lack of knowledge that is widespread at the local authority level, it is difficult for many District Assemblies to appreciate the importance of children's rights, and this limits their ability to incorporate these principles into their medium-term plans. This lack of knowledge is also evident among national level politicians. Speaking in the mid-2000s, a representative of a central government agency informed me that there are some MPs who did not even know what was in the country's Children's Act, which many of them had voted into passage in 1998 (KI6, Interview, 27 February 2006, Accra, Study 1).

This lack of knowledge and awareness is reproduced among the general public, where there remain sections of the society who do not know about the Children's Act and the Convention on the Rights of the Child. However, given the work of government and civil society agencies, including the media, the proportion of people who lack a complete awareness of children's rights has dwindled in recent decades. The bigger issue, perhaps, relates to those who are aware, but remain opposed to, the principles underpinning global norms. Specifically, this relates to those who reject the concept of children's rights due to the fact that they see it a threat to the very premise on which Ghanaian cultural values, such as respect and reciprocity, are based. Such attitudes emerged in my first study on children's rights in Ghana (Study 1) where, among some sections of the population in my study sites, the idea of children, or indeed, anyone, having rights *a priori* was often met with rejection by many of the adults I interviewed. According to several participants in the different focus group discussions and interviews that I organized, "We do not want Western children here in Ghana." Implied in this statement is the belief that 'Western' children are disrespectful as a result of rights they have been 'given'. Hence, the belief was expressed that rights result in the production of disrespectful and wilful children who are quick to challenge and disobey the authority of their parents and caregivers and who have been given too much power by the dominant children's rights framework. The anger felt towards the concept of children's rights in some sectors further became apparent in my interview with a chief in one of my study sites in Central Accra in Study 1:

> 'We have enough problems with children without giving them their rights. They should straighten up, go to school, and look after us when we are old. Children's rights are a luxury that only people in London and New York can enjoy. But in [name of community], the basic things are not being taken care of. When you have provided basic things [costs of schooling, medicine] then you can sit down and ask them for their opinions. Because of poverty levels and problems, we do not have

time to discuss these things. We do not have time to ask children their opinions unless they are going to be able to bring money. When I have to worry about where I am going to get my next pay from, I cannot be asking my child for his opinion. ... Besides, you need to enforce things on children. If you leave them, they will do the wrong thing.' (Community Leader 1, Interview, 16 December 2005, Accra, Study 1)

What is interesting about this statement is the assumption that the notion of children's rights better aligns with the lives of children in the US, a country which has yet to ratify the Convention, primarily as a result of conservative sentiments which fear the loss of parental power in rearing their children which are not too dissimilar from the sentiments expressed by some sections of the population in Ghana. These sentiments expressed by this traditional leader were more recently foregrounded in interviews with key informants in Study 6. This shows the extent to which almost 18 years following the interview with a traditional leader in one of my research sites, this resistance to the concept of children's rights persists within sections of the population:

'There is some level of aversion for the term "rights" by a good percentage of the population. A good percentage of the Ghanaian population perceive child rights as alien to them and therefore, [it] is an imposition. Child rights, according to most Ghanaians make children stubborn and difficult to control because it gives too much power and freedom to the child. Some aspects of child rights are perceived [as] anti-cultural, e.g. [provisions on] corporal punishment and therefore [they] are resentful to the average Ghanaian.' (KI3, 1 February 2023, Study 6)

'A good part of the challenge is the fact that many people are still sceptical about child rights ok; some people talk of it in a very derisive way like "Yah you get up and talk of child rights, child rights, this is what has made the children become disrespectful", you know, so for these people it's like reducing indiscipline in society to the presence of child rights.' (KI2, 1 December 2022, Study 6)

What emerges from these comments is an understanding that children's rights are synonymous with principles underpinning discursive understandings of child participation as articulated in the Convention, which causes rejection and anger. This differential reaction to aspects of children's rights, depending on whether they centre around socioeconomic rights or civil and political rights, is further noted by another key informant in Study 6:

'Ghanaians are ready to accept children's rights, but then there is still a gap as to, er, how to let children enjoy these rights. When you mention education, every parent wants the child to go to school, when you mention health, every parent wants the child to have, er, you know, maximum level of health for their children, but there are certain areas that adults don't want to understand when it comes to children's rights. It's, erm, like adults do not want to share the same space with children when it comes to participation and that is an area that probably we may have to do more advocacy.' (KI1, 11 November 2022, Study 6)

This interpretation of children's rights leads to a belief that the concept is about children being empowered, rather than about the provision of basic needs such as education and food, clothing and shelter, which are also rights as conceptualized within dominant frameworks. Instead, when basic rights such as education and food are focused on, there is much more understanding and acceptance by communities because they are perceived as needs that communities have been striving to provide for their children since time immemorial as prescribed by tradition, culture or religion. Tine and colleagues (1998) also made a similar observation – that while there is much misunderstanding of what children's rights mean, there is considerable willingness to promote the fulfilment of children's needs. It is arguably these interpretations of children's rights, which foreground ideas of participation, agency and empowerment, that have facilitated the progress of the protectionist interpretation of the concept of children's rights which has been adopted and utilized by government and civil society actors to engage communities in children's rights discussions and in programmes seeking to encourage a change in attitudes and behaviours. For instance, this association between rights and empowerment of children has led to a hesitance among professionals to frame social justice concerns relating to children in the language of rights. This is supported by McCrystal and Manful (2011) who found, in a study centred around eliciting the views of professionals who are mandated to ensure the rights of children to legal protection in the country, that social work professionals viewed the work they do through the prism of solely protecting children without any consideration of rights-based framing. Using this strategy has also enabled professionals to draw a linkage to traditional patterns of child-rearing and key socialization values that families can identify with, which has also contributed to whatever change in attitudes and practices that has been documented.

Conclusion

This chapter has traced the emergence of the systematic development and expansion of the framework of children's rights as globally articulated within the policy and public discourses in Ghana, especially in the period following 1979. In addition to highlighting the initiatives undertaken, it analyses the role of the president of Ghana (a military ruler who later transformed himself into a civilian leader) during the period when a significant number of the child-focused legislation, policies and initiative were introduced. While over 40 years later this has resulted in greater scrutiny of practices vis-à-vis dominant rights discourses, there remain economic and cultural challenges to the implementation of child-focused laws. Beyond the lack of resources, a central problem that has been identified is an understanding of children's rights that has developed among some groups that perceives rights as synonymous with civil and political rights, which are seen as a threat to cultural norms relating to children's (and indeed, adults') position in society and adult–child relations more generally.

6

Exploring the Multiplicity of Childhoods and Child-Rearing Practices in a Pluralistic Society and the Implications for Children's Rights

Introduction

Having established the historical context of Ghana, especially in relation to the development of dominant children's rights discourses not only in legal and policy discourses, but also within public consciousness, I now want to return my attention to the ideas I had started to develop at the end of Chapter 3 and explore the impact of the country's historical legacy on the plurality of childhood experiences that are identifiable and their implications for children's rights.

Before turning my attention to Ghana, it is important to situate this discussion within a broader African context in order to illuminate the point that Ghana is not unique in relation to this idea of plurality and variability in childhoods and family life more generally. In fact, it is now widely accepted that sub-Saharan Africa is a continent of multiple heritages. Within the region three traditions have been observed as intersecting with each other and together, shaping the beliefs and lifestyles of individuals and communities. These traditions pertain specifically to the respective worldviews of:

1. the diverse Indigenous groups that can be located on the continent;
2. Islamic religion and culture, and
3. Western, primarily Europeanized Christian, traditions.

This state of affairs is a product of a series of developments which are critical to the history of many countries on the continent, most notably: Indigenous cultural norms and values which have been transmitted from generation to generation for thousands of years; Arab incursions on the continent from the early 7th century onwards, which led to mass conversions to Islam in societies across the continent, especially in the North, Sahel, West, East and Horn; evangelization by European missionaries from the 15th century onwards which sought to civilize and convert to a Europeanized form of Christianity, especially through the institution of the school, Indigenous peoples they considered to be primitives living 'ungodly' lifestyles; formal colonization of much of the continent, which was accompanied by the introduction of a cash economy and, in turn, led to a huge desire by Indigenous groups for white-collar jobs and as a result, Western academic education; and the more recent intensification of global processes which has led to the circulation of goods, capital, ideas, media and people. The resulting outcome of these multiple heritages intersecting with each other in the region is the emergence of now politically independent countries in which a diversity of experiences and realities coexist as part of what Ali Mazrui (1986) has termed Africa's 'triple heritage'.

The manifestations of a plural society: the context of Ghana

Ghana, a country of a little over 30 million people currently, is a notable example of the way these multiple influences intersect and impact a society and its peoples. In fact, due to the recognition of Ghana as a society comprising multiple heritages, the concepts of pluralism and duality have long been deployed to explain Ghanaian society and the behaviours of its peoples, most notably in relation to its legislative, political, institutional and religious frameworks. This pluralism can also be identified in the social and cultural aspects of the way people live their lives and approach issues such as healthcare. Much of this confluence of traditions has been documented by local scholars over the decades, such as Awusabo-Asare (1990), Assimeng (1999) and Atiemo (2012). A common thread in all this scholarship produced is that Ghanaian society is dynamic, comprising both internal and external factors which coexist, sometimes complementarily but more often than not, inconsistently, leading to contradictions and tensions in worldviews, behaviours and practices.

This plurality can be seen in myriad ways in the composition of the society. The first relates to the numerous ethnic groups that are located in Ghana today who were all forced to come together to form the Gold Coast colony in the period after the Berlin Conference of 1884–1885 which was hosted by the first chancellor of the newly constructed Germany, Otto von Bismarck. This conference represented what became known as the 'scramble for Africa' as it resulted in the partitioning of the continent by a number of European countries – most notably Britain, France, Germany, Belgium and Portugal (see, for example, Pakenham, 1991). The resulting outcome of this partitioning in the area now known as Ghana was the creation of borders that separated people belonging to the same ethnic group across four different countries. Specifically, it led to whole communities or families being divided between the Gold Coast, a British colony, and three French colonies – Togo (in the case of the Ewe and Mole-Dagbani), Côte d'Ivoire (in the case of the Akan and Mole-Dagbani) and Burkina Faso (in the case of Mole-Dagbani).

The creation of the Gold Coast in this way means that today, it is hard to determine the exact number of ethnic groups that comprise contemporary Ghana. However, writing at the turn of the millennium Awedoba (2002: 40) tentatively put forward the suggestion that 'if linguistic units are anything to go by, the 45 to 50 languages of Ghana should suggest a large number of ethnic groups'. Of these various linguistic units, it is possible to identify four major ethnic groups who are distinguished largely by language, as well as political, social, and other cultural institutions (see Figure 3). The Akan (comprising the subgroups of the Asante, Brong, Akyem, Akwapim, Fante, Ahanta, Nzema, Denyikra and Akwamu) constitute almost half of the country's population (45.7 per cent) and were historically located along the coast in the southwest, as well as further inland in the east and what can be described as the middle belt. The second largest group originate from the northern part of the country, the Mole-Dagbani (comprising the Mamprusi, Mossi, Dagomba, Gonja and Dagaba) who form 18.5 per cent of the population. The Ewe (12.8 per cent) and Ga-Dangme (7.1 per cent) inhabit parts of the southern and eastern belts of the country. In addition

Figure 3: Population by major ethnic groups

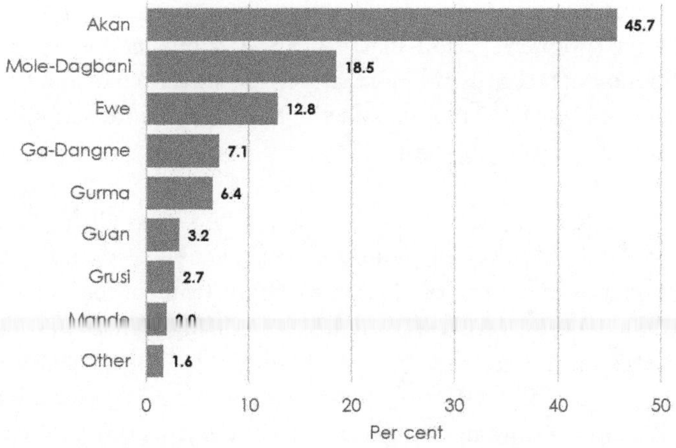

Source: Ghana Statistical Service (2022)

to these, there are smaller groups such as the Gurma (6.4 per cent) and Guan (3.2 per cent) who are seen as Indigenous to some parts of what is now known as Ghana – the northeast and south respectively. However, as a result of improvements in transport facilities and urbanization, most parts of the country have become ethnically mixed, with recent decades witnessing enormous rates of migration from largely rural areas to urban conurbations, especially those in the Greater Accra (mainly Accra, Tema and Ashaiman), Asante (Kumasi and Obuasi) and Western (Bibiani, Tarkwa and Prestea) regions. This movement of people around the country has also led to increased intermarriage between groups, making not only the regions, but also their people, ethnically mixed.

Added to these groups, external influences have entered this area over several centuries. First, the Islamic religion entered this area from the direction of the Sahel, mainly through Mande and Hausa traders and Fulani jihadists wading incursions across West Africa. The migration of these groups, which can be traced back to the 10th century, was facilitated by the trans-Saharan trade routes (Ardayfio-Schandorf, 2006). Second, Western European political, educational, legal and religious values, including Christianity, which although Eastern, re-entered[1] the continent in what can be described as a Europeanized form, through traders, soldiers, missionaries and colonial government officials who came with the purpose to exploit the resources of the country and to convert its people to Christianity from the 15th century onwards (Ardayfio-Schandorf, 2006; Atiemo, 2006). Atiemo, for instance, explains the extent to which foreign religions, especially Christianity, have shaped the nature of the pluralism that can be identified in Ghana:

> The encounter with the West did not involve only the imposition of foreign political structures. It also involved a more disruptive variable – the Christian religion, which together with Islam altered the religious and cultural landscape of many Ghanaian communities. In effect, the transition to a modern nation-state has been accompanied by a growing phenomenon of religious pluralism, which has relativised the previously dominant traditional religious systems that underpinned traditional state structures. (Atiemo, 2006: 365)

The incursions of Europeans into the area now known as Ghana, including through eventual political and economic control, also exposed the country to other societies and peoples, including those from other non-Western contexts. For example, Afro-Brazilians, who had been manumitted or who had escaped enslavement, arrived, in batches, in the Gold Coast from 1829, as part of a bilateral agreement. Settling in Jamestown, they integrated themselves among the Ga-Dangme[2] people who were the primary inhabitants of this area and became known as the Tabom (Schaumloeffel,

2008). Another noteworthy example is the significant number of Lebanese and Syrians who started arriving in the colony in order to escape hardships at home in the latter part of the 19th century at a time when all three territories were colonized by Britain.

Further, the intensification of global processes in the 20th century and its implications for economies, politics, cultures and peoples has also impacted Ghanaian society. Migration is a notable example, as over recent decades immigrants from numerous countries have arrived to settle in Ghana, especially in urban areas. While most are from other countries in the sub-region (Nigeria, Togo, Burkina Faso, Benin, Côte d'Ivoire, Liberia, Sierra Leone, Mali), other immigrants have come from further afield, such as India and China and a range of countries in Europe and the Americas, with most relocating to Ghana for the purpose of exploiting business opportunities.

The legacy of the intermeshing of worldviews on lifestyles and behaviours in Ghana

The resulting outcome of this enmeshing of peoples, traditions and cultures in Ghana is the existence of a plethora of worldviews and practices, some of which overlap and cause contradictions. This has led Atiemo (2012: 88) to argue that being Ghanaian cannot refer to any uniform beliefs or practices which every Ghanaian shares. Instead, he makes the case that '[a]nything that can be referred to as Ghanaian culture must be hybrid containing elements from the traditions of the various Indigenous societies, Western European and Arab Islamic sources'. This hybridity is exemplified in a variety of ways, especially in relation to family life. A good example relates to marriage, which can be contracted in Ghana based on customary or civil laws, or a combination of both. In fact, the majority of people preparing for marriage in Ghana today draw upon both traditions as they make arrangements for their nuptials (Woodman, 2003). While the customary wedding is designed to bring together the two families, the wedding informed by civil law is centred more directly on the two individuals. Related to marriage practices both monogamy and polygyny continue to coexist in the country. While polygynous marriage arrangements can be established from the outset, in some cases, marriages based on monogamy can eventually become polygamous in nature over time. Thus, the influence of Christianity has not replaced the practice of polygamy even among so-called Christians. This is a point that Thérése Locoh (1994) makes in relation to Ghana's neighbour, Togo. Specifically, she argues that with increased schooling in urban areas, the spread of Christianity, the rapid increase in interactions with Western countries and the diffusion of the means of communication, Western notions of monogamy have entered into the culture of Lomé, the capital city. Among the urbanized elite, she claims, there are those who adopt the nuclear family model either under the influence of Christianity or as a result of a desire to be 'modern'. However, this notwithstanding, Locoh (1994) maintains that polygyny persists, especially in rural areas where, at the time she was writing, the most common marital status among women over the age of 20 was that of a wife married to a polygynous man with whom she co-resides. However, this persistence is not just limited to rural areas. She further asserts that as individuals have moved from rural to urban areas and their lives have changed in other ways, the institution of polygyny has adapted to suit changing conditions. This is evident in cases of men whom she describes as 'theoretically monogamist' but who have an informal wife/mistress. This adaptation has led Karanja (1994, cited in Cheal, 2008) to argue that keeping mistresses who do not reside with their husbands in their primary nuclear household and, instead, become part of a secondary household, represents an attempt by elite men in these contexts to reconcile their desire for Western ideals of modernity (Christianity and monogamy) with their continued admiration, albeit expressed differently, for the African practice of polygyny.

These assertions made by Locoh (1994) are also evident in Ghana. Findings gathered from some participants in Study 5, all of whom started primary school before the achievement of independence in 1957, indicated the extent to which being a Christian did not necessarily represent a wholesale replacement of cultural norms and practices in many families. Instead, respondents talked about how, within their families, various aspects of their culture were practised alongside the Christian values they also claimed to adhere to. For instance, nine out of 18 participants in that study were born within families that were already Christian and had been for a few generations. However, at the same time, these families into which some of my participants were born were also polygamous. For instance, one of my participants from Central Accra provided the following information about his father: "My father was a polygamist. He married four women, including my mother, married them at different intervals, but without divorcing anyone, but my mother left him because he married another woman. So, she left and so I was the only person born [to mother and father]." However, later on in the same interview he stated that: "My father was a Methodist before even I was born. He was a leader and a teacher, Sunday school teacher. He was a leader and a Sunday school teacher [repeated]. Even my grandmother [father's mother] was a Methodist" (Participant 4; male; year of birth: 1930; region of origin: Greater Accra; interviewed 21 June 2018, Accra, Study 5).

Another participant, also from Central Accra, explained when talking about the religion of his family, that: "We are all Methodists. ... Er, my grandfather, my father's side, and [on] my mother's side too my grandmother was the first to become a Methodist. They were all Methodist." However, at the same time, in explaining the living arrangements in his family, which spread across three different households, he informed me that: "No [his parents living separately was not because of the breakdown of their marriage] because by then he [father] had married another wife. The second wife was then living with her mother somewhere. So [my] mother was here, [the] second wife was there and [my]father was somewhere else" (Participant 5; male; year of birth: 1933; region of origin: Greater Accra; interviewed 21 June 2018, Accra, Study 5). Thus, in this way Christianity and its insistence on monogamy coexisted with the age-old practice of polygyny. An individual, primarily a man, could be both a Christian and have several wives whom he has married under both civil and customary law, respectively. This coexistence remains evident in contemporary Ghana either in its traditional form, or in a more adapted form, which may or may not adhere to customary law.

Another example relates to kinship ties which have been well documented in anthropological literature focusing on sub-Saharan Africa (for example, Fortes, 1949; Evans-Pritchard, 1951). What emerges from the literature based upon these various, primarily anthropological studies, is the high degree of mutual support (Fortes, 1949; Evans-Pritchard, 1951; Goody, 1973, 1982; Alber et al, 2010), interdependence, cooperation and reciprocity that exist within a lineage or kinship group whether they follow a matrilineal or patrilineal descent pattern (La Ferrara, 2003; see also the discussion in Chapter 3, this volume). This results in a situation whereby the production, distribution and circulation of goods, resources, wealth and assets are shared within this grouping. It is this circulation of goods, resources and mutual support and interdependencies that tie family members in what Fortes (1949) once called a 'web of kinship'. In relation to Ghana, Ardayfio-Schandorf puts it well when she states:

> Within the indigenous culture, families lived together, worked together, owned property jointly, and took responsibility for the upbringing and enculturation of the young together. There was a high premium on childbearing, and polygyny was even encouraged under certain circumstances. The communities in which people lived were smaller, and communality reigned. Thus, apart from procreation, economic cooperation and production within the family, socialization, and caregiving to family members as well as the enculturation of the young were tasks usually performed not only by the biological parents but also the extended family. (Ardayfio-Schandorf, 2006: 132)

These ties binding kinfolk together continue to be important for individuals in Ghana (MacLean, 2011) due to the persisting emphasis placed on mutual obligation and support, cooperation and solidarity. This prioritization of bonds among kin are not only as a result of the lack of an effective state welfare system in a context of the lack of resources, but also due to the recognition of the importance of the benefits of fostering connections and trust among kinfolk in particular (Tsai and Dzorgbo, 2012).

However, in recent decades enormous widespread social, economic and political transformations have had an impact on attitudes, behaviours and family practices (Kaye, 1962; Aboderin, 2004; Oppong, 2006). These shifts can be summed up as consisting of urbanization (Gugler and Flanagan, 1978; Goody, 1989; Oppong, 2006); colonial rule which introduced a cash economy, leading to the opportunity for individuals to accumulate personal wealth which they could use to cater for their own needs (Little, 1953; Azu, 1974); new laws introduced by colonial governments and maintained by post-colonial governments relating to inheritance and property relations (Allman, 1997); the formation of state employment and its attendant compensation programmes which assumed the existence of a nuclear family model (Fapohunda, 1987; Goody, 1989); Christianity and the work of different denominations of missionaries who, in their teachings, foregrounded conjugal family bonds while disapproving of polygyny (Allman, 1997); the advent of the institution of the school and the new forms of knowledge it introduced as well as the careers to which it could lead (Kaye, 1962; Ardayfio-Schandorf, 1996; Twum-Danso Imoh, 2020); and new norms about parenthood and childhood promoted by media images which have entered into community consciousness, leading to a change in understanding of what it means to be 'modern'.

These demographic changes have led to more individualistic pursuits and a loosening of bonds and notions of mutual obligations and reciprocity among kin in sections of Ghanaian society (Aboderin, 2004; Oppong, 2006). In relation to reciprocity, Ming-Chang Tsai and Dan-Bright Dzorgbo's (2012) study found that some individuals had retreated from social exchanges that have historically been central to the notion of reciprocal obligations among kin, leading to the production of a small number of self-reliant families in the country. Related to this is the increasing visibility of family units in urban areas in particular that, ostensibly at least, appear to be nuclear-based – centred around two married adults living with, and assuming the role of primary carer for, their biological children.[3]

The impact of nuclear family formation on kinship bonds has been noted by numerous scholars. Writing more generally about Africa in the 1960s, Marris (1966) claimed that when nuclear families relocated away from their extended family members, the frequency of visiting decreased and mutual aid declined (in Kayongo Male and Onyango, 1984). Within the context of Ghana this shift was noted by Kaye (1962: 135), who in the early 1960s, observed that some educated married couples preferred to live by themselves on 'European patterns', instead of as a part of an extended family household. He further noted that 'this must have a great effect on the nature of the relations between themselves and their children'. He attributed this not only to the influence of Christianity and urbanization, but also to formal education. Writing several decades later, Ardayfio-Schandorf (1996) identified how school-based education, alongside Christianity, had, in the years since independence, led to a strengthening of relations between spouses and, in turn, between them and their children at the expense of relations with kin.

This increasing visibility of nuclear family bonds and its impact on relations with kin is further supported by findings from Study 3 which sought to adopt a life history approach to explore continuity and change in child-rearing practices within three or four generations in four Ghanaian families. This emphasis on prioritizing nuclear family bonds over those with kin were especially noted in two families: Family A, which consisted of four generations, an elderly woman aged 87, her 62-year-old daughter, her 38-year-old granddaughter and her 15-year-old great grandson; and Family B which comprised three generations, an elderly woman aged 88, her 71-year-old daughter and her 25-year-old granddaughter. Within Family A the foregrounding of nuclear family bonds became evident during the interview with the second-generation participant, Madam Manubea, who married a man who worked for a government agency in a port town far away from their natal village and whose job came with accommodation. It is in this government-owned bungalow miles away from their village that Madam Manubea and her husband raised their six children. The composition of the family was noted by her daughter, Abena, age 38, who was the fourth child and eldest daughter: "[W]e lived with only mum and dad, so we didn't stay with aunties and uncles. It wasn't like that. It was very much a nuclear family." This lack of kin within the social network established by this family is further seen when Abena acknowledges that while they experienced a communal style of living as they were growing up in their neighbourhood, this was "not with family, but with neighbours", many of whom were also associated with the government agency that employed her father. Hence, these living quarters provided by government for employees led to a situation whereby members of this family were physically distanced from their extended family. In fact, as she was growing up, she hardly went to her parents' village. Instead, the relatives (except her maternal grandma) would visit them and go back:

> 'Apart from my first year at secondary, I had not been really going to [name of village]. I did not know it. Rather, sometimes they would visit their sister [her mother]. So, they would rather be coming to [town where she grew up], rather than us going to [name of village]. ... But my grandma never visited. My grandpa did once. He was coming to Accra because he had a linkage with the *Gas* [Ga-Dangme] so he would

come for *Homowo*[4] and then he would visit us in [name of town] and then go back. My father's mother would come and visit sometimes but not my mother's mother. She never visited us in [name of town] when I was growing up. I don't remember her ever ever.' (Interview, 17 August 2013, Cape Coast, Study 3)

It was not until it was time for her to attend secondary school that she finally became acquainted with the village. This was because the school – a boarding school – was near her parents' natal village. However, as she was younger than her classmates, her father was concerned about her becoming a boarder and being mistreated by other students. Therefore, he only agreed to let her attend that school if she could register as a day student for the first year. It is within this context that Abena came to live with her grandmother for one year and became acquainted both with her and the village. However, once she became a boarder from her second year of secondary school onwards, her visits to the village became less frequent as she would go to the town where she grew up to spend each school holiday with her parents and siblings. Therefore, it seems that while the extended family was present in Abena's childhood, it was the relationship between the parents and the children which was paramount in this family unit. This emerges clearly in her account of the time spent together as a family or the time they spent specifically with their father due to the nature of their mother's occupation:

'We did a lot [have family time]. Sometimes in the evening when mum is around we would sit and chat and they would give us stories, you know; because we were not coming to the village they would tell us stories about their own upbringing, some of their experiences and all that so we used to ... and because mum may be at the market and will not return early, when we finish eating, we would spend a lot of time with dad; we chat, sometimes we would go out, not often though, but sometimes, there was this big base – a drinking spot/ restaurant – and we would go and sit there and just have bottles of Coke and Fanta and [we] would feel so happy.' (Interview, 17 August 2013, Cape Coast, Study 3)

While ensuring that their children had an awareness of their culture and village of origin, this statement demonstrates the extent to which this family's structure was very much based on a nuclear family unit, with bonds between parents and their children being prioritized above all other kinship ties. The relationship between the father and children in this family was especially notable due to the time he appears to have invested in the relationship.

In Family B the shift to foregrounding nuclear family bonds started to occur as part of the socialization process adopted by the first-generation participant,

MULTIPLICITY OF CHILDHOOD CONCEPTUALIZATIONS

88-year-old Madam Akosua who had been fostered out to her aunt from the age of about two until she married her husband in her late teens and proceeded to have 11 children. Her husband had been educated through primary and secondary school and attended a teacher's college. Therefore, he was a teacher and catechist and later trained to become a Methodist pastor. Once they were married, she came to live with her husband in what she calls a 'mission house' owned by the church, which was within the same region in which she was born and reared, but in a different town. Here, as she informed me, "[I]t was just me and my husband. No family members were there." She further added that, after she had her first child "[W]hen he [husband] came back from school he would come and look after the baby so if I had something to do, I could go and do it" (Interview, 6 August 2013, Central Region, Study 3). Given their separation from the rest of their extended family due to her husband's occupation, which resulted in frequent transfers and relocations, this family spent a lot of time together. Madam Akosua gave an insight into this aspect of their family life when she explained how she and her husband raised their children:

> 'We used to have morning devotions at home and during the morning devotions we would admonish our children to have good behaviour so that later wherever they find themselves as adults, they would respect authority and they would work well wherever they find themselves. ... Also, he [husband] taught the children to play the organ, so all the children know how to play the organ. What he used to do was that early in the morning he would call one of them and tell him to play a particular tune and that tune is what we would use for our morning devotion. Through that the children rehearsed until they perfected the act of playing the organ.' (Interview, 6 August 2013, Central Region, Study 3)

This was further supported by her daughter, Auntie Serwaa, who underscored the close bonds that existed within the family as they were growing up: "We are all one. We were all one. We respected each other. We are related to each other as a bond family. We were free with everybody. Very free to talk. Everybody is a friend to everybody" (Online interview, 25 June 2013, USA). The data from this family, similar to Family A, highlights the close relationship parents sought to develop with, and between, their children, through building in specific times of the day which were structured in a way to foster closer ties within this unit.

This weakening of bonds with the extended family also emerged in a later study undertaken in 2018 (Study 5) when one of my participants, on reflecting on how he and his wife raised their children, revealed the lack of interaction with their respective hometowns:

137

'Unfortunately. It is unfortunate, for instance, we were not sending them to our village. Even the mother would not take them to [name of wife's village] and me too, I didn't bother to take them to my side. It was only when I was installed as a Chief that they attended my installation.' (Participant 7; male; year of birth: 1931; region of origin: Eastern; interviewed 23 June 2018, Accra, Study 5)

While migration and urbanization can be pointed to as factors underpinning this disconnect between these families and their kinfolk, there is also a need to consider the possibility that the reduced interaction was due to an active decision by these couples to parent their offspring in a different way from previous generations – possibly as a result of both Christian values and formal education, both of which foregrounded nuclear family bonds. The role parents played in this disconnect emerges in the language from the previous statement in which the participant uses expressions such as "we were not sending them", "the mother would not take them", "I didn't bother to take them". Underpinning this language is a reluctance, or a lack of a desire on behalf of these parents, for their children to develop a certain level of familiarity with, and knowledge about, their villages and towns of origin.

This shift towards more closer bonds within a nuclear family among sections of the population does not necessarily mean that value is no longer placed on kinship bonds or the concept of communalism in Ghana (MacLean, 2011; Tsai and Dzorgbo, 2012). For many, ties with kinfolk continue to be valued, not only as a result of the support system they provide in the absence of effective welfare services or due to the weakness of state institutions (Nsamenang, 2002); they continue to persist because the kinship group continues to play a role in identity formation and the development of a sense of belonging. However, these bonds among kin have changed in nature and scope over time, leading to a situation whereby more individuals make their own decisions and choices about their lives, including who they marry and how they raise their children. Added to this is the emergence of groups among whom familial bonds within kinship groups have indeed declined in favour of the development of strong bonds within friendship groups along with their attendant reciprocal exchanges (MacLean, 2011). The key point to be made here is that in the contemporary period these different family forms and the values that underpin them are all identifiable and coexist in Ghana, leading to different experiences of family life.

Implications of interlocking worldviews for childhood construction and children's lived experiences in Ghana: the example of transitions to adulthood

Against this backdrop of duality and pluralism – both historical and contemporary – any statement underscoring the plurality of lifestyles or childhoods in Ghana seems somewhat obvious. What outcome other than plurality can emerge in the construction of childhood and children's lived experiences of growing up from this enmeshing of peoples, cultures (including those external), religions (including those external) and landscapes (see also Nsamenang, 2004)?

This plural environment shapes understandings of childhoods, transitions to adulthood and the realities of children's lives in a number of ways. Attitudes and practices around determining the transition from childhood to adulthood presents a good illustration of the multiplicity of realities that exist. Puberty rites, for example, have historically played a critical role in the transition from childhood to adulthood for many ethnic groups in this context:

> Precolonial education in both Ghana and Mozambique was largely based on oral traditions, and young people were taught about, and initiated into, the community and its values by various members of the community, in particular elders (Ndege 2007; Adu-Agyem and Osei-Poku 2012). Apprenticeships and initiation rites formed important means of educating young people, the latter being crucial to marking the transition of childhood to adulthood. Initiation rituals were performed separately for girls and boys, and were geared to teaching them about appropriate (female/male) conduct and behaviour, and the duties associated with various social positions within the community (Ndege 2007). (Miedema and Oduro, 2017: 73–74)

While some ethnic groups have puberty rites for both boys and girls as part of an Indigenous way of educating young people as they made their transition to adult male and female status – a process which is pivotal in a society where rigid distinctions continue to be made between masculinity and femininity – some only have puberty rites for girls (Miedema and Oduro, 2017). For this group, in particular, rites of passage ceremonies were intended to celebrate their readiness to bear children and prepare them to become 'good' wives and mothers (Glozah and Lawani, 2014; Miedema and Oduro, 2017).

Although there are similarities in how puberty rites are structured between ethnic groups, especially those for girls, the exact details of their organization demonstrate their distinct features. Among the Akan, for example, who hold puberty rites for girls only, the transition to adulthood for this group historically included a rites of passage ceremony called *Bragoro* which took place over a period of a week normally around the end of January or early February, soon after a girl's menarche (Sarpong, 1977; Arthur and Mensah, 2021). The ceremony was seen to facilitate the entrance of girls into the activities of their community as individuals with full adult status as the week was used to mark the fact that they were ready to bear children as well as prepare them to become 'good' wives (Sarpong, 1977; Miedema and Oduro, 2017; Boateng and Agyeman, 2018; Arthur and Mensah, 2021). The actual rite involved girls who had experienced their menarche being presented to the Queen Mother of the community who would undertake a physical inspection to check that they were still virgins and were not pregnant (Hale, 2013). Historically, failing this test would have led to the girl (and the man who impregnated her in the case of pregnancy) being ostracized by the village (Boateng and Agyeman, 2018). This can be attributed to the high value placed on the morality of womanhood in Akan society.

Central to the rite was the ritual bathing in a river near the village. This was followed by a grooming process which involved the initiate having her nails trimmed before being dressed in white cloth, with her upper body left bare and adorned with jewellery and beads on various parts of the body, including her waist and ankles (Hale, 2013). On her return from the river the girl was enthroned on a stool in a public space near her house (Sarpong, 1977; Hale, 2013) as an older woman placed an egg in her mouth, which she had to swallow whole, an act which symbolized her fertility. Biting the egg instead of swallowing it whole signified biting the seeds of her womb and, thus, implied future infertility. The girl was then welcomed as an adult by all in the village. As part of the last step in this rite of passage ceremony, the initiate, now recognized as a woman, performed a thanksgiving ritual by walking around the whole community to give thanks to all its members.

A similar age-old elaborate rite of passage identifiable in Ghana can be found among the Krobo people who were historically located in the southeastern part of the country. Known as *Dipo*, it is probably the most well-known rite of passage ceremony in the country, having been subjected to great scrutiny and documented by academics (local and foreign) as well as tourists who still travel to observe the annual ritual which continues in some communities. Like *Bragoro*, *Dipo*, which takes place annually over a period of ten days between March and June, is a ritual that marks the transition to womanhood for girls who are in the early stages of puberty and are associated with the shrines of different 'traditional' priests (Steegstra, 2005). The timing for a girl to undergo *Dipo* is not associated with her menarche, but like *Bragoro*, fertility is central to the ritual as it is a taboo for a girl to become pregnant before the rites take place (Steegstra, 2005). In fact, determining the virginity status and pregnancy possibility of girls is a key element of the process (Glozah and Lawani, 2014). A girl who is found to be pregnant becomes a social outcast who is seen as impure. The way their virginity is verified involves girls being made to sit and rise repeatedly on a sacred stone. The rationale behind this is that if a girl is not a virgin, she will become stuck to the stone on the third count. As failing this test can lead to rejection by families, girls strive to do all they can to ensure their chastity prior to the initiation due to the fact that among the Krobo,

Dipo is not seen as just a puberty rite; instead it is a rite which reaffirms an individual's identity as Krobo.

A pivotal element of the rite involves girls being taken away from their home for a period of seclusion alongside older women. During this time, they are taught about their role as adult married women and instructed in the development of key skills such as cooking, cleaning and sweeping, as well as skills which could enable them to generate income such as basket-weaving and pottery-making. Similar to the *Bragoro* rites of passage, ritual bathing plays a key part in this process as bathing in the river is seen to cleanse both body and spirit. This ritual ends with a ceremony with girls parading through the village, bare-chested with their bodies adorned with expensive beads and other jewellery and the lower parts of their body covered in expensive cloth. This parade serves to enable initiates to declare their virginity to their community and demonstrate that they are ready for marriage (Glozah and Lawani, 2014).

While such puberty rites for girls continue to exist, there has been a reduction in the number of families that continue to follow these rituals over the course of the last 100 years or so. This is especially the case in relation to *Bragoro*, which is no longer observed by most Akans although there remain some communities among the Asante, a subgroup of the Akan, who continue to adhere to the ritual. Interestingly, in recent years Queen Mothers in some Asante villages have started to explore the possibility of resurrecting the practice in communities where it has died out. This is largely because they see it as a strategy to curb perceived promiscuity among girls and young women (Antwi and Okyere-Manu, 2018). However, any resurrection has only been evident in a small number of cases. This is quite dissimilar to the practice of *Dipo*, which stands out in discussions of rites of passage rituals in Ghana largely as a result of its enduring nature within Krobo society.

The decline noted in adherence to rites such as the *Bragoro* among certain groups such as the Akan can be largely attributed to widespread conversions to Christianity and Islam, which, in turn, result in the creation of new value systems within some families and leads them to distance themselves from, and disapprove of, local practices (Ardayfio-Schandorf, 2006). Consequently, such families do not allow their daughters to engage in rituals of this nature either at all or not in their conventional forms as they see it as 'ungodly'. Even in relation to *Dipo*, which continues to be a well-known practice in contemporary Krobo society, Steegstra observed a change in the practice:

> Throughout my fieldwork, I had numerous conversations with Krobo people about tension felt between Christianity and *dipo*. I often encountered the views – held by Krobo Christians from different denominations – that *dipo* is not celebrated today as 'in the olden days,' and that *dipo* has become 'more pagan' and is deemed 'outmoded' and 'immoral.' *Dipo* is seen as inimical to 'development' in a world where

Christianity is linked with 'enlightenment' and 'modernity.' Christianity has become the dominant religion in Southern Ghana where most people now call themselves Christians. A few old Presbyterians families originating from the first Krobo converts have abstained from *dipo* since generations and strict Christian church members do not want to be associated with *dipo*. The rites represent 'paganism' and therefore local Christian churches do not allow their followers to participate in the rites. Nowadays, especially adherents of Pentecostal churches criticize the rites. (Steegstra, 2005: 2)

This creation of a new value system, and indeed, a new culture, created by Christianity, in particular, is a theme that has emerged in my own research. For instance, in Study 5, which focused on the impact of British colonial rule on constructions of childhood, several participants talked about how they grew up in families that ensured that they kept away from so-called traditional practices due to the fact that they did not correspond with Christian teachings. According to one of my interview participants who was born to a family that had converted to Christianity several generations before she was born:

'We were in the [church] choir, and we were given that sort of training where we weren't supposed to go and visit friends and walk around town ... unless you are sent to go and buy something, you had no business entering a store – to do what? You couldn't, so we sort of led restricted lives. You can't go here, you can't go there and there was this idea of, there are certain practices we shouldn't engage in; for example, we used to see fetish priests and priestesses dancing and so on. We were not supposed to even look that way because it was completely devilish, satanic you know, that sort of thing. Anyone who goes to church shouldn't go anywhere near such things. That was the sort of training we had. And up to, er, the time when you were really grown up and on your own you felt that anyone who even went to stand and watch this sort of thing is not a Godly person. It is a taboo. And then you also had stories about members of the family, some of them being devils, witches and wizards. Don't eat from this house. Don't go there. Don't associate yourself with anyone from that house, that sort of upbringing, because the people indulged in, erm, witchcraft and all sorts of things; even though there was no proof, you dare not challenge anyone. So, you grew up with the fear that your Auntie, your cousin, your uncle, your grandmother, especially [laugh] if your great grandmother is alive, then she is a witch; to be alive at this age she's a witch – that was the sort of upbringing we had.' (Participant 1; female; year of birth: 1943; region of origin: Western; interviewed 14 June 2018, Accra, Study 5)

This also emerged in an interview with a respondent from Central Accra who makes a distinction between a culture created by Christianity to which believers were expected to adhere in order to maintain what he calls their "prestige" in society, and the culture that informed the value system and behaviours of their fellow community members who had not made a similar religious conversion:

'When they were bringing me up, we go to church on Sundays in the morning, in the afternoons we come to Sunday school. There, they teach us how to read the Bible, study the Bible well and we should go out to do evangelism. There, we started to follow our father's or grandfather's footsteps to become a Christian. They taught us, I wasn't alone oh, I was there with my brothers and sisters, they taught us how we should go about studying the Bible, teach us, er, the way Christ came to be and how we should, I mean, the, the, er, er, I could say, how we should treat our brothers and sisters who are next to us and people outside. You see they taught us how to evangelize. Being a Christian, we don't go much about the culture [of their community]. Being a Christian, we don't have to. We were taught not to go to, to, this, to follow these our cultures. When something is happening outside like this, we all kept [stayed] indoors. Being a Christian, we don't have to follow their footsteps. At present as I am sitting down here if anything is happening outside, a cultural thing, I don't go near [it]. So, [our] parents don't follow these steps, so they don't teach us. As for *Homowo* they cook in the house, and they call all of us to participate. That is all. Apart from *Homowo* we didn't do anything else. Not much. It is only these folks, the fisher folks, who really enjoy *Homowo* because it is part of their culture [laugh]. They rather enjoy the *Homowo* festival much more than we, the Christians. Well, of course, we were taught, being a Christian, we were taught not to follow their footsteps so that we don't lose our prestige.' (Participant 5; male; year of birth: 1933; region of origin: Greater Accra; interviewed 21 June 2018, Accra, Study 5)

In some instances, this conversion to Christianity, and the culture that participants associated with it, meant a separation between children and their parents in cases whereby the latter, unlike their children, had not undergone the same religious conversion or schooling experience. This emerged in an account of a participant in Study 5 whose aunt came to take him from his parents' home to live with her in another town for the purpose of sending him to school which involved him becoming baptized:

'During that time as I was a student, I was not mingling with them [parents], with that their [parents'] culture because in the school we were taught different thing. They [parents] also are holding their culture, so I am not used to their culture. If they [parents] are doing their culture, I leave them alone. Then I concentrate on my schooling. So, I don't know much about Krobo culture. Yeah, I know some, but the deepest ones that the chiefs and people do, that one, I don't know.' (Participant 8; male; year of birth: 1941; region of origin: Eastern; interviewed 16 June 2018, Tema)

This process of religious conversion and civilizing Indigenous populations with a focus on children involved the development and implementation of a series of strategies by missionary groups, which set the individual apart from his or her community. In her study on the Basel Mission's schools in the Gold Coast (present-day Ghana), Koonar (2014) found that 'through their education at Basel Mission Schools, their eventual Baptism and their training and work experience at the mission stations, African children were being carefully prepared for a future that emphasized colonial and missionary values and attempted to reduce the influence of African communities'. This was done because of the fear among many missionary groups that the lifestyle and ways of living that were inherent to diverse African communities were incompatible with the core principles of being a 'Good Christian' and, ultimately, would result in 'evident damage to their souls' (Koonar, 2014: 78). As a result, Basel missionaries in the Gold Coast and elsewhere advocated for segregated communities in the areas in which they operated, including entirely segregated villages, which would allow Christian converts to live separately from the rest of their natal community. This desire to keep children apart from their communities led to a situation whereby 'the young members were trained to be members of the minority Christian community rather than members of the community as a whole' (Martin, 1970: 50, cited in Ofori-Attah, 2006: 419). This strategy of the Basel missionaries and its impact on children was further identified by a participant in Study 5 who grew up within a region in which Basel missionaries were especially active:

'Children were expected to come to Church on Sundays, er, you could get into trouble at school if you were found indulging in fetish rites. In many of the places [parts of the town] they had, there was some kind of segregation. The Christians lived at their own part, usually called Salem, er, the idea was to protect them from the idol worshippers. So, in many of the towns where Presbyterians established ministries you'll find [a neighbourhood], sometimes called *schoolmu* in Twi, because that is where the schools were built, or sometimes [it will be called] Salem. So, if you go to Akropong today you can ask about Salem, and they'll show you. So, there was a strong Christian slant, erm.' (Participant 6;

male; year of birth: 1944; region of origin: Eastern; interviewed 22 June 2018, Accra, Study 5)

Therefore, what emerges here is the extent to which in addition to the cultures associated with the various ethnic groups that had existed in this locale for generations, the spread of Christianity in this context created an additional culture informed by the principles of this religion. While for some this new religion has come to coexist with more traditional practices such as polygyny, for others becoming a Christian and the status it afforded an individual resulted in the need to reject more local beliefs and their attendant practices and milestones. Added to these groups were those families, such as that of Participant 5 (Study 5), whose accounts of his childhood outlined in relation to this point as well as in the discussion about the polygynous arrangements in which he grew up (see earlier discussion in this chapter), did not mean the end of polygyny even though it signified a withdrawal from elements of Ga-Dangme culture and spirituality.

Beyond religion a key development that has influenced the attitudes of some families towards such practices is formal education and the role it has come to play in marking the transition from childhood to adulthood. A key rationale behind the ceremonies underpinning the rites of passage rituals described earlier was to show off newly recognized 'women' to prospective husbands from their community and demonstrate that they were ready for marriage. However, in contemporary Ghana this declaration of marriage readiness by pubescent girls is no longer perceived as relevant or desirable in many families in communities where such practices can be identified as they now seek to access formal education for both their sons and daughters up until the completion of, at least, secondary school, and possibly beyond. Therefore, the notion of their daughters going through this practice, which normally takes place between the ages of 12 and 14, but sometimes at age 11, no longer seems necessary. What this means is that this value placed on formal education serves as a deterrent for many families and may have also altered the way they perceive, and construct, markers to monitor the transition from childhood to adulthood for their daughters.

This notwithstanding, it is also important to note that the options available to families in relation to these practices are not framed in binary terms – adhering to the practice or not. For example, in the case of *Bragoro* there also exist Akan families who have adopted a compromise between tradition and modernity by adapting the approach for the 'modern' period which aligns well with their educational and religious sensitivities. This adaptation consists of feeding their daughters, upon their menarche, a meal called *Eto*, a sacred dish consisting of mashed yam mixed with onions and palm oil which is served with a boiled egg placed on top of the yam. While it can be served on various special occasions, its significance here relates to the fact that it is used to celebrate an individual's status as an adult woman after her first menstruation, with the boiled egg symbolizing fertility. For those who continue to participate in the ritual itself they have sought to modify the practice by ensuring that the breasts of girls are covered at the very least (Arthur and Mensah, 2021). Therefore, in relation to puberty rites, there exist various attitudes and realities. For some these practices persist while for others these are scorned due to religious beliefs and formal education. For some, too, they adopt a hybrid approach which sees them adhere to the principles underlying a particular rite of passage while adapting the practice in order to bring it in line with new values they have adopted as a result of religion or formal education (Hale, 2013; Arthur and Mensah, 2021).

These diverse approaches to marking the maturation of girls upon their menarche is an indication that contemporary Ghanaian society is caught between multiple legacies which continue to shape how lifestyles are constructed and realities are experienced, including those relating to children. The first relates to norms that have been transmitted from generation to generation since the pre-colonial period. The second involves values that have been imbibed because of a more recent historical event – colonialism and its attendant missionary engagement. These two legacies intersect at a crossroads and create a situation whereby the relationship between communities in Ghana and global and dominant human rights principles are varied, fluid and inconsistent. Specifically, this hybridity leads to the production of individuals whose outlook incorporates both traditional and Westernized and/or Islamic values, picking and choosing which cultural heritage to adopt and which to flout at any one time (Twum-Danso, 2008). This point is supported by Howard (1986: 23), who observes that 'people are quite adept at being cultural accommodationists; they are able implicitly to choose which aspects of a "new" culture they wish to adopt and which aspects of the "old" they wish to retain'.

The question then becomes: what does this all mean for dominant children's rights principles? Simply put, it shows that there can be no singular interaction between children's lives and dominant children's rights in any context. In Ghana, given the plurality that underpins all facets of the society, including those relating to the sphere of the family and the child-rearing practices adopted, there are not only varying attitudes about child rearing and the treatment of children, but there are also diverse lived experiences of growing up within this context, including in relation to dominant children's rights principles. Specifically, while practices such as *Dipo*, which continues in some Krobo communities today, challenge dominant children's rights norms and ideals and have been subject to numerous campaigns seeking to end the practice, there also exist families belonging to the same ethnic group who no longer mark the transition between childhood and adulthood through a rites of passage ceremony, preferring instead to draw on milestones relating to formal education which they now use to measure the ending of childhood. However, to further show the breadth of the lived realities versus children's rights scenarios that exist in Ghana, this chapter has also shown how for some families the adoption of new ideas and values does not necessarily lead to a wholesale replacement of their culture; instead, they seek to combine these new ideas with norms associated with their Indigenous culture, leading to some kind of hybridized outcome whereby the lifestyle people adopt reflects aspects of both (see Twum-Danso Imoh, 2019). By using the notion of hybridity to describe this third possibility I do not mean to convey a sense of peaceful coexistence. While some families may find a way of striking harmony between these norms, others too end up with lived realities or adopting child-rearing practices which are characterized by contradictions and significant amounts of 'chopping and changing' in their worldviews, behaviours and practices, depending on the issue at hand. Sometimes these worldviews are dependent on the objective they are seeking to achieve at a given time. Therefore, the plurality of this context, as with other contexts, results in a multiplicity of experiences.

Conclusion

This chapter has highlighted the extent to which the multiple heritages underpinning Ghanaian society shape the plurality of existences or realities that can be identified in the country in the contemporary period, including in relation to understandings of childhood and its termination. While for some families the dynamics of their lifestyle are shaped by one heritage more than the others, many adopt worldviews, behaviours and practices that reflect a hybridity in how they perceive, understand and experience the world around them. This results in multiple childhood and children's rights experiences or possibilities.

7

The Plurality of Childhoods and the Significance for Rights Discourses: An Exploration of Child Duty and Work Against a Backdrop of Social Inequality

Introduction

Embedded in understandings and indeed, accounts, of childhoods in Ghana and in other contexts in Africa has been the notion of children's duties or responsibilities, which primarily manifest themselves not only in the behaviour expected of children within the context of the family, but also through the work tasks they undertake. Some of this work in which children engage generates income for themselves or their family alongside – or independent of – other household members. This particular aspect of the work children undertake has generated much academic and policy attention over recent decades due to its perceived hazards as well as its implications for children's development, wellbeing and formal educational trajectories. Abebe sets out the crux of dominant policy concerns about child work well when he states:

> Accordingly, children's participation in work – although paradoxically amplified by and increasingly subordinated to the global political economy – is seen as a hindrance to achieving children's rights and realizing the millennium development goals such as ensuring the universal enrolment of children in schools by 2015 (United Nations, 2007). Article 32 of the CRC emphasizes the right of children to be prevented from 'performing any work that is likely to interfere with their education', while Article 28 expresses the conviction that children have the right to be educated and that primary schools should be made

free and compulsory for that purpose. What these Articles suggest is a denigration of work contrasted with an idealisation of the potential of schooling (Ansell, 2005). By claiming that the state knows what is in the best interests of the child, the CRC not only diverts attention away from families and communities who sustain children's protection and provision (however refracted), it also denies children the right to benefits arising from work appropriate to their age. (Abebe, 2013: 86)

While it is this paid work in which children engage that has received the bulk of policy and academic attention, children also undertake other forms of work that ensure the maintenance of the household – cooking, cleaning, washing clothes and utensils, yard work, taking care of siblings, running errands, and working on the farm to grow produce to feed the family. Using the work children do as an analytical lens this chapter seeks to explore the plurality of childhoods within the context of Ghana

Situating child work within Ghanaian notions of personhood and its attendant mutuality of duty within and between generations

Although many accounts of children's work in Ghana exist and some of these make linkages to the notion of children having duties to their families and communities, very little of this literature traces the value placed on children working (whether in – or outside – the home) to the historical construction of personhood within this context and its implications for the constructions of both childhood and social relations.

In Ghana, as elsewhere in sub-Saharan Africa, communitarian principles, which have already been discussed in earlier chapters of this volume (see Chapters 3, 4 and 6), historically shaped social relations (Gyekye, 1996, 2013). The centrality of principles underpinning communalism within the societies that make up the country now known as Ghana resulted in a situation whereby notions and behaviours that reflect interdependence, cooperation, sociability, mutual assistance as well as mutual obligation and reciprocity were foregrounded. Among the Akan of Ghana, an ethnic group, which constitutes the single largest linguistic group in the country (see discussion in Chapter 6, this volume), their beliefs were historically based upon a worldview which takes, as its departure point, the principle that human beings are communal and social by nature. These behaviours make up what Ghanaian philosopher, Kwame Gyekye (2013: 233), describes as a 'morality of duty' among the various subgroups that comprise the Akan who come from societies that can now be found in both Ghana and Côte d'Ivoire. According to this viewpoint, human beings are seen as being created by the supreme being, *Nyame*, in the sky. However, 'when a person descends from heaven he descends into society' (Gyekye, 1996: 36; see also Asante, 2009). Therefore, while human beings are created by God, which is an indication of the value and recognition of the individual as a unit of society among the Akan, it is believed that they are born into a human community. As members of the human community, individuals are not seen as self-sufficient. Instead, it is believed that they need assistance and the goodwill of others to fulfil their own basic needs and personal objectives (see also Twum-Danso Imoh, 2022). As such, then, a human being cannot 'live in isolation because he is naturally oriented towards other persons and must communicate with them to be in relation to them' (Gyekye, 1996: 36). The limitations to the self-sufficiency evident in individuals result in what Gyekye (2013: 23) calls the 'morality of a shared life', which demands mutuality or reciprocity 'as a moral mandate in a world in which human beings, weak and limited in many ways, are subject to vulnerable situations'. This illuminates the relational character of human beings. The principles or values underpinning this worldview were expected to be evident in how individuals related to each other. Specifically, within this context there was an understanding that individuals not only had duties towards each other, but also possessed rights they were entitled to claim from one another (see also Cobbah, 1987; Gyekye, 1996, 2013).

These expected behaviours from individuals as a result of communitarian principles do not only relate to *intra*generational relations. They also shape, and inform, *inter*generational relations. In effect, these principles signify that adults and children depend on each other in order to achieve their wellbeing and personal objectives as well as broader household or family needs. This illuminates the interdependence between adults and children as, bearing in mind communitarian principles, both are expected to not only receive care from each other, but also to provide care to one another (Coe, 2016; Twum-Danso Imoh, 2022). In effect, the ability and, indeed, the expectation to provide care is associated not only with the status of parenthood (however defined), but also with the status of childhood. Given the interdependence that characterizes this relationship, and the reciprocal obligations that underpin it, I have argued elsewhere (Twum-Danso Imoh, 2022: 451) that 'it may be more appropriate to discuss more equally the dependency associated with both phases of life instead of primarily associating childhood with dependency'.

This mutuality of duty was captured briefly by a female child participant in Ga Mashie (Study 1) who stated that "[Y]our mother has to help you and you must help your mother" (focus group discussion [FGD] with Ga Mashie out-of-school children II, 10 February 2006, Study 1). This brief statement captures the essence of the reciprocal obligations or mutual duty that both parties have within an adult and child relationship. Therefore, while childhood was recognized as a period of dependency by many participants in this particular study, this state of dependence did not signify an inability of children to provide support, care and assistance to key adults in their lives both in the house and in their business. This understanding of personhood and its implications for intergenerational relations requires us to problematize the association of the term caregiver with those who are recognized as adults in their society. The consequence of shifting this understanding results in a construction of childhood as a phase of life in which individuals within this status group are both productive and competent and able to provide care and assistance to others, including those who are defined as 'adults' as part of a relationship of interdependence. This understanding provides the foundation upon which a deeper appreciation of the value placed on the notion of children's duties and responsibilities can be acquired. In particular, this conceptualization of childhood provides an explanation for the significant role work tasks of various kinds play in childhood socialization processes in this context.

While the notion of children having duties has caused some consternation within international policy circles and among some academics (see Van Bueren, 1995; Nsamenang, 2004; Abebe, 2013), one exception in the global policy arena is the African Charter on the Rights and Welfare of the Child, the first regional charter on children's rights. Despite the similarities between the Charter and the Convention, the Charter, in its attempt to foreground what it calls 'African cultural values', also makes provisions relating to the notion of children having responsibilities to their family and communities (see discussion in Chapter 3, this volume). This provision reiterates the principles articulated in the 1981 African Charter on Human and People's Rights (the Banjul Charter) which stipulates that all individuals have responsibilities towards their family, society and the state. Within the child-focused Charter, in particular, the idea is that the concept of children possessing responsibilities helps 'educate others in the potential value of children's contribution to society, a potential contribution that is often overlooked' (Van Bueren, 1995: 24). Therefore, in accordance with the Banjul Charter, Article 31 of the African Charter on the Rights and Welfare of the Child imparts duties on children: every child has responsibilities towards his family and society, the state and other legally recognized communities, including the international community. Specifically, it states that children have a responsibility to work for the cohesion of the family, to respect parents and elders at all times and to assist them in cases of need.

In Ghana the importance of children's duties emerges in the accounts of several scholars who illustrate the extent to which the work that children are expected to undertake from an early age is seen as a form of learning (see Kaye, 1962; Nukunya, 2003; Twum-Danso, 2008, 2009; Adonteng-Kissi, 2018a, 2018b; Twum-Danso Imoh, 2022). Therefore, in this context children are expected to assist their parents in all tasks that will be expected of them as adults – be they in the household, on the farm or at sea. This is not only an expectation of parents, but also of customary law (see Mensa-Bonsu and Dowuona-Hammond, 1996). These expectations are part of an intergenerational contract centred around reciprocity whereby there is an understanding that by caring for the latter, parents expect children to reciprocate when they are able to do, not only later on as adults, but also as children through fulfilling their end of a bargain centred around the mutuality of duty (see Twum-Danso Imoh, 2022).

Despite the rapid social change that has affected Ghanaian society in wide-ranging ways over the last few hundred years, evidence gathered indicates that work continues to be a key element of the construction of childhood for diverse demographic groups in Ghana and, consequently, continues to inform attendant socialization strategies adopted by families. This is supported by Sackey and Johannesen who, writing in 2015, posit that:

> In contemporary Ghana children still grow and develop as members of a family and a local community. It is as family and community that their needs are fulfilled, and as family and community members that they are obliged to also perform certain duties. To sum up, children in Ghanaian communities typically see themselves, and are also seen as capable members in their families and communities' development processes. (Sackey and Johannesen, 2015: 449)

This understanding of the role of children, which can, in turn, be attributed to the construction of childhood and personhood more generally, informs behaviours in relationships between individuals, including those that are intergenerational. The resulting outcome of these beliefs creates a situation whereby emphasis is placed by adults and children in all the studies I have undertaken in Ghana on childhood being a phase of life centred around 'responsibility', 'duty' and 'work':

> 'Children must work.' (FGD with Nima school children IV, October–December 2005, Study 1)

> 'Children have to help parents in everything they are doing.' (FGD with school children at Sempe II Primary, 1 February 2006, Study 1)

> 'We are supposed to help my mother with the household chores and also in selling her things, be obedient and respectful. If we don't do that, we get punished.' (Abena, female, age 13, Pokrom Nsabaa, 2009, Study 2)

Therefore, all children in multiple studies I have undertaken were very conscious that as part of their role as 'children' in their families they were expected to support and provide assistance to their so-called caregivers. This emerged through the ways most child participants in Study 1 discussed their understanding of the meaning of childhood and the roles of children within the family or the community (Twum-Danso, 2008, 2009; Twum-Danso Imoh, 2020). In the same study all children interviewed were able to easily, and without hesitation, produce a long list of their responsibilities in the household as well as in their community more generally. Specifically, they identified their duties as running errands for parents and other adults, contributing to the maintenance of the household by sweeping the compound and its interior, weeding, fetching water to use to wash clothes and utensils, helping mother or other female adults to cook, looking after younger siblings and helping parents in whatever business that is dominant in the domestic economy in which they live, such as farming, fishing and petty trading (see Twum-Danso, 2008, 2009; Twum-Danso Imoh, 2022). In some cases, these duties included earning money independently to contribute to the maintenance of their family or to provide for themselves and by so doing, easing the financial pressures facing their family.

Errands, which children of all genders run for adults in their household as well as others within the community, feature significantly in the work in which children participate. As two children in different FGD sessions (Study 1) put it, "when they [children] are sent, they should go" (FGD with Ga Mashie children V, 1 February 2006; FGD with Ga Mashie children III, 8 February 2006, Study 1). In two different FGDs for the same study other child participants made explicit the extent to which reciprocity as a norm underpinned the running of errands:

> 'They treat us as children, so they send us and we go and they like us.' (FGD with Ga Mashie out-of-school children II, 10 February 2006, Study 1)

> 'Because children go on errands for people sometimes these people will take them to hospital when they are sick.' (FGD with Ga Mashie out-of-school children III, 20 February 2006, Study 1)

The important role of errands in child-rearing approaches is foregrounded by Sarpong (1974: 70) who, in his explanation of the behaviour expected of children, illuminates not only the priority placed on errands undertaken by children, but the need for them to run such errands happily without grumbling or frowning. As he goes on to explain, children are 'ideally expected to be respectful, charming, and smiling when in the company of adults, ready to go, without hesitation, on the errands they are sent on by adults'.

The running of errands is seen as so central to the work that children are expected to undertake within families that sanctions are imposed if they do not obey or do not run the errand effectively. This emerged in data gathered for Study 2:

'[The last time I was punished was when] my mother sent me to go and buy something and I lost the money. When I came back and told her about it, she said I was playing on the way that's why I lost the money and [she] made me squat and stand repeatedly for a while.' (Akorkor, female, age 10, Dodowa, August 2009, Study 2)

'He [my father] called me and asked me and asked me to buy something for him around 10pm. I refused to go, and he punished me.' (Mawuena, female, age 15, Bukom, August 2009, Study 2)

For some, the amount of time spent on errands on which they were sent by family members interfered with their schooling and resulted in them getting into trouble with teachers:

'[The last time I was punished at school was] today – I was late for school because my grandmother sent me to take her things to the market before going to school. The teacher on duty saw me when I was, when I was going to my classroom, so he called me and gave me three lashes. I felt sad because I explained to him that it was not my fault that I came to school too late.' (Kweku, male, age 14, Pokrom Nsabaa, August 2009, Study 2)

The findings demonstrate the linkage between physical punishment as a disciplinary tool and the construction of childhood which has, embedded at its core, the notion that children, even those who are quite young, are capable of fulfilling duties within the family.

For children, these chores which enabled them to meet their reciprocal obligations to adults in their family fostered feelings of a sense of belonging as well as strengthened their position to make claims against adults for their own needs (see Twum-Danso Imoh, 2022). Interestingly, in discussing their role in the community children prioritized the importance of receiving education; for these children, this education was not only about attending school, but also about receiving training in household chores, such as cooking, cleaning, sweeping the compound, weeding/yard work, fetching water and using it to wash utensils and clothes, and looking after siblings. This is because they understood that by behaving like a 'good' child through their behaviours and fulfilling their responsibilities, they can make a request for their own needs which a 'good' adult would struggle to refuse. This is supported by Hardgrove (2017: 44) who, in her study focusing on children's lives in post-conflict Liberia, made the following observation about the caregiver and child relationship: 'Children were at the beck and call of their elders, but by fulfilling their obligations the younger ones earned the right to make certain requests of them. If unmet, these requests would appear equally shameful for the older superiors.' Therefore, what emerged from the data gathered from a number of my studies is that children have a clear understanding that the caregiver–child relationship is one based on mutual support, assistance and reciprocity. Further, they understand that this expectation is embedded in not just the understanding of parenthood, but also in their understanding of what childhood constitutes.

Preparing children for adult roles: the gendered nature of socialization processes

In line with gender constructions in Ghana which are rigidly constructed (see Adomako-Ampofo, 2001; Boateng et al, 2006; Adomako-Ampofo and Boateng, 2007; Adinkrah, 2012; Adjei, 2016), the socialization of children, including their responsibilities and the work expected of them, remains highly gendered in many families. For instance, Adjei (2016), although focusing on violence against women rather than gender socialization *per se*, claims that due to the belief that an individual can 'fail' to meet all the accomplishments required to be recognized as a man or a woman in this context, significant emphasis is consequently placed on teaching children of different genders the ideal gender roles and behaviours as prescribed by their society (see also Adomako-Ampofo, 2001; Adomako-Ampofo and Boateng, 2007). These responsibilities and behaviours expected of each gender are imbibed from an early age as children and young people are expected to undertake chores and display attitudes and behaviours that correspond with the roles they will be expected to adopt upon achieving adulthood. Adomako-Ampofo, who has, in various papers (Adomako-Ampofo, 2001; Boateng et al, 2006; Adomako-Ampofo and Boateng, 2007), been instrumental in shedding light on the gender socialization process in Ghana, discusses the extent to which the socialization of girls, especially after they have reached adolescence, is centred around training them for the role they will assume upon marriage, which is largely domestic while their male peers are trained to assume leadership roles due to the belief that they will eventually become heads of families which requires them to be able to make major decisions. The resulting outcome of this process, she argues, is that boys are taught to be strong individuals who can lead, and control, women, while the latter are taught to accept, and submit themselves to, this control (Adomako-Ampofo, 2001; Adomako-Ampofo and Boateng, 2007). Deviation from roles and behaviours being taught is, it is claimed, not encouraged and sanctions and punishments await those who do not conform, with boys often being punished more harshly than girls (see also Geoffrion, 2013).

These gender norms consequently informed the duties of children within the context of households. The gendered nature of children's work and its role in the socialization process was well outlined by a number of adults in Study 1 and Study 4, with girls undertaking roles which require them to be in the house while boys engage in job roles that tend to be outdoors and require strength and leadership. The attributes emerging from these studies all align with broader dominant constructions of each gender in this context:

'All children know their work depending on their sex – if it is a girl she cooks and gives her father food and boys will sweep, clean the father's shoes, bath, and go to school. If the girl is the only girl in the family, they will keep her at home while male children go to school, and she will look after the family and help mother to sell. Among the fishermen and farmers, they keep male children from school to help the father in fishing or farming. When a girl is the first born, she is expected to help look after her younger brothers and sisters.' (FGD with Ga Mashie Elders, 8 February 2006, Study 1)

'At home, we assign the females to chores related to the kitchen, like cooking, washing, sweeping, fetching of water and the like. And also, in a house where there are sheep and goats, we allow the males to take charge of them because we want them to assume that leadership role. So, at home, we give the supervisory roles to the males and give the engaging roles to the females … ahaa!' (FGD, male, age 27, single, Christian, Abura, 2015, Study 4)

'As for females their duty has to do with sweeping, the boys fetch water, the girls wash clothes, prepare food when they are a bit mature. So, the girls, in the course of time, support the house. And the boys also, their work is to weed around the house when it is bushy. So, they also have their roles that they play – pounding of *fufu*[1] is the role of the boys. And the ladies' role is sweeping, fetching water and preparing food to support the house.' (FGD, female, age 58, widowed, Christian, Assin Fosu, 2015, Study 4)

Children themselves illuminated the extent to which their experience of chore allocation was gendered within the context of their families. In Study 2 and Study 4 a number of children outlined their roles in their families:

'Every day when I wake up, I sweep, go to the stream to fetch water and bath; in the evening I help my mother [aunt] to cook in the kitchen. When I get up, I sweep the room I sleep in, sweep my father's [uncle's] room and the compound. On school days I only sweep the compound and bath and go to school. When I come back, I go to the stream whilst my mother is boiling the cassava on the fire. By the time I finish fetching the water, the cassava will be well cooked, and I come and punt [pound] it. After that we all eat, bath and I will learn and go to bed.' (Pokrom Nsabaa, diary participant, age 16, female, October 2009, Study 2)

'What I need do is, I must sell when I wake up in the morning. I must cook, bath my siblings, I must also have my bath and wash my clothing. ... They [boys] must go to fetch water or clean the room or if there are some other jobs in the house he will do it ... because the male is strong and brave, so there are certain jobs women should not do.' (Amina, age 14, Jukwa child interview, 2015, Study 4)

'We [boys in his house] fetch water, pound *fufu* and they send us.' (Assin Fosu boys group activity 2, 2015, Study 4)

Underpinning these statements are assumptions about masculinity and femininity as these socialization strategies seek to ultimately prepare children for the roles society expects them to adopt upon the attainment of adulthood.

Children's ability to undertake work as a measurement of maturity and competence

This work that children are expected to undertake as part of the socialization process is not ad hoc. Instead, children's duties, which primarily centre around work either within the house or outside of the house as part of a broader family enterprise, are seen as an important part of preparing children for their roles as adult men or women, especially for the roles they will be expected to assume upon marriage. Given this end goal of the socialization process, the work in which children engage provides adults with the opportunity to monitor their progress and make judgements about their maturity (see also Twum-Danso, 2009; Sackey and Johannesen, 2015; Adonteng-Kissi, 2018a, 2018b). Therefore, chores are constantly monitored by adults within the family who gradually increase children's responsibilities as they prove their competence in a particular skill or task until it is clear that they are able to engage in tasks that are normally reserved for adults. In concrete terms this means that while the experience of responsibility begins early, it is usually allocated in accordance with the physical size, competence and abilities of the child. According to a child participant in Study 1: "You get special treatment as a child. If you are a child in the house, you would not get as much responsibility as [your] older brothers or sisters. A child is not supposed to do hard work" (Ga Mashie out-of-school children I, October–November 2005, Study 1).

As they grow older and stronger the responsibilities increase and become more difficult and specialized until they finally attain adulthood. Therefore, while a girl may begin helping her mother in the kitchen from a young age, she may not be given the responsibility for cooking for an entire household until she is much older. Oppong, writing in the 1970s, outlines in detail the gradual assumption of responsibilities on the farm for boys in Dagbon, northern Ghana:

> By 5 years or so a small boy can begin to care for his father's or uncle's chickens. By age 12 or more a boy is old enough to herd the cattle, which is a job beneath the dignity of a grown man. One criterion of maturity for boys is the ability to make 100 yam mounds in a day. When he has achieved this a boy may be given his own hoe to show he is now a farmer and the use of a piece of land of his own to cultivate in his spare time. From the produce of this with his father's or guardian's permission, he may begin to accumulate a few livestock of his own, chickens at first, later a goat and so on. Thus, the assumption of the roles of farmer and housewife are very gradual and graded according to increasing maturity and skill. (Oppong, 1973: 52–53)

A more recent example is provided by Adonteng-Kissi, who describes the following process among the Asante:

> Children accompany their parents to farms to work as a means of passing on basic farming skills to them. They begin to gain insights into their parents' farming activities and become acquainted with the simple tasks of farming such as weeding, pod plucking, pod gathering and heaping, scooping of cocoa beans, carting of fermented beans, and drying of beans. Children's farming activities also include carrying water for spraying, and carting of dry beans to sale hubs. ... Tilling of the land and harvesting of crops which are harder work begin a little later when children are around 10 years of age. (Adonteng-Kissi, 2018b: 56–57)

This assessment of children's competence in undertaking chores as part of evaluating or determining maturity has been noted in other contexts (see Serpell, 1993; Ncube, 1998; Nsamenang, 2004; Lancy, 2012). These skills form the basis of what David Lancy (2012) calls 'the chore curriculum', a term he uses to demonstrate that children's work within families involves careful thinking and close monitoring to ensure that the responsibilities allocated to children are always commensurate with their abilities and enable them to become self-sufficient and effective contributors to the domestic economy. This linkage between children undertaking tasks and the gradual maturation process is key to understanding the importance of children having duties or responsibilities in contexts across the continent, including Ghana. These duties, which primarily centred around work, either within, or outside of, the house were seen as an important part of preparing children for their roles as adult men or women and providing adults with the opportunity to monitor their progress and make judgements about an individual child's maturity and competence.

Children's paid work and labour

The work in which children in Ghana engage goes beyond household duties as many participate in income-generating activities in order to contribute to the sustenance of the family or for themselves (Hilson, 2010; Okyere, 2012, 2013a, 2013b; Adonteng-Kissi, 2018a, 2018b; Lambon-Quayefio and Owoo, 2018; Twum-Danso Imoh and Okyere, 2020; Okyere et al, 2023; Yeboah and Egyir, 2023). According to the most recent population and housing census, there are approximately 230,000 (3.2 per cent) children aged between five and 14 years who are engaged in economic activity in Ghana (Ghana Statistical Service, 2022). The evidence shows that there is a substantially higher proportion of children economically active in rural areas (5.7 per cent) compared to urban (1.0 per cent). The prevalence of rurality in rates of children's economic activities is further borne out by the fact that the regions with the highest proportion of children aged five to 14 who engage in economic activity are: Oti (20.8 per cent) where children's economic activity is more than six times the national average of 3.2 per cent; North East (11.4 per cent), Savannah (9.9 per cent); Upper West (9.3 per cent); Northern (8.6 per cent); and Upper East (6.1 per cent) (Ghana Statistical Service, 2022). The high incidence of children engaged in economic activity is not a new phenomenon. In relation to forms of work that have now been prohibited by law, Okyere and his colleagues illustrate, in a recent book chapter, the extent to which the number of children engaged in such work has remained high or has increased over a nine-year period:

> In 2003, a survey by the Ghana Statistical Service (GSS) showed that over one million children under 13 years were working despite being prohibited from economic activities (Ghana Statistical Service, 2003). An estimated 242,074 children aged 13 to 17 years were engaged in exempted activities such as mining, fishing, stone quarrying, and others. Hence, approximately 1.3 million children or 19 per cent of the then estimated 6.4 million children in Ghana were engaged in activities prohibited by national and international policies. About a decade later in 2012, data from the Ghana Living Standards Survey (GLSS) estimated that the number of children aged 14 years or younger who were

involved in prohibited children's work was almost 1.5 million (Ghana Statistical Service). Methodological differences and other factors such as lack of information on the percentage increase or decrease in the population of children do not permit direct comparisons to be made between the 2003 and 2012 data. (Okyere et al, 2023: 208)

In rural areas much of this income-generative work consists of farming, while in urban areas the work children engage in includes hawking, domestic work, porterage, fishing and quarrying, and small-scale mining or artisanal mining (Hilson, 2010; Tetteh, 2011a, 2011b; Ofosu-Kusi and Mizen, 2012; Okyere, 2012, 2013a, 2013b; Omoike, 2013; Adonteng-Kissi, 2018a, 2018b; Lambon-Quayefio and Owoo, 2018; Mizen, 2018; Seyram Hammoo et al, 2018; Afriye et al, 2019; Ansong, 2020; Gatsinzi and Hilson, 2022; Okali et al, 2022; Okyere et al, 2023). Some of this work in which children engage has been classified as representing the worst forms of child labour which Lambon-Quayefio and Owoo (2018: 1592) list as: 'head porters (*kayayei*), child domestic labour, ritual servitude (*Trokosi*), commercial sexual exploitation, quarrying and small-scale mining (galamsey), fishing and cash-crop agriculture'. In a more recent publication Okyere and colleagues (2023: 207) set out a table outlining the type of work children undertake in the country that has been targeted for regulation or elimination by government (see Table 1).

While there is evidence to show that some children are pressurized or coerced by adults in their family to undertake some forms of work, including those considered to be hazardous or detrimental to their education, wellbeing and development, others make an active decision to engage in diverse forms of work (Okyere, 2012, 2013a, 2013b; Twum-Danso Imoh and Okyere, 2020). For some this decision to find work is also made alongside a decision to migrate from their rural homes to larger towns and cities which provide more opportunities for earning an income that they can use for themselves or their families (Hashim, 2005; Kwankye, 2012; Ofosu-Kusi and Mizen, 2012; Ofosu-Kusi, 2023). The desire for work, especially that which takes the form of apprenticeships, has been pointed to as a driving factor behind the independent migration of children from primarily the northern regions due to the poor quality of school-based education in these areas and the inability of many parents to cater for their children's needs, which leads them to drop out of school and migrate in search of work to urban conurbations such as Accra and Kumasi (Hashim, 2005; Kwankye, 2012; Ofosu-Kusi and Mizen, 2012). As Okyere, in his various publications (Okyere, 2012, 2013a, 2013b; Twum-Danso Imoh and Okyere, 2020) has asserted, for the children who participated in his doctoral study which focused on artisanal mining in Kenyasi, a neighbourhood of Kumasi in the Asante region, it was not a case of choosing between school or work. Instead, for this group they

Table 1: Children's work targeted for regulation or elimination in Ghana

Sector/industry	Activity
Agriculture	Producing cocoa★, including land clearing, using machetes and cutlasses for weeding, collecting cocoa pods with a harvesting hook, breaking cocoa pods, working in the vicinity of pesticide spraying, and carrying heavy loads★ of water.
	Production of palm oil★ and cotton, including weeding, harvesting, and acting as scarecrows.
	Herding livestock, including cattle, hunting★, and work in slaughterhouses.
	Fishing★, including for tilapia; preparing bait, nets, and fishing gear; launching, paddling, and draining canoes; diving for fish; casting and pulling fishing nets and untangling them underwater; sorting, picking, cleaning, smoking, transporting, and selling fish; cleaning and repairing nets; and building and repairing boats.
Industry	Quarrying★ and small-scale mining★, sometimes for gold, including using mercury, digging in deep pits, crushing rocks by hand, carrying heavy loads★, and operating machinery★.
	Manufacturing and working in sawmills★.
	Construction and bricklaying or carrying brick.
Service	Domestic work★.
	Transporting heavy loads as *kayayei*★.
	Work in transportation★, activities unknown.
	Electronic waste and garbage scavenging★, including sorting scavenged items★ and transporting items for sale★.
	Street work★, including begging★, small-scale vending, and working at restaurants or bars★.
Categorical Worst Forms of Child Labour★★	Commercial sexual exploitation, sometimes as a result of human trafficking.
	Forced labour in begging; agriculture, including herding; fishing, including for tilapia; artisanal gold mining; domestic work; and street work, including vending and carrying heavy loads, each sometimes as a result of human trafficking.
	Forced ritual servitude for girls known as *trokosi*, including domestic work for priests.

Notes: This table was originally published in Okyere, S., Frimpong Boamah, E., Asante, F. and Yeboah, T. (2023) 'Children's work in Ghana: Policies and politics', in Sumberg, J. and Sabates-Wheeler, R. (eds), *Children's Work in African Agriculture: The Harmful and the Harmless,* Bristol: Bristol University Press. It has been reproduced here with the permission of the editors.

★ Determined by national law or regulation as hazardous and, as such, relevant to Article 3(d) of ILO C. 182 (1999).

★★ Child labour understood as the worst forms of child labour per se under Article 3(a)–(c) of ILO C. 182 (1999).

strongly assert that in order to be able to go to school and pay for all the attendant costs, they needed to work, an activity most of them engaged in during the long school vacations. Thus, far from school and work being polar opposites in the child labour debate, for these children, they were, in fact, more complementary than policy makers and children's rights advocates at both national and global levels have, hitherto, been prepared to acknowledge.

Moving beyond poverty-based explanations of child work

The work in which children engage both within, and outside, the home has often been explained through the lens of poverty which has foregrounded narratives centred around the reliance of families on children's labour as part of survival strategies in the context of poverty (Hilson, 2010; Sackey and Johannesen, 2015; Okyere et al, 2023). While a poverty-centred analysis has primarily been applied to the work in which children engage outside of the home (see Hilson, 2010; Adonteng-Kissi, 2018a, 2018b; Gatsinzi and Hilson, 2022), the rationale of poverty has also been deployed to explain the work in which children undertake within the home to support the sustenance of the family. Laird, for instance, makes the case that:

> In light of the fact that households are multiply deprived of utilities (70% of the population do not have access to electricity; only 21% of the population has pipe borne water), children, specifically girls, are recruited to undertake the time-consuming and monotonous tasks of collecting water and firewood, disposing of human waste, and assisting with washing and cooking. It would simply not be possible for an adult to complete these tasks alone; without completion basic survival needs could not be met. It is the labour of girls, which replaces the refrigerators, the cooker, and the washing machine of homes in developed countries. (Laird, 2002: 897)

Therefore, according to this argument, without the collective action of all family members in labour the multitude of poor families risk destitution, as adults alone cannot complete the tasks that need to be undertaken in a household for a family to survive.

This framing, which links children's work of different types to poverty as a driving factor, is not without validity. However, the question that needs to be asked is whether more affluent families who do have refrigerators, cookers, microwaves, washing machines and dishwashers in households which, in turn, draw on a regular supply of electricity, even if it is via a generator or a solar panel, place the same level of emphasis on the need for children to undertake work as part of socialization processes? This exploration of work in the lives of children in more affluent families is important to consider if we are to develop a holistic picture of childhoods in Ghana. Failure to consider the work experiences of this group means that we simply produce accounts of children's lives in this context through the lens of the work that poor children undertake – both unpaid and paid. While this focus is important and very valuable, it only provides us with an incomplete understanding of the association between the notion of work and the conceptualization of childhood in this context. In her research with street and working children in Vietnam, Rachel Burr (2006) noted the way foreign non-governmental organization workers overlook the plurality of lifestyles that children experience in both Vietnam and in the countries that comprise the so-called 'West'. This led her to pose the following question: 'Why should a Western child be assumed to be indulged and spoiled? Is it always the case that a Vietnamese child is bred to work?' (Burr, 2006: 81). She concludes that these perceptions overly exaggerate the distribution of wealth in the West and stereotype the form that childhood takes in the South. This question that Burr asks is also relevant to sub-Saharan African contexts. In relation to Ghana specifically, the question becomes: to what extent are all Ghanaian children 'bred to work'?

Before attempting to answer this question, it is important to provide some economic context which has resulted in increased differential experiences in relation to income within the Ghanaian population and the implications this may have for the type and intensity of work in which children engage. In doing this, it is worth taking a step back to dwell on the regional context before honing in to focus on Ghana more specifically. Africa has long been recognized as the poorest continent in the world and continues to be so today. Although the region's extreme poverty rate in 1981 (43.1 per cent) was almost equivalent to the average for the rest of the world (42.8 per cent) based on a poverty line of US$1.90 per day, by 2015 the extreme poverty rate in Africa was 35.5 per cent and, hence, was 6.8 times the average for the rest of the world (ISS Today, 2022). At the outbreak of the COVID-19 pandemic approximately 445 million Africans (34 per cent) lived below the poverty line. The impact of the pandemic has subsequently resulted in approximately 30 million additional people falling into extreme poverty (that is, living on less than US$1.90 a day) (ISS Today, 2022). The significance of this is that based on current trends the continent is unlikely to meet the UN's Sustainable Development Goal 1 – ending poverty in all its forms – for 97 per cent of the population – by 2030.

These dire statistics notwithstanding, the status of Africa as the poorest continent does not encapsulate all the experiences and lifestyles that can be identified in the region. Put quite simply, Africa's status as the world's poorest continent does not make all Africans poor. For instance, while economic conditions in Africa, like elsewhere in the world, are currently precarious due to COVID-19 and the Russian invasion of Ukraine which remains ongoing, after more than two years, at the time of writing, it is worth noting that during the 2000s a number of countries on the continent experienced rapid economic growth. For example, in 2014 the International Monetary Fund estimated that Ethiopia, a country we continue to associate with famine and starving children so weak and emaciated that they are unable to lift a hand to bat away the hungry flies hovering around their limbs, was the world's fastest growing economy at more than 10 per cent (Oxfam, 2015). This was followed by other countries such as Congo, Côte d'Ivoire, Mozambique, Tanzania and Rwanda – all also growing at rapid rates within a similar timeframe. Much of this growth during this period was driven by natural resources, an increase in commodities exports and growth in the tourism sector in a number of countries (see also Twum-Danso Imoh, 2016).

In the case of Ghana, in particular, the country experienced increasing growth rates of over 7 per cent per year on average between 2005 and 2009 when it dropped to 4 per cent, the lowest growth in nine years as a result of the 2008 global economic crisis. There was a slight resurrection in 2011 as economic growth increased to a peak of 15 per cent as a result of commercial oil production and export. This growth had been further strengthened, in 2010, by the attainment of middle-income status (Cooke et al, 2016). However, by 2013 the economy had declined to 7.6 per cent (Aryeetey and Baah-Boateng, 2016; Cooke et al, 2016). The key point to underscore is that during this period, inequality worsened in the country, with the Gini coefficient rising from 37 in 1992 to 42.3 in 2013 according to data gathered from the Sixth Ghana Living Standards Survey. Levels of consumption demonstrate well the inequality between the wealthiest and poorest in the society:

> Looking at consumption levels, we see that the gap between the poorest 10% and the richest 10% of the population has been on the rise and has also increased since 2006. The wealthiest decile now consumes 6.8 times the amount than the poorest 10%, up from 6.4 times in 2006. We also find that average consumption of this wealthiest group increased by 27% between 2006 and 2013, whereas for the poorest it only increased by 19% – meaning that growth for the richest group was over 1.4 times greater than for the poorest in this period. Equally, we find that the shares of total national consumption vary substantially between rich and poor. The wealthiest 10% consume around one third of all national consumption, whereas the poorest 10% consume just 1.72%. This means that even if the Gini has not notably increased since 2006, other evidence suggests that inequality between the poorest and wealthiest has indeed increased. (Cooke et al, 2016: 2)

AN EXPLORATION OF CHILD DUTY AND WORK

These inequalities created by the uneven impact of economic growth in the decades following the turn of the millennium have led to the persistence and worsening of poverty among some sections of the population in both urban and rural areas (Cooke et al, 2016). As a result of the increase in inequality and its ramifications for the poorest in society, much attention has, quite rightly, been paid to the lives of those adversely affected by the worsening inequalities visible in the country.

What has been less discussed are those groups who have benefited from the periods of economic growth the country has witnessed, especially in the years following the advent of the new millennium. The benefits that economic conditions have brought to bear for these groups is important to consider if we are to fully understand how inequality has operated within this context and resulted in differential outcomes for diverse groups of people depending on income/social status and geographical location. An example that illustrates well the need to maintain a focus on both sides of the inequality line in a given context is the recent case of Nigerian politician, Ike Ekweremadua, former deputy president of the Nigerian senate,[2] and his wife, Beatrice. In March 2023, the couple was found guilty, in a British court, of facilitating the travel of a 21-year-old street trader from Lagos to London for the purpose of exploiting him to donate his kidney for their 25-year-old daughter whose long-term medical condition was deteriorating. In recounting the details of the case following the guilty verdict, an article by BBC News, which outlines the background of the two young people at the centre of the case, throws into sharp relief the extent to which inequality insidiously shapes the lives of young Nigerians leading to quite different outcomes even if their paths may cross along the way:

Student Sonia Ekweremadu appeared to have an ideal life – wealthy parents at the heart of Nigeria's political system and a place at a leading UK university – but she was also desperately sick and needed a kidney transplant. Her dad, Ike Ekweremadu, paid fixers, and middlemen thousands of pounds to arrange a donor. Daniel, whose real name cannot be reported for legal reasons, grew up in a big family in rural Nigeria, without running water or electricity. Aged 15, he was selling mobile phone accessories from a barrow in the capital Lagos and sending money home. In 2022, aged 21, he walked into a police station near Heathrow, tired, homeless, and terrified. He told police he had run away because people wanted to take one of his kidneys. While Daniel pushed his barrow, at the other end of the Nigerian social ladder, Ike Ekweremadu and his wife Beatrice grew increasingly worried about their daughter's health. The Ekweremadus approached a middleman, Dr. Obinna Obeta, who in July 2021, had himself received a kidney donation, using his connections to make it happen: a Nigerian doctor

165

friend in Cambridge organized fundraising, a young donor was found in Nigeria, and the private operation took place at London's Royal Free Hospital. The Ekweremadu family wanted Dr. Obeta to repeat the process for Sonia. Dr. Obeta asked his donor to find someone willing to provide a kidney for Sonia. He suggested Daniel. Daniel claimed Dr. Obeta had promised to bring him to Britain and never mentioned a kidney transplant. 'I will live in his house, and he will get work for me. He asked me not to tell people that I'm coming to the UK,' Daniel told the court. When Dr. Obeta asked Daniel to undergo medical tests, Daniel thought they were for a visa application. His UK visa was granted in January 2022. Good news, Daniel thought. Dr. Obeta's help was as if 'from God,' he said. Once in London, however, he had to sleep on Dr. Obeta's sofa and says the doctor used him as a houseboy. Behind the scenes, Ike Ekweremadu, communicating through his brother, a doctor, was being asked to pay Dr. Obeta nearly £2,000. Daniel was to receive £6,000 for a kidney, while the operation, at the Royal Free private wing, would cost £80,000. (Symonds, 2023)

This example illustrates exceptionally well, in many respects, the different walks of life individuals experience growing up within the same country on the continent and the extent to which this leads to different experiences of childhood as well as different life chances. Interestingly, despite this dissonance between their experiences and lifestyles, there are still ways that their lives overlap. In the case outlined here this is evident in the way the life of an individual from a poor community is seen as expendable in efforts by the affluent to ensure their own wellbeing.

This example also demonstrates the extent to which the financial benefits that individuals have accrued as a result of unequal dynamics of their country's economy filter down to their children. This consequently impacts the childhood they experience, primarily characterized by: the technologies they use either for play or communication; their use of social networking sites to interact with their peers and others; their access to satellite TV (and hence, American programming and advertising); and the various ways they spend the leisure time they have at their disposal (Twum-Danso Imoh, 2016). Added to these is the issue of quality education. In the case of Ghana, while there are more children enrolled in both basic and secondary schools compared to 20 or even ten years ago, children from wealthier families are able to access a significantly better quality of education than those attending public schools, which strengthens their position to advance their educational journeys and embark on lucrative careers in future (see Adu-Boahen, 2022).

These affluent children are part of a small group whose transition to adulthood occur in what Western discourses around children's rights would consider a 'timely' manner. This transition to adulthood, which fulfils expectations of global social policies and international organizations, is addressed by anthropologist Alcinda Honwana (2012: 5), who, in her discussion on 'waithood', claims that while some young people attain adulthood too soon and others experience delayed adulthood, 'waithood manifests itself differently among a small group of elite youths who are generally able to afford a good education in private schools and abroad and are often well connected to networks of the powerful that facilitate their access to secure jobs'. Therefore, while some children may be seen as not being able to access 'childhood' due to the need for them to engage in paid work, possibly hazardous, which may have implications for their formal education, there exist a small group of children whose familial circumstances mean that their transition from childhood to adulthood meet all milestones in ways, and within timeframes deemed appropriate by global children's rights discourses and frameworks.

In returning to the question of whether all Ghanaian children are 'bred to work', the data I have gathered from groups of children who come from more affluent families in Ghana leads me to put forward 'yes' as a brief answer. This is due to the fact that analysis of the data from this group demonstrate the extent to which, similarly to children from less affluent neighbourhoods in urban or rural areas, work remains an important aspect of the socialization of children from these families. The work in which this group of children engage, which primarily takes the form of house chores, highlights their contributions to the household. For example, in Study 2, which focused on the physical punishment of children, diary entries completed by children attending a private international school in an affluent suburb of Accra reveal the importance of duties and responsibility in shaping their upbringing:

> I am 13 years old. I'm a boy. I am in JHS2. I'm quite strong and handsome and tall. I'm a kind person, friendly, caring, and hard working. My weaknesses are that I like laughing and teasing people younger or older than me and I'm quite lazy. I live with my two sisters, father, stepmother, stepsister, maid, and uncle. There are five children in the house. My father is an engineer, my uncle is in university, my stepmother is also an engineer. The woman I live with cares for me lot. She is my step mum. ... On weekends I wash my clothes, iron, go to church, help in preparing dinner and lunch, go on errands for my parents and uncle and watch TV most of the time. I also do my homework and read over my notes. (Ekow, male, age 13, October 2009, Study 2)

> I am a girl of 12 years. I do like to talk. I am the first born of my family. I am in JHS 2 at [name of school]. My strengths are studying, working with all my might, and obeying my responsibilities. My weaknesses

are laziness, watching of TV. I live with my father, aunties, uncle, cousins, and friends. I live at a noisy surrounding since it is near the street. The aunties I live with in my household are my father's elder sisters and my uncle is my father's in law. There are four children in the house including me. There are seven adults in my household, one teenager and five dogs. My father works as a businessman with a Masters degree. ... I was last punished on the 29th of January 2009 for not completing my chores for the day. I was punished by my father. He lashed me very hard, and this caused bruising on my hands, legs and back. I was crying very much, and I was still being whipped. My father was very angry with me, and this made me think I would be sick if he continued to lash me. My bigger sister came to my aid. She pleaded on my behalf and told my father that it would not be repeated again. My father told me after the punishment the reason why he had to lash me. He told me that all those chores were given to me to finish on that day because the next day we were going to go to the hospital to visit my sick grandmother. He later apologized for beating me like that. (Nana Adwoa, female, age 12, October 2009, Study 2)

These accounts provide an indication of the extent to which the notion of children having duties, manifested through their undertaking of specific work tasks within the household, remain an important part of socialization strategies to integrate the young into more affluent families, with sanctions attached to tackle the perceived failure by children to fulfil the role expected of them. It further demonstrates the value that continues to be placed on Indigenous understandings of learning within such families. Additionally, it underscores the importance of traditional notions of personhood and their attendant expected behaviours on constructions of childhood within these families – emphasizing mutual obligations and duty, responsibility, and respect within the relationship between adults and children. Therefore, the findings illuminate the extent to which for these families who have the resources to pay for expensive private international schools as well as a house with running water, regular supplies of electricity, a house help and a washing machine, Indigenous forms of learning centred around the duties to children remain valued alongside the emphasis they place on formal education. This is perhaps driven by the gendered nature of the society in which they live whereby children are expected to undertake chores that will prepare them for the roles they will undertake as married men or women in future (see Adomako-Ampofo, 2001; Boateng et al, 2006; Adomako-Ampofo and Boateng, 2007). This need to prepare children to become 'good' wives or 'good' husbands cuts across social and economic groups. The significance of this is that regardless of social status or income, families seek to prepare

AN EXPLORATION OF CHILD DUTY AND WORK

their children to become the kind of adults their society expects them to become, especially upon marriage.

Nevertheless, the accounts of child work by children from affluent families does demonstrate a difference when compared to those of children from poorer families in this context. Specifically, the accounts of more affluent children show that while work features in their everyday lives, it does not play as significant, or as intense, a role in their daily schedule of activities as it does for children from less affluent families. Therefore, while work may remain an important socialization tool across most family types and status groups in this context, the nature and intensity of the work varies. This is especially notable in the accounts of two boys living in two different cities in Ghana and who participated in two separate studies I conducted. The first example comes from a boy aged 15 in 2009 who was attending a private international school in Accra during fieldwork for Study 2. In the diary exercise he completed, which was accompanied by a set of questions, he outlined his personality, home life and perspectives as well as his experiences of physical punishment (not only as someone who has been physically punished, but also as an individual who has administered physical punishment to a younger child). In the process he shed light on key activities he undertakes at home including chores he undertakes and the role of his father in the socialization process:

Presently I am in JHS2A, I have also reached the peak of writing my BECE[3] exams. I aspire to, someday, be a scriptwriter and have my name on the Hollywood walk of fame and provide a huge number of block buster movies. The sound of 'camera, lights, action' always draws my attention. My personality can be described as funky, funny, and fabulous. I always like to add a sense of humour in everything I do. I love to be all over the place. I laugh so hard in certain cases and people think I am insane. I live in a big mansion with my family. Father, mother and five children. Also, my grandma, cousin and aunt live with us. ... I am the youngest child. We gather to attend a church in my district every Sunday. Everybody has a television set to entertain in his/her room. My dad controls inspection in the house for constant neatness. We all get on well, nicely and have good times. We also iron our clothes every Sunday evening. ... On a normal day everyone is up and doing his/her chores. We take our baths and eat our breakfast. We spend some time watching television and chatting or playing. Sometimes we go out to watch films in cinemas to relax our minds and brains and attend certain parties at times. We also go on site to my dad's land to work and I must say it's a wonderful experience. We come back home, eat our dinner [and] watch television. We sometimes crack jokes, and we are off to bed. In my family every child has the same right as the other. My dad whips when necessary. Chores are being done and clothes are washed. Anyone found loitering when everybody is working is given some punishment. We are treated fairly and equally. My dad sometimes is very lenient on us [and] listens to our views; he is not autocratic. These past two weeks all the children were given a break from doing so many chores and my dad let my mom increase the food we get every day. My dad also decided to take us to a hotel to have fun. We swam and ate a buffet of food. We relaxed and felt very very comfortable. At the hotel where we lodged, he made them give us royal treatment and everyone had his/her private room. Golf was played by the children and also table tennis. (Fiifi, male, age 15, 2009, Study 2)

The second example, drawn from a semi-structured interview undertaken for Study 3 in 2013, also comes from a 15-year-old boy living in the Central Region of Ghana who had recently completed basic education and was waiting to start senior secondary school:

'I'm a 15-year-old boy who loves music a lot and I just completed junior high school. During my leisure time I like to play lawn tennis, ride my bicycle, play my instruments. I play the piano and the trumpet. For the piano I was being tutored at home. The trumpet I was in a school band, so I played with them. I am in a family of six; I have three other siblings besides me, and I have two parents, my daddy, and my mum. I am the eldest. And we have a helper who helps us. Typical Saturday – normally cleaning, a bit of cleaning, putting the house in order; having breakfast together sometimes when Daddy and Mummy are all at home and [we] have quiet time sometimes. ... And sometimes we go to the primary school; we have a field day to train/exercise our bodies. We run. I play tennis with my friends and other guys come to the court. When I used to be in school [he had just completed basic school and was waiting to start senior secondary school], I normally slept after school, then did my homework and sometimes watch TV and I was very serious with my academics, so I had time that I used to learn. ... Sometimes we go on family vacation at beach resorts and come together and share experiences [and] play games together. As a family we come together normally in the evenings when everyone goes to work and comes back. We sit together and watch the news. After that we do what you have to do. If you want to go and read, you go. If you want to play games. ... We are very lucky compared to them [parents]. Because Daddy tells me he used to go to school barefooted, walking miles to school and we, we can just walk down the, our school is just down here [gestures at the window with his hand]. Sometimes we even go in a car. And we are really lucky. And Mummy said when she was a kid, she had only one school uniform but we, we have so many, so many uniforms, footwear, so many. I am satisfied, really satisfied. I know compared to my parents and everything, I know I am lucky, and God has blessed us.' (Yaw, male, age 15, Family A, 17 August 2013, Study 3)

This work that these boys do, which I acknowledge may be less than their female counterparts in their respective families, illustrates that although their chores are an important part of their everyday lives, it is only a relatively small part of how they structure their day. As such it does not take away from the time they spend on other activities, including homework set by school or leisure activities in which they participate with other family members or with their friends.

The extent to which work differs in the upbringing of children based on social status is noted by Andre and Hilgers, who, writing about sub-Saharan Africa more generally, assert that:

> In families from the upper and middles classes, there is a stronger separation between the realm of family and the sphere of labour, between the realm of adults and children, to the point that children are barely perceived as producers or providers to the domestic income. This is so, even though in middle-class homes work-related activities such as fetching water or washing clothes are still, according to the lines of the seniority system, deemed valuable activities for children since they have strong socializing virtues. (Andre and Hilgers, 2015: 125)

Using this as a starting point they proceed to argue that the lives of children who are seen as producers through the work they do and those who are not as a result of the status of their families 'is a key feature distinguishing social groups, their relationship to the world and their perceptions of labour' (Andre and Hilgers, 2015: 125). What this suggests is that instead of exploring the working lives of primarily poor children, the experience of work can be deployed as a lens through which to explore differential experiences between social groups, especially in relation to childhood and growing up (see Twum-Danso Imoh, 2016).

Conclusion

Drawing on the phenomenon of work (both paid and unpaid), this chapter has established that while work is a key feature of childhood socialization in Ghana regardless of socioeconomic status, partly as a result of understandings of personhood which proceed to inform socializing practices, the intensity of the work in which children in poorer families engage is substantively different from those from more affluent areas. Therefore, work can be utilized to distinguish the experiences of social groups and the childhoods individuals experience within these differing groups. What this means, then, for research purposes is that work can be used as a unit of analysis through which the social stratification of a given society and its significance for the pluralities of childhood conceptualizations and lived experiences, including in relation to dominant children's rights discourses, can be explored.

8

Implications of the Pluralities of Childhood Conceptualizations and Lived Experiences in the Global South for Studies of Children's Rights

Countering the portrayal of the South as the problem location for children's rights

The preceding chapters, which were centred around Ghana as a case study, have foregrounded two subject areas. The first relates to the evolution of children's rights discourses and their attendant laws and policies in Ghana. The second focuses on an exploration of the pluralities of childhood conceptualization and children's lived experiences in Ghana, especially in relation to transitions from childhood to adulthood, understandings of family life and implications for child-rearing practices, and, finally, the notion of children having responsibilities within the household, manifested through the work they undertake both within and outside the home. In discussing these issues, the chapters also considered their implications for children's experiences of the principles underpinning dominant and global discourses relating to children's rights. The question this leads me to now pose is: what insights does this Ghana example offer to the broader study of children's rights, not only in contexts in the South, but also more generally?

Over the years the implications of this plurality of childhood understandings and experiences in a given context in Ghana – even in quite sparsely populated communities – has led me to ask questions about the bulk of the literature that focuses on the intersections between Southern childhoods and dominant children's rights discourses as these have overwhelmingly sought to illuminate the tensions, resistance and inapplicability of dominant discourses of rights and their principles within these contexts. A notable example of such a focus in the literature is evident in Hanson and Nieuwenhuys' (2012) edited collection centred around the framework of 'living rights' with a focus on reconceptualizing children's rights with particular regards to international development. In justifying their focus, the editors explain that most of the case studies illuminated in their edited volume are drawn from contexts in the South: 'Because, as we explain below, it is there that the contrast between legal principles and daily practices makes it dramatically clear that an alternative conceptualization of children's rights, that goes beyond issues of implementation, is necessary' (Hanson and Nieuwenhuys, 2013: 3–4).

It is important to note at this point that I do not question the validity of the concept of living rights, which is underpinned by the premise that laws are not sufficient units of analysis in trying to understand both the articulation, and experience, of rights, as children and their families 'craft these concepts of rights as they actively engage with issues that confront them in contexts in which they live' (Hanson and Nieuwenhuys, 2013: 3). This argument very much resonates with my own thinking about dominant discourses of rights. The questions I *do* raise about Hanson and Nieuwenhuys' volume's framing relate more to the articulation of its conceptual framework in an edited collection which draws only on case studies from the South. This hesitation I have about the volume's focus is due to the fact that the 'daily practices' of groups of children and their families within specific populations in contexts in the Global North can be pointed to as *also* making it 'dramatically clear' that alternative formulations of children's rights are needed. A notable example is Gypsy, Roma and Traveller groups whose contemporary practices, perspectives and attitudes around childhood conceptualization and socialization are still, for a significant number of families, as discussed in the Introduction, informed by age-old social and cultural norms and values despite the impact of the intensification of social change in the societies in which they inhabit (Levinson, 2008; Introduction, this volume). Thus, drawing on case studies from both the North and South, especially based on the realities of children who experience childhoods at the margins of their society, would provide invaluable insights into alternative conceptualizations of rights or new framings of claims for social justice which may not actually draw on the lexicon of rights at all. Simply put, Northern-based researchers (of any heritage) seeking to challenge hegemonic children's rights discourses or justify the need for alternative conceptualizations of children's rights do not need to cast their attention to faraway lands to find diverging perspectives and realities of children's lives and the ways they interact with dominant rights principles. These are identifiable within the very locales in which they live and work.

Focusing on only contexts in the South in the search for alternative formulations of rights reinforces a binary framing of children's rights discourses in relation to the Global North versus the Global South within the multidisciplinary field of childhood studies, especially when discussions of childhoods move beyond national contexts (see Twum-Danso Imoh, forthcoming 2024a). By drawing on contexts in the South in a bid to reconceptualize the notion of children's rights results in these contexts continuing to be perceived as the locus of the 'problem' in debates about children's rights. Kenyan human rights academic, Makau Mutua (2016), has made a note of this tendency to draw a linkage between obstacles to human rights and portrayals of the South. In particular, he has argued that human rights scholars have tended to observe only deficits in the Global South, which he attributes to the 'short comings of an international order that is characterized by multiple asymmetries and, in setting standards, produces a cultural bias in favour of the North' (in Liebel, 2020: 130).

While seeking to explore how the lives of many children in the South are at odds with dominant rights discourse can offer important insights that facilitate the advancement of alternative conceptualizations of children's rights, these are not the only experiences and perspectives that are identifiable within contexts in the South. At the same time as exploring how children and their families may conceptualize the concept of children's rights in alternative ways, including in ways that do not deploy the language of rights, there is also a need to consider that for some groups of children within the same locations, conceptualizations of childhood and their experiences of growing up indicate a considerable amount of synergy with dominant children's rights discourses and their attendant laws and policies. Therefore, for some children in the South, just like for some in the North, their 'lifeworlds' correspond rather closely with codified laws drafted in Geneva.

The West and the rest: destabilizing the concept of 'the West' as an analytical lens through which to critique dominant children's rights discourses

The existence of degrees of synergy, or alignment, between children's lived experiences and rights discourses and principles in contexts in the South, attributable to history, and the positioning of individuals and groups relating to social and economic structures, requires us to move beyond critiques of the 'Western-bias' of dominant discourses of children's rights, as today, the legacy of the entanglements between Southern or 'non-Western' contexts and Western Europe and North America continue to influence many aspects of social, economic and political structures.

They specifically force us to question what we mean by the terms 'Western' and 'non-Western'. As a term that was invented in the early modern period and expanded upon during the course of the 17th century, the concept of being 'Western' has long been recognized as applying to cartographically – or geographically – delineated locations, typically located in the Western hemisphere as well as being characterized by the following features: the traditions of Ancient Greece and Rome;[1] Christianity in a form which had become adapted to correspond with European ways of life; and the Enlightenment from the 17th century onwards (Kurth, 2003). Beyond referring to a geographical place or societies that are believed to share common traditions, it has also come to be seen as an idea. In interrogating the concept of 'the West' and 'the rest' Stuart Hall (1996) makes a distinction between 'the West' as referring to a group of countries linked by traditions or cartographical positioning and 'the West' as an idea which emerged within a specific set of historical circumstances affecting certain societies located in the Western hemisphere but was also reinforced by the growing 'Western' identity that started being deployed in those societies. Hence, as Hall puts it:

> We know that the West itself was produced by certain historical processes operating in a particular place in unique (and perhaps unrepeatable) historical circumstances. Clearly, we must also think of the *idea* of 'the West' as having been produced in a similar way. These two aspects are in fact deeply connected, though exactly how is one of the big puzzles in sociology. We cannot attempt to resolve here the age-old sociological debate as to which came first: the idea of 'the West' or western societies. What we can say is that, as these societies emerged, so a concept and language of 'the West' crystallized. And yet, we can be certain that the idea of 'the West' did not simply reflect an already-established western society: rather, it was essential to the very formation of that society. (Hall, 1996: 187;emphasis in original)

While the idea of the West may have emerged within broader processes that sought to bind together certain European countries and facilitate their self-perception as one unit with a shared culture and religion, it also played a functional role in tightening these bonds. This was done through the establishment of a political system which ordered the world in a particular way as well as the creation of a system of knowledge production which prioritized ways of knowing and being which centred around the value and belief systems of European societies. As a concept that consists of an idea as well as a geographical place, 'the West' came to be understood, over time, as a label to refer to countries which share a certain level of development and reflect, in their structures and lifestyles, urbanized, secular, modern and capitalist principles or values (Hall, 1996). While many of these were located in Europe, the term was also used to refer to other countries – the US, Canada, Australia, New Zealand (Kurth, 2003) – all countries that had previously been colonies of Britain and had witnessed significant European settlement. In more recent decades other countries such as Japan have come to be included in this notion of 'the West' despite its Eastern location, thereby showing the extent to which the concept of 'the West' has long been understood as a complex and fluid set of ideas (Hall, 1996). Within childhoods – and children's rights – studies specifically, the term 'the West', when deployed in publications, conference papers and teaching, normally as part of an argument seeking to critique dominant children's rights principles, is often used to denote societies in Western Europe and North America and, on occasion, Australia and New Zealand.

Despite the fluidity that has, hitherto, existed in concepts of 'the West', limits have been carefully imposed on how far this label can be stretched. For example, while 'the West' has, over the years, come to incorporate countries such as Japan, New Zealand and Australia, other countries, some of which are physically located in the Western hemisphere and have also witnessed mass European settlement as a result of colonization, have been excluded from being defined as being part of 'the West'. Notable examples are countries in Latin America where the state of being Western can be identified within the fabric of many aspects of the social and cultural structures of countries in the region as a result of over 400 years of, primarily, Spanish and Portuguese colonization, which not only saw the decimation of millions of Indigenes and the transportation of approximately four million[2] enslaved Africans to the region, but also witnessed the migration and settlement of millions of Europeans in these contexts. This latter phenomenon is worth noting as it continued after the ending of the transatlantic slave trade and the achievement of independence of countries in the region from Spain and Portugal respectively, leading to 13 million Europeans migrating to Latin America between 1879 and 1930 (Sánchez Alonso, 2007). The significance of this for discussions on children's rights can be explained thus. Despite the diversity of these countries in terms of language, population and area size, economy, ethnic composition and role in relation to the world economic order following independence, this dynamic of peoples and the power imbalances and inequality that came to underpin these societies resulted in the articulation of the concept of children's rights for some groups of children, mainly those who were White and had European ancestry, at a similar period of time that these same discourses were also being consolidated in Western Europe and North America. As Szulc and Cohn explain:

> One recurring feature across South America is shared with both North America and Western Europe: from the very beginning, the status of child has been reserved for a particular segment of the underage population. While childhood was applied to individuals who would be socialized and granted protection by the family and educational institutions, minors – those not included in childhood and regarded as potentially dangerous – would be the object of social and crime

control at different level of society (García Méndez 1993, Alvin and Valladares 1988). (Szulc and Cohn, 2012: np)

This problematizes the concept of what it means to be 'Western'. Specifically, the question to be posed is as follows: given that debates around children's rights were being deployed for certain groups of children in Latin America around the same time as similar framings were being constructed in Western Europe and North America, how useful is it for us to continue referring to children's rights as 'Western', usually defined with Western Europe and North American geographical boundaries or populations in mind?

This problematization can further be extended to even contexts which are not located in the Western hemisphere and do not possess a colonial history characterized by European settlement, but yet demonstrate evidence of 'the West' as an idea in lifestyles, values, belief systems and aspects of their cultural norms. Thus, this suggests that 'the West' as an idea can even be found among populations in contexts which do not necessarily reflect the same level of development or which, while rapidly urbanizing, remain largely rural. This is evident in Ghana, for instance. The question here is: what can be considered 'Ghanaian' culture after approximately 500 years of contact with Western European and North American societies which is ongoing and which has taken the form of trade, conversion to a religion which, although Eastern in origin, re-entered the continent of Africa after it had been 'Europeanized' in many ways, school-based education centred around curricula aligned with the norms and values of European societies, political subjugation with its introduction of a range of laws and policies, travel and migration (both inward and outward) for both education and economic factors, and interactions with various forms of media? In answering this question, the religious and formal education element must be given special attention due to the cultural transformation they set in motion for sections of the population. In particular, both formal education and Christianity resulted in new ideas about what was 'proper' education, what was 'proper' family relations and 'proper' family life filtering into existing social structures and relationships, not just between a husband and his now one (official) wife, but also between parents and children (Ardayfio-Schandorf, 1996; Allman, 1997). The components of this cultural shift led to new behaviours underpinned by the concept of individualism among sections of the population. Additionally, they created a situation whereby the values, religion and domestic economies of the Indigenous peoples were devalued. Given these transformations and their enduring legacy in contemporary society how can we define 'Ghanaian' culture today? What would we include in this definition? And how are we to be certain that the elements we seek to include in our attempt to define 'Ghanaian' culture' are actually Indigenous to the peoples inhabiting the area now known as Ghana (itself created by forcing together diverse ethnic groups into one colony to be ruled by Britain)? How can we make sure that what is referred to as 'Ghanaian' culture today is not a hybridized outcome which not only draws on Indigenous values, but also on those imported through centuries of encounters with European peoples, cultures, norms, values and general ways of life (see Atiemo, 2012)?

The implications of these questions I am asking for children's rights is that they indicate the existence of groups in Ghanaian society who have long imbibed 'Western' values and norms and for whom the concept of children's rights is not an alien notion being imposed into their lives. Therefore, for this group 'Western' ideas and values are not dislodging more traditional norms and practices and creating havoc on their existing belief system (at least not for their generation) due to the fact that their belief systems already align with the ideas underpinning the concept of children's rights in several ways.

These questions I raise about Latin America and Ghana respectively throw into sharp relief the extent to which the idea of 'the West' has been expanded into a range of societies which do not share all the characteristics that have tended to be associated with societies that are labelled as 'the West'. Instead, the notion and state of being 'Western' has for a long time been evident in the construction of social relations identifiable within many communities in diverse parts of the world which have, hitherto, been labelled as 'non-Western'. As a result of this development, a continued critique of dominant children's rights discourses and their attendant laws and policies for their 'Western-bias' or 'Western' origins becomes somewhat of a moot point because the state of being 'Western' or the idea of 'the West' has taken root within the social structures and value systems of certain groups within a diverse range of countries. Its identification within the structures and social relations of these societies is evident not only through the articulation of norms and values, but also in the existence of so-called 'Western-bias' within sections of Indigenous populations in these societies who have come to prioritize, for example, formal education over Indigenous forms of education (see, for example, Dei and Simmons, 2011). In Ghana, this is evident through the value placed on the English language, as opposed to more local languages, in government policy and the socialization processes many families adopt which foregrounds English as the primary mode of communication over and above Indigenous languages (see, for example, Adika, 2012; Nyamekye and Baffour-Koduah, 2021).

It is worth noting that the other side of this argument about the extension of the idea of 'the West' is the presence of significant communities representing 'the non-West' or 'the rest' in the cities and towns of countries considered to be part of 'the West' (Hall, 1996). This further raises questions about what the concept of 'the West' can possibly mean in the contemporary period given that within urban areas of countries typically defined as 'Western' can be found large numbers of Africans, Caribbeans, Asians and South Americans whose presence can be seen not only through the demographics of these cities and towns, but also through the way their presence and lifestyles shape these societies socially, culturally and linguistically. As Inda and Rosaldo (2008: 21) posit, 'the interesting thing about migrants nowadays is that, in general, when they move across national boundaries, they do not simply leave their "homelands" behind'. Rather, they are able to forge social relations that link together their homes and host societies across vast distances. Thus, not only has the idea of 'the West' travelled to contexts which do not share all the characteristics that we associate with 'Western' societies, but also cultural norms and values of societies in the 'the rest' have also been de-territorialized and found their way into contexts in 'the West'. This, in turn, has an impact on constructions of cultures and identity formation among host populations in these societies. This emerges in an account of a young White reggae fan from Birmingham's ethnically diverse Balsall Heath neighbourhood who participated in a study undertaken in the late 1980s by cultural theorist, Dick Hebdige:

> There is no such thing as 'England' any more … welcome to India brothers. This is the Caribbean! … Nigeria …! There is no England, man. This is what is coming. Balsall Health is the centre of the melting pot, 'cos all I ever see when I go out is half Arab, half Pakistani, half Jamaican, half Scottish, half-Irish. I know cos I am [half Scottish/half Irish] … who am I? Tell me who I belong to? They criticize me, the good old England. Alright where do I belong? You know I was brought up with blacks, Pakistanis, Africans, Asians, everything, you name it … who do I belong to? … I'm just a broad person. The earth is mine … you know we was not born in Jamaica … we were born here, man. (Hebdige, 1987: 158–159, quoted in Inda and Rosaldo, 2008: 24)

While this quote is somewhat overstated, it does reinforce the point that immigrants and the importing of cultural identities that they bring with them shape and influence the contexts to which they migrate. Thus, again, what can 'the West' or being 'Western' mean when large numbers of 'the rest' can now be found in primarily the towns and cities of countries that have, hitherto, been included in the definition of 'Western' countries?

Related to this is the point that the overt focus on the 'non-Western contexts' in discussing the challenges to children's rights also has consequences for the study of childhoods and children's rights in contexts in the so-called 'West'. Specifically, it results in insufficient scrutiny being paid to the ways cultural and social norms as well as economic factors in contexts in the 'the West' result in the variability and plurality of intersections between children's lived realities and dominant rights discourses within these locales. The issue of culture is especially interesting because lack of scrutiny of diverse 'Western' cultural and social norms leads to the cultures of some of these societies becoming either invisible or being made to appear synonymous with the culture of human rights almost as if all aspects of modern 'Western' cultures and 'human rights' culture were one and the same phenomenon. In this way the diversity of cultures that exist in modern Western contexts, which do not all align with human rights principles, are overlooked. This highlights the need to problematize the extent to which the term 'Western' applies to all countries labelled as 'Western'. Simply put, which Western countries are we thinking of, or referring to, when we talk about the 'Western' origins or 'Western' bias underpinning the dominant concept of children's rights? This is important to consider due to the vast differences that have long existed within societies labelled 'Western'. In effect, the question that needs to be asked is whose 'Western' traditions counted in the development and articulation of dominant children's rights discourses? This point is further sharpened when one considers the middle-class roots of the development of dominant rights principles in contexts in 'the West'. What this means, in effect, in relation to children's rights is that the homogenization of particular ideas about childhood and their position in society is experienced, and responded to, in different ways by distinct groups of children and their families within the so-called 'West'. Therefore, the consequence of the homogenization of the legacy of one historical, geographical, class-based and cultural context in the shaping of childhood is the creation of conflict between the notion of childhood articulated in global policies on one hand and the differing legacies of constructing childhoods, family relationships and definitions of children's rights, not only among sections of the population in countries that have been referred to as 'the non-West', but also among 'non-middle-class' populations within contexts that have typically been referred to as 'the West' (Sandin, 2014; Holzscheiter et al, 2019).

Centring middle-class values as a unit of analysis to interrogate dominant children's rights discourses

Despite the importance of the middle-class origins to the development of dominant children's rights principles both in the so-called 'West' and more globally, it is more often than not only mentioned in passing in analyses of childhoods and children's rights, almost as an aside that needs to be briefly acknowledged before researchers dwell more substantially on the 'Western' origins of these discourses which they appear to take greater issue with. As a concept which emerged from the child-saving movement of the 19th century, the class-based principles underpinning the dominant children's rights framework requires much more interrogation, especially in relation to how it intersects with the lives, practices and attitudes of lower-class children and their families in both the North and the South. In particular, there is a need to recognize that the conceptualization of childhood embedded in international treaties and policies such as the Convention articulates a middle-class vision of how childhood should be understood.

Furthermore, given the fact that today, there are groups in 'non-Western' contexts who support dominant children's rights discourses at the same time that there exist those in these same contexts whose cultures or socioeconomic status grouping continue to be in resistance to such dominant discourses, it may be more worthwhile to devote more substantial attention on not simply 'the Western-bias' of dominant rights discourses, but also their middle-class origins. In particular, it would be crucial to explore the impact of the intersections between both geographical- and class-based locations on shaping attitudes towards, and experiences of, rights as the concept 'travelled' across contexts. This approach that foregrounds a class-based analysis may provide an entry point that sheds light on how dominant rights principles 'other' poor and marginal children's lives regardless of whether they live in contexts in the Global North or in the Global South. Such an analysis needs to not only consider the lives of children whose childhoods are characterized by poverty, deprivation and marginalization, but also those whose more affluent status and stronger linkages to both economic and cultural capital in the locales in which they inhabit produce different outcomes when they interact with dominant children's rights norms – at least in relation to certain rights, most notably survival/provision and development rights. By bringing this more affluent group of children's lives under greater scrutiny in the South as well as in the North researchers will be able to identify, more closely, the ways rights discourses, and indeed, policies and laws have been deployed as a disciplinary tool to regulate and intervene in the lives of poor children and their families (Holzscheiter et al, 2019).

This focus on the lives of children living in poor and marginalized communities in childhood research not only has consequences for children and their families within such socioeconomic groups; it also has implications for many children from more affluent families whose experiences of, and access to, dominant children's rights principles have been overshadowed. This is probably most obviously notable in relation to a range of protection rights as articulated in dominant children's rights frameworks. Specifically, in relation to the Global North, a number of authors have underscored the challenges of ensuring protection rights for children within affluent families due to the economic, educational and cultural capital of their parents (O'Brien and Salonen, 2011; Segado Sánchez-Cabezudo and López Peláez, 2014; Sánchez-Cabezudo et al, 2016). In relation to the UK, Bernard (2018) asserts that middle-class parents undervalue the role, expertise and power of social workers and used their social capital and education to dispute the interventions of professionals in child protections cases involving their children. This leads Bernard, in a later publication (Bernard and Greenwood,

2019: 345), to conclude that a challenge to developing interventions that can adequately protect the rights of middle-class children is the 'highly-resistant parents who have the economic, social, and cultural capital to resist their interventions'. Similarly, Carmi and Walker-Hall (2015) claim, in relation to child protection processes, that affluent parents use their status, confidence and assertiveness to block professional intervention within their families. The resulting outcome is that children's rights violations, as defined by dominant children's rights norms, among such groups often do not come to light until it is too late. Therefore, by deploying the concept of children's rights as a tool to govern and indeed, discipline, poor and marginalized children and their families, middle-class children are made somewhat invisible. Perhaps this is because this group of children was never the subject of children's rights norms and frameworks (despite repeated and vocal claims about the universality of children's rights) as their childhoods were never deemed to be faulty and in need of 'fixing' through laws, policies and interventions framed in the language of rights.

Foregrounding holistic understandings of children's experiences of rights in the North and South

In effect what this discussion has pointed to is that not only can dissonance in attitudes and experiences of dominant children's rights discourses be found in the South due to cultural norms and economic factors, but they can also be identified in the North – also as a result of cultural norms and economic circumstances. Similarly, in relation to the ways that some children's lives correspond closely with dominant rights discourses (or at least some aspects), these can be found in both contexts in the North and the South due to the positioning of the lives of these children and their families within the historical, social and economic structures of their society. The implication for childhood researchers is that there is a need to adopt a more holistic approach in the study of children's rights outcomes and possibilities. While the literature relating to contexts in the North does quite well in producing this balanced picture of the varied ways dominant children's rights intersect with a range of children's lives (although it can be argued that even in this context there is a tendency for the dynamics in Anglophone countries to be foregrounded in the bulk of the literature which is attributable to the dominance of the English language in academic knowledge production), in contexts in the South this holistic approach to analysing the interactions between the variety of children's lives that exist and dominant discourses of children's rights is lacking.

This is despite the fact that 100 years after the first international codified treaty on the rights of the child, there now exist a diversity of attitudes and experiences of children in relation to children's rights in different contexts in the South. While some of these attitudes and experiences are completely at odds with the dominant discourses surrounding the notion of children's rights to the extent that some of these children and their families may not express their claims for social justice in terms of the language of rights, other experiences do exist that illuminate varying levels of dissonance and synergy with dominant and global children's rights principles. The paucity of more balanced literature focusing on the lives of different groups of children in a given context, especially in the South, is problematic. This is especially important because by focusing disproportionately on the lives of poor children in the South while adopting a more balanced approach to the study of childhoods in the Global North, which considers the lives of middle-class children to some degree (although there is a tendency to focus more on the lives of poor children in this context also), leads to the production of knowledge which reinforces binary thinking between the North and South. Therefore, there is a need for more scholarly work focusing on the South, in particular, which adopts a holistic approach to elicit the daily lived experiences of diverse groups of children and proceed to draw on that to:

1. interrogate the various ways they intersect with dominant children's rights principles;
2. explain the factors that underpin this variation in experiences and attitudes; and
3. reflect on what these plural experiences of childhood conceptualizations and lived realities in relation to the intersection with children's rights reveal about wider social structures and relationships.

Towards a concept of a continuum in exploring the plurality of childhood experiences within a locale

In trying to access the variability of children's lives in relation to dominant children's rights norms and principles in diverse contexts in the South, the concept of a continuum which connects the local to the global may provide a useful framing which helps to explain the wide range of everyday lives and their intersections with dominant children's rights norms in such contexts (Twum-Danso Imoh, 2019, 2020). While at one end of the continuum are realities of childhoods and children's lives that are in stark contrast to the global ideals embedded within dominant rights norms and discourses as defined by global institutions, at the other end can be identified lived experiences that correspond quite closely with such global conceptualizations, ideals, norms and principles in numerous respects. In between these two polar opposites are points along the continuum which reflect realities of, and attitudes towards, childhoods and their interactions with dominant children's rights discourses that combine both global and

IMPLICATIONS FOR STUDIES OF CHILDREN'S RIGHTS

local conceptualizations to varying degrees of intensity (Twum-Danso Imoh, 2019, 2020). If we adopt a continuum approach then it would be important to explore these differing positions on the continuum in a given locale and reflect on the plurality of lived experiences of, and attitudes towards, dominant children's rights principles with increasing levels of intensity as you approach either end of the continuum, not just those that are polar opposites to each other, but also those that are situated in these in-between points on the continuum – all in equal measure.

Such continuum thinking requires us to adopt an approach within locales which enables us to consider the intersection between dominant and global children's rights discourses and principles and children's realities through an analysis that considers numerous intersecting variables that may have implications for children's experiences of different aspects of the rights framework: social status, gender, geographical location, family type, education of parents, and so on (Hecht, 1998; Hollos, 2002; Rizzini and Barker, 2002; Punch, 2003; Holt and Holloway, 2006; Naftali, 2014; Twum-Danso Imoh, 2016). These variables are important to consider as differences between groups within a particular context informs understandings and perspectives of childhoods and proceed to shape the everyday experiences of growing up for different groups of children. This was well highlighted by the discussion on child work, which can be acknowledged as a cultural norm embedded in Ghanaian socialization processes but manifests itself not only in terms of tasks required for children to undertake, but also with regards to level or degree of intensity (see Chapter 7, this volume).

It is important to note that the conceptualization of these intersections between children's lived realities and dominant children's rights norms as a continuum does not suggest a smooth or stable interaction between distinct groups of children positioned along the continuum and dominant children's rights discourses and principles (see Twum-Danso Imoh, 2020). Given the colonial legacy evident in most countries in sub-Saharan Africa (as well as elsewhere in the South), we have to pay attention to the contradictions and tensions that are bound to underpin these conceptualizations and understandings (Nieuwenhuys, 2012). Such tensions were well noted in Chapter 6 which explored the plurality in lifestyles in Ghana, including those relating to child-rearing and transitions to adulthood. Thus, these interactions between the local and the global as they relate to children's lives and dominant children's rights discourses and principles are unstable and fluctuate, often depending on the specific rights issue under discussion (see Twum-Danso Imoh, 2020). A good example in the context of Ghana perhaps relates to the right to formal education versus the right to protection from physical punishment. While certain groups of children may be firmly positioned at one end of the continuum in relation to their experience of the right to formal education due to the fact that their parents prioritize this entitlement and ensure that they achieve a good quality education, the position of some of these same children in relation to the right to protection from physical punishment may not be similarly assured (see also Twum-Danso Imoh, 2020). Therefore, we need to recognize the highly fluctuating nature of this intersection between rights and daily realities even in the experience of an individual child in a given locale. These ideas are aligned with Dembour's (2001: 56) work on the universality and cultural relativity of human rights in which she puts forward the idea that individuals take an in-between position, which, she argues, 'is not a middle position that would represent a happy compromise, putting at rest, once and for all, the debate concerning the respective strengths of universalism and relativism'. Instead, for Dembour, this in-between position is reflective of the motion of a swinging pendulum as:

> [I]t is a position which makes sense of the fact that a moral agent is inevitably drawn into a pendulum motion. Thus, as one accepts being drawn toward relativism, there is a moment when, getting as it were too close to it, one is compelled to revert towards universalism and vice versa. The image of the pendulum indicates that the in-between position I advocate is unstable. (Dembour, 2001: 56)

Thus, within the continuum there is movement, fluidity, fluctuations which result in tensions and conflict as well as conflicted individuals whose attitudes and experiences appear to 'chop and change' from one rights issue, as codified by international law, to another (see also Howard, 1986; Twum-Danso, 2008; Twum-Danso Imoh, 2020; Chapter 3, this volume).

The benefit of the continuum approach I am proposing can be seen in two distinct ways. First, such approach will not only highlight the extent to which income inequalities that exist *within* regions and countries in the South inform differential experiences and outcomes of childhoods in relation to dominant rights discourses, but it will also throw into sharp relief broader dynamics relating to the social stratification and structures that underpin these societies, such as power and its machinations, which compound a range of inequalities between peoples. This is important to consider because often we discuss social and income inequality by focusing on one side of the coin or the picture – those who bear the brunt of unequal societies (see also Rosemberg, 2005; Introduction, this volume). With regards to childhoods in the South, this focus leads to an intense scrutiny of the lives of poor children with the view to highlighting the inequalities that exist in a given society. However, at the risk of pointing out the obvious, if a dynamic or situation is unequal that means there is another side to explore. Again, in the study of Southern childhoods, this refers to children whose lives are characterized by certain privileges. Without exploring both sides of the coin can we truly develop a comprehensive understanding of inequality, how it is operationalized and the numerous ways it insidiously shapes the lives of individuals in a given context and influences the experiences of dominant rights principles for diverse groups of children? To hammer home the point, it is worth drawing on the example of discussions about, and strategies to tackle, racial equality where the focus is often on the experiences of people of colour in relation to racial inequality without sufficient attention being paid, at the same time, to Whiteness, White privilege and the White supremacist system, which are all factors which drive, and benefit from, this inequality. If we only focus on the experiences of people of colour, we will obtain many insights into, and indeed accounts of, their experiences of racism, prejudice, discrimination, microaggressions, disenfranchisement and oppression more generally. However, if we *additionally* scrutinize systematically, as part of our analysis, Whiteness and White privilege we will gain a significantly deeper understanding of the institutionalization of racial inequality and the insidious ways it affects all aspects of a society on a daily basis. It is this holistic or whole-systems picture that I am arguing for in relation to studies of children's rights.

Second, by adopting the concept of a continuum as a framework for childhood and children's rights research in the South, this approach will also reveal commonalities between particular types of childhoods and certain groups of children in the Global South and their counterparts in the Global North in relation to not just age, but also socioeconomic status (see Twum-Danso Imoh, forthcoming 2024a). Further, this approach will pave the way for the creation of spaces which facilitate discussions about connections as well as comparisons between contexts in the Global North and the Global South. This consideration is important to take into account because as Hecht (1998), Goldstein (1998, cited in Prout, 2005) and Rizzini and Barker (2002) have all noted in relation to Brazil, for instance, analyses of the lives of middle-class or more affluent children reveal the extent to which the realities of these groups of children demonstrate that they share more experiences with children from a similar background in countries in the North such as the US than with the poor and marginalized children who may live in close proximity to them. Hecht, who makes a distinction between the 'nurtured', pampered childhoods of middle-class children in Recife (northeastern Brazil) with their poor counterparts whose childhoods are centred around 'nurturing' their household, highlights the extent to which the nature of these middle-class childhoods is experienced in ways that even exaggerate, almost in caricature form, the middle-class childhoods that can be found in the Global North:

> Painted in broad strokes, the nurtured childhood of the rich in Brazil has much in common with the ideal of contemporary middle-class

> childhood in Europe and North America. But it exaggerates the forms. Not only are nurtured children not expected to contribute to the family income, they are not expected to clear their dishes from the table, make their beds, or clean their rooms. These are the tasks of maids and, on occasion, mothers. It is not enough to sleep late during summer vacation; many very rich, nurtured children (particularly from cities thousands of kilometers to the south of Recife such as Sao Paulo, Curitiba, and Porto Alegre) are shipped off in groups for several weeks at a time to Florida for a sort of luxury summer camp experience where they stay at five-star hotels, shop for exotic electronic gadgets, and make the obligatory stop at Disney World. (Hecht, 1998: 83–84)

This demonstrates that there is value in exploring how the lives of different groups of children in the Global South connect and differ from those of their counterparts in the Global North. In concrete terms, then, a holistic approach requires that studies that seek to illuminate connections or comparisons between children in the North and South must centre around those with almost 'like-for-like' experiences which allow for the consideration of variables such as socioeconomic background as these inform childhood experiences in both Northern and Southern contexts. However, at the same time, such studies seeking connections and comparisons must tread cautiously in order not to oversimply any commonalities identified (see also Punch, 2015; Twum-Danso Imoh, forthcoming 2024a).

To realize an approach to childhood and children's rights research which centres around the notion of a continuum, several structural issues will need to be addressed. Most noteworthy will be the need for more collaboration between scholars focusing on children's rights research in contexts in the North and South because while some researchers individually research contexts located in both world areas, they are few and far between. This is due to the fact that most childhood researchers, from an early stage in their career, make a decision to focus on either contexts in the South or the North in their research agendas. Hence, to be able to identify more connections or comparisons between like-for-like groups in both world areas more collaboration between researchers will be required – at least until such a time when childhood researchers feel equipped (methodologically, conceptually and ethically – both in terms of research and their own personal ethics) to regularly design research studies that cut across multiple sites covering both the North and South. The other structural issue relates to funding. Although some funding schemes are centred around open calls which invite researchers to submit research proposals on a topic of their choosing as long as it is excellent, original and methodologically rigorous, a good number of schemes are developed with a specific topic or research population in mind. In relation to calls centred on the South, most of these adopt a deficit lens with a focus on poor marginalized populations whom researchers then need to foreground as they design their own proposals if they want to secure much sought-after funding which is critical to their career progression. This, in turn, influences the angle researchers take to explore a given topic within a Southern context, leading to the proliferation of studies presenting rich data on an aspect of the lives of those whose daily realities are characterized by poverty, marginalization and a range of deprivations. This, then, has consequences for the focus of the publications that emerge from these studies, which are then consumed not only by other academics, but also by students and members of the public. Therefore, while much of this book has centred on the need for childhood researchers to reflect on the approach they adopt to the study of childhood and children's rights in both the North and South, it is critical to note that any change researchers can bring about will be limited until these broader structural issues are addressed.

Notes

Introduction

[1] While there are numerous reasons behind the decision by the British colonial government to move the capital from Cape Coast, in the Central Region, to Accra, one reason put forward by Kilson (1974: 1) was that it was because of the latter's drier climate.

[2] The double shift system of basic education in Ghana consistently operated in urban areas from the early 1960s when policy makers introduced Ghana's first Education Act (1961), which sought to make basic education more accessible and, hence, making it free as well as compulsory. This system was developed as a response to the significant demand for formal education in the years since independence in 1957. The Education Act 2008 stipulated the abolishment of this system of schooling in almost all public basic schools under their jurisdiction in the 2009/2010 academic year. However, in more recent years some district assemblies have reintroduced the system as a result of COVID-19. According to this system, pupils attend classes either in the mornings or afternoons in alternative weeks for a specified duration of time, usually two weeks.

[3] *Ampe* is a game played by two or more players and can look more like a dance than a game. The leader and another player jump up at the same time, clap, and thrust one foot forward when they jump up. If the leader and the other player have the same foot forward the leader wins a point. If they are different, then the other player becomes 'it' and plays against the remaining players. If the players are in a circle, the leader moves along the inside of the circle, playing against others in turn. If they are in a line, the leader moves on down the line. If only two players are playing, they keep score until a certain number of points determines the winner (www.apmenmultimedia.com, accessed 27 November 2022).

Chapter 1

[1] In this early period discussions about the emerging conception of childhood centred around upper- and middle-class boys. The gendered and class-based nature of this understanding of childhood at this time is discussed later on in this chapter.

[2] Thomas Spence (1750–1814), an English advocate of common land ownership wrote a pamphlet entitled the 'Rights of Infants, explicitly ascribed to children's natural rights on full participation of the fruits of the earth' (in Liebel, 2012: 30).

Chapter 2

[1] While Jebb has long been framed as the founder of the Save the Children movement, more recent accounts have sought to correct this narrative by documenting how the original founder of the organization was actually her sister, Dorothy Buxton (Baughan and Fiori, 2015).

NOTES

Chapter 3

[1] The vision of a human being produced at this time had a bias towards White men, especially those who owned land. This highlights the narrow scope of who exactly was included in understandings of who was human in early conceptualizations of the human rights discourse (du Toit, 2013).

[2] The Nigerian Child Rights Act was passed at the federal level in 2003. However, due to the federal structure of the country, it is only effective if State Assemblies also enact it. Thirteen years after the passage of the Act, in May 2016, 23 out of 36 states had passed the Act. Of the remaining 13 that had not, 12 were based in the North. Since then, there has been some progress as, as of May 2023, 34 states had passed the Act. The two remaining states that have not passed the Act are, again, based in the north of the country: Kano and Zamfara (https://independent.ng/states-and-the-child-rights-act-3/, accessed 25 May 2023).

[3] Renamed the African Union in July 2002.

[4] Kwame Nkrumah was not only the first president of Ghana; he was also instrumental in the development of Pan-African ideology in Africa and the establishment of the Organization of African Unity (now known as the African Union) in May 1963. This led to him to be seen as an influential figure across the continent.

[5] See Chapter 8 for a fuller discussion of this issue.

Chapter 4

[1] The Yaa Asantewaa War of 1900, also known as the War of the Golden Stool, is named after the Queen Mother of Edweso (Asante region), Nana Yaa Asantewaa, who led the Asante in combat against the British whose Governor was making demands for additional tributes from the Asante on behalf of the British Queen. In particular, the Governor's demands centred around the Golden Stool, which is both symbolic and sacred to the Asante. Given the fact that the King of the Asante (the Asantehene), Nana Agyeman Prempeh I, and other leading chiefs had already been sent into exile in the Seychelles by this time, it was Nana Yaa Asantewaa, Queen Mother of Edweso, who, at the age of 69, rallied Asante resistance to the British. The Asantes' eventual defeat by the British facilitated Britain's expansion and consolidation of the area they controlled and called the Gold Coast.

Chapter 5

[1] £33 approximately as of 22 December 2023.

[2] PNDC Law 42, passed in January 1982, suspended the Constitution, and gave the military regime wide ranging powers over the peoples of Ghana.

[3] The African Charter on the Rights and Welfare of the Child does not feature much in public or policy discussions around children's rights in the country. The relatively low level of attention it receives can be seen by the fact that while the Convention and African Charter were adopted just within nine months of each other (November 1989 and July 1990), Ghana's approach to ratifying each of these treaties was rather distinct. While Ghana rushed to ratify the Convention less than three months after it was adopted by the UN General Assembly, in the case of the African Charter it took 15 years before the government ratified it in 2005 (although it signed it in 1997 which shows its intent to ratify). That the ratification of the Charter took place in 2005 means that it took place under a government which was not led by Rawlings. This is a further indication of the extent to which Rawlings' efforts to gain support for his programmes were very much centred around Western governments and agencies.

[4] The Multiple Indicator Cluster Surveys (MICS) are household surveys to provide internationally comparable, statistically rigorous data on the situation of children and

women in countries around the world. The survey was developed by UNICEF but is administered by national governments. The first survey in Ghana was conducted in 1995 and 1996 and the most recent were launched in 2016 and completed in 2018. In total there have been six MICS surveys conducted.

5 In these MICS, physical punishment is defined as: shaking, hitting or slapping a child on the hand/arm/leg; hitting on the bottom or elsewhere on the body with a hard object; spanking or hitting on the bottom with a bare hand; hitting or slapping on the face, head or ears; and hitting or beating hard and repeatedly. Severe physical punishment is understood as: hitting or slapping a child on the face, head or ears; and hitting or beating a child hard and repeatedly (Ghana Statistical Service, 2019).

Chapter 6

1 I phrase it in this way because Christianity existed in parts of Africa before the arrival of European missionaries and traders in the 15th century. Arriving first in North Africa in the 1st or 2nd century AD (before the Arab conquest of North Africa), it spread both West and East from Alexandria (in present-day Egypt). In relation to the East in the 4th century AD, the Ethiopian king, Ezana, made Christianity the official language of his kingdom. Further, St Augustine, who is recognized as 'bringing' Christianity to the Anglo-Saxons in the 6th century AD, was born in North Africa. While his father is acknowledged to have been Roman, his mother is described as a Berber who are one of the Indigenous groups of northern Africa. Factoring in this early history is critical to understanding that Christianity was not new to parts of Africa at the time European missionaries arrived in the 15th century to 'civilize and convert' the Indigenous people of the continent.

2 The Ga, or the Ga-Dangme, people are an ethnic group found in Ghana and Togo who speak a dialect of the Kwa branch of the Niger-Congo languages. Descended from immigrants who travelled down the Niger River and across the Volta, the Ga-Dangme came to settle in the southern part of the country along the coast of Guinea, creating six independent towns (Accra, Osu, Labadi, Teshi, Nungua and Tema).

3 While pre-colonial Ghanaian societies had a more fluid understanding of sexuality (Geoffrion, 2018), in contemporary Ghana the understanding of a nuclear family centres around two adults of the opposite sex and their biological children. This is because laws against sodomy (which thereby makes homosexuality illegal), first introduced under British colonial government in 1892, remained unchanged in much of the post-colonial period and are now being discussed with the view to making them more stringent.

4 *Homowo* derives from two Ga-Dangme words, 'homo' meaning hunger and 'wo' meaning to hoot at. Therefore, *homowo* means 'hooting at hunger'. This festival, celebrated annually in August, seeks to commemorate the period when the ancestors of the Ga-Dangme people overcame hunger when they first migrated into the area they are now associated with – the Greater Accra region. According to the narrative, during their migration from the Niger River, the Ga-Dangme people experienced famine and severe hunger. However, upon settling in this area they found the strength to farm the land and called upon their ancestral spirits through libation to bless their new farms so they could grow food in its abundance. In response, a period of rainfall ensued, allowing their crops to grow. Their cattle also multiplied and, as fisher folk, they were able to catch a lot of fish in the seas alongside the coastal areas where they had settled. To celebrate this victory over hunger, they prepared a special meal made from unfermented corn powder called *kpekple* and palm nut soup with fish. As they ate the dish they hooted at, and ridiculed, hunger and poured libation to the gods as well as provided them with an offering of food. Since then, every year during the *Homowo* festival, Ga-Dangme people come together

NOTES

to celebrate overcoming this adversity through sharing *kpekple* and palm nut soup in a festival which brings families together.

Chapter 7

[1] *Fufu* is popular dish in Ghana typically made from mashed cassava and/cocoyam or plantain that is served in a round or oval shape alongside a variety of soups.

[2] The Senate is the upper chamber of Nigeria's bicameral legislature, the National Assembly which, is charged with drafting the country's laws.

[3] The Basic Education Certificate Examination (BECE) is the main examination to qualify students for admission into secondary and vocational schools in Ghana and is written after three years of junior secondary education. Passing this exam enables students to advance to senior secondary schools or to vocational courses.

Chapter 8

[1] These accounts situating the concept of the West within Ancient Greek and Roman culture have conventionally not considered the extent to which both civilizations were multicultural in many respects.

[2] Source: www.slavevoyages.org/assessment/estimates (accessed 3 June 2023).

References

Abebe, T. (2007) 'Changing livelihoods, changing childhoods: Patterns of children's work in rural southern Ethiopia', *Children's Geographies*, 5(1): 77–93.

Abebe, T. (2013) 'Interdependent rights and agency: Children's role in collective livelihood strategies in rural Ethiopia', in Hanson, K. and Nieuwenhuys, O. (eds), *Reconceptualising Children's Rights in International Development: Living Rights, Social Justice, Translations*, Cambridge: Cambridge University Press.

Abebe, T. (2022) 'African futures and childhood studies in Africa', in Abebe, T. (ed), *African Futures and Childhood Studies in Africa*, Dakar: CODESRIA.

Abebe, T. and Tefera, T. (2014) 'Earning rights: Discourses on children's rights and proper childhood in Ethiopia', in Twum-Danso Imoh, A. and Ansell, N. (eds), *Children's Lives in an Era of Children's Rights: The Progress of the Convention on the Rights of the Child in Africa*, Abingdon and New York: Routledge.

Abebe, T. and Ofosu-Kusi, Y. (2016) 'Beyond pluralizing African childhoods: Introduction', *Childhood*, 23(3): 303–316.

Abebe, T. and Biswas, T. (2021) 'Rights in education: Outlines for a decolonial, childist reimagination of the future – commentary to Ansell and colleagues', *Fennia*, 199(1): 118–128.

Aboderin, I. (2004) 'Decline in material family support for older people in urban Ghana, Africa: Understanding processes and causes of change', *Journal of Gerontology*, 59B(3): S128–S137.

Addo-Fenning, R. (2013) 'Ghana under colonial rule: An outline of the early period and the interwar years', *Transactions of the Historical Society of Ghana*, 15: 39–70.

Aderinto, S. (2015) *Children and Childhood in Colonial Nigerian Histories*, New York: Palgrave Macmillan.

Adichie, C.N. (2009) 'The danger of a single story', *TED Talk*, July, www.youtube.com/watch?v=D9Ihs241zeg (accessed 14 October 2009).

Adika, G.S.K. (2012) 'English in Ghana: Growth, tensions, and trends', *International Journal of Language, Translation, and Intercultural Communication*, 1: 151–166.

REFERENCES

Adinkrah, M. (2012) 'Better dead than dishonoured: Masculinity and male suicidal behaviour in contemporary Ghana', *Social Science and Medicine*, 74(4): 474–481.

Adjei, S.B. (2016) 'Masculinity and spousal violence: Discursive accounts of husbands who abuse their wives in Ghana', *Journal of Family Violence*, 31: 411–422.

Adomako-Ampofo, A. (2001) 'The socialization of Ghanaian adolescents and their gendered sexual role-expectations and sexual culture', Annual Meetings of the African Studies Association, Houston, Texas, 15–19 November.

Adomako-Ampofo, A. (2005) 'Collective activism: The Domestic Violence Bill becoming law in Ghana', *African and Asian Studies*, 7: 395–421.

Adomako-Ampofo, A. and Boateng, J. (2007) 'Multiple meanings of manhood among boys in Ghana', in Shefer, T., Ratele, K. Strebel, A., Shabalala, N. and Buikema, R. (eds), *From Boys to Men: Social Constructions of Masculinity in Contemporary Society*, Lansdowne: UCT Press.

Adonteng-Kissi, O. (2018a) 'Parental perceptions of child labour and human rights: A comparative study of rural and urban Ghana', *Child Abuse & Neglect*, 84(208): 34–44.

Adonteng-Kissi, O. (2018b) 'Causes of child labour: Perceptions of rural and urban parents in Ghana', *Children and Youth Services Review*, 91: 55–65.

Adu-Boahen, E. (2022) 'Understanding the learning gaps between private schools and public schools in Ghana', *International Journal of Social Economics*, 49(9): 1277–1301.

Afriye, L., Saee, B. and Alhassan, A. (2019) 'Determinants of child labour, practices in Ghana', *Journal of Public Health from Theory to Practice*, 27: 211–212.

Aitken, S.C. (2001) 'Global crisis of childhood: Rights, justice and the unchildlike child', *Area*, 33(2): 119–127.

Alber, E., Häberlein, T. and Martin, J. (2010) 'Changing webs of kinship: Spotlights on West Africa', *Africa Spectrum*, 45(3): 43–67.

Allman, J. (1994) 'Making mothers: Missionaries, medical officers and women's work in colonial Asante 1924–1945', *History Workshop*, 38: 23–47.

Allman, J. (1997) 'Fathering, mothering, and making sense of "Ntamoba"', *Africa: Journal of the International Africa Institute*, 67(2): 296–321.

Allman, J. and Tashjian, V. (2000) *'I Will Not Eat Stone': A Woman's History of Colonial Asante*, Oxford: James Currey.

Alston, P. (ed) (1994) *The Best Interests of the Child: Reconciling Culture and Human Rights*, Oxford: Clarendon Press.

Ameh, R. (2004) 'Reconciling human rights and traditional practices: The anti-*Trokosi* campaign in Ghana', *Canadian Journal of Law and Society*, 19(2): 151–172.

Amua-Sekyi, E.T. (1998) *Ghana: Education for Girls*, Women's Center at Eastern Washington University.

Andre, G. and Hilgers, M. (2015) 'Childhood in Africa between local powers and global hierarchies', in Alanen, L., Brooker, L. and Mayall, B. (eds), *Childhood with Bourdieu*, Basingstoke and New York: Palgrave Macmillan.

An-Na'im, A. and Hammond, J. (2002) 'Cultural transformation and human rights in African societies', in An-Na'im, A. (ed), *Cultural Transformation and Human Rights in Africa*, London and New York: Zed Books.

Ansell, N. (2010) 'The discursive construction of childhood and youth in AIDS interventions in Lesotho's education sector: Beyond global–local dichotomies', *Environment and Planning D: Society and Space*, 28: 791–810.

Ansell, N. (2016) *Children, Youth and Development*, 2nd edn, London and New York: Routledge.

Ansong, A. (2020) 'SDGs and elimination of child labour in the cocoa industry in Ghana: Can WTO law and private sector responsible business initiatives help?', *Forum for Development Studies*, 47(2): 261–281.

Antwi, J. and Okyere-Manu, B. (2018) 'Bragro as an Akan African indigenous knowledge system pedagogical system: An ethical critique', in Okyere-Manu, B. and Moyo, H. (eds), *Intersecting African Indigenous Knowledge Systems and Western Knowledge Systems: Moral Convergence and Divergence*, Pietermaritzburg, South Africa: Cluster Publications.

Archard, D. (1993) *Children: Rights and Childhood*, London and New York: Routledge.

Archibald, S. and Richards, P. (2002) 'Converts to human rights? Popular debate about war and justice in rural central Sierra Leone', *Africa: Journal of the International Africa Institute*, 7(3): 339–367.

Ardayfio-Schandorf, E. (1996) *The Changing Family in Ghana*, Accra: Ghana Universities Press.

Ardayfio-Schandorf, E. (2006) 'The family in Ghana: Past and present perspectives', in Oheneba-Sakyi, Y. and Takyi, B. (eds), *African Families at the Turn of the 21st Century*, Westport and London: Praeger.

Ardayfio-Schandorf, E. and Amissah, M. (1996) 'Incidence of child fostering among school children in Ghana', in Ardayfio-Schandorf, E. (ed), *The Changing Family in Ghana*, Accra: Ghana Universities Press.

Ariès, P. (1962) *Centuries of Childhood: A Social History of Family Life*, Harmondsworth: Penguin.

Arthur, P. and Mensah, A. (2021) 'The rhetoric of "Bragoro": The philosophy behind Akan traditional concept of marriage', *Journal of Mother-Tongue Biblical Hermeneutics and Theology*, 3(2): 32–34.

Aryeetey, E. and Baah-Boateng, W. (2016) *Understanding Ghana's Growth Success Story and Job Creation Challenges*, www.brookings.edu/wp-content/uploads/2016/07/Understanding-Ghanas-growth-success-story-and-job-creation-challenges.pdf (accessed 28 February 2023).

REFERENCES

Asante, M.K. (2009) 'Personhood', in Asante, M.K. and Mazama, A. (eds), *Encyclopaedia of African Religion*, Los Angeles, London, New Delhi, Singapore and Washington, DC: SAGE.

Ashford, H. (2019) 'The Red Cross and the establishment of maternal and infant welfare in the 1930s Gold Coast', *The Journal of Imperial and Commonwealth History*, 47(3): 514–541.

Asomah, J. (2015) 'Cultural rights versus human rights: A critical analysis of the *Trokosi* practice in Ghana and the role of civil society', *African Human Rights Law Journal*, 15(1): 129–149.

Assimeng, J.M. (1999) *Social Structure of Ghana: A Study in Persistence and Change*, Accra: Ghana Publishing Corporation.

Atiemo, A. (2006) 'International human rights, religious pluralism and the future of chieftaincy in Ghana', *Exchange*, 35(4): 360–382.

Atiemo, A. (2012) '"Punish my husband but not so hard": Religion, customary values, and conventional approaches to human rights in Ghana', *Religion and Human Rights*, 7(2): 71–93.

Awedoba, A.K. (2002) *Culture and Development in Africa with Special References to Ghana*, Accra: Institute of African Studies, University of Ghana Legon.

Awusabo-Asare, K. (1990) 'Matriliny and the new intestate succession law of Ghana', *Canadian Journal of African Studies/La Revue Canadienne des études Africaines*, 24(1): 1–16.

Azu, D. (1974) *Ga Family and Social Change*, Leiden: Afrikastudiecentrum.

Balagopalan, S. (2002) 'Constructing Indigenous childhoods: Colonialism, vocational education and the working child', *Childhood*, 9(1): 19–34.

Balagopalan, S. (2014) *Inhabiting 'Childhood': Children, Labour and Schooling in Postcolonial India*, New York: Palgrave Macmillan.

Barra, M. (2022) 'Childhood at latitude zero: Revealing São Tomé and Príncipe children's play culture', *Journal of the British Academy*, 10(s2): 83–109.

Baughan, E. (2013) '"Every citizen of empire implored to save the children!": Empire, internationalism, and the Save the Children Fund in inter-war Britain', *Historical Research*, 86(231): 116–137.

Baughan, E. and Fiori, J. (2015) 'Save the Children, the humanitarian project, and the politics of solidarity: Reviving Dorothy Buxton's vision', *Disasters*, 39(2): 129–145.

Benwell, M.C. (2009) 'Challenging minority world privilege: Children's outdoor mobilities in post-apartheid South Africa', *Mobilities*, 4(1): 77–101.

Bernard, C. (2018) *An Exploration of How Social Workers Engage Neglectful Parents from Affluent Backgrounds in the Child Protection System*, London: Goldsmith University of London, https://www.basw.co.uk/resources/exploration-how-social-workers-engage-neglectful-parents-affluent-backgrounds-child (accessed 1 February 2022).

Bernard, C. and Greenwood, T. (2019) '"We're giving you the sack": Social workers' perspectives of intervening in affluent families when there are concerns about child neglect', *The British Journal of Social Work*, 49(8): 2266–2282.

Bhopal, K. (2011) '"This is a school, it's not a site": Teachers' attitudes towards Gypsy and Traveller pupils in schools in England', *British Educational Research Journal*, 37(3): 465–483.

Bilyeu, A.S. (1999) '*Trokosi* – the practice of sexual slavery in Ghana: Religious and cultural freedom vs. human rights', *Indiana International and Comparative Law Review*, 9(2): 457–504.

Boateng, F. and Darko, I. (2016) 'Our past: The effect of colonialism on policing in Ghana', *International Journal of Police Science & Management*, 18(1): 13–20.

Boateng, A. and Agyeman, F.A. (2018) 'Back to our roots: Using puberty rites of the Akans of Ghana as cultural tools for promoting traditional ideals of womanhood in classroom contexts', in Asimeng-Boahene, L. and Baffoe, M. (eds), *African Traditional Oral Literature and Visual Cultures as Pedagogical Tools in Diverse Classroom Contexts*, Charlotte: Information Age Publishing.

Boateng, J.K., Adomako-Ampofo, A., Flanagan, C.C., Gallay, L. and Yankah, J. (2006) *Gender Socialization of Pre-teen Youths in Ghana: Alternative Approaches for Extension*, AIAEE 22nd Annual Conference Proceedings, http://www.aiaee.org/attachments/article/901/070.pdf (accessed 12 July 2016).

Boyden, J. (1997) 'Childhood and the policy makers: A comparative perspective on the globalization of childhood', in James, A. and Prout, A. (eds), *Constructing and Reconstructing Childhood: Contemporary Issues in the Sociological Study of Childhood*, 2nd edn, London and New York: Routledge Falmer.

Brydon, L. and Legge, K. (1996) *Adjusting Society: The World Bank, the IMF and Ghana*, London and New York: Taurus Academic Studies.

Buah, F.K. (1998) *A History of Ghana*, 2nd edn, Oxford: Macmillan Education.

Burman, E. (1994) 'Innocents abroad: Western fantasies of childhood and the iconography of emergencies', *Disasters*, 18(3): 238–253.

Burman, E. (1996) 'Local, global or globalized: Child development and international child rights legislation', *Childhood*, 3: 45–66.

Burman, E. (1999) 'Morality and the goals of development', in Woodhead, M., Faulkner, D. and Littleton, K. (eds), *Making Sense of Social Development*, London and New York: Routledge.

Burman, E. (2016) '"It shouldn't happen here": Cultural and relational dynamics structured around the "poor child"', in Hopkins, L. and Sriprakash, A. (eds), *The 'Poor Child': The Cultural Politics of Education, Development and Childhood*, London and New York: Routledge.

REFERENCES

Burr, R. (2002) 'Global and local approaches to children's rights in Vietnam', *Childhood*, 9(1): 49–61.

Burr, R. (2006) *Vietnam's Children in a Changing World*, New Brunswick: Rutgers University Press.

Cammaert, J. (2015) '"I want to follow Kwaku": The construction of self and home by unfree children in the Gold Coast c.1941', *Journal of African History*, 56(3): 373–378.

Cantwell, N. (2011) 'Are children's rights still human?', in Invernizzi, A. and Williams, J. (eds), *The Human Rights of Children: From Visions to Implementation*, London and New York: Routledge.

Carmi, E. and Walker-Hall, N. (2015) *Serious Case Review Family A*, Kingston LSCB, https://kingstonandrichmondsafeguardingchildren partnership.org.uk/media/upload/fck/file/SCR/Family%20A%20Seri ous%20Case%20Review%20Report%20November%202015.pdf (accessed 1 February 2022).

Cheal, D. (2008) *Families in Today's World: A Comparative Approach*, London and New York: Routledge.

Cheney, K. (2007) *Pillars of the Nation: Child Citizens and Ugandan National Development*, Chicago and London: University of Chicago Press.

Clark, C. and Cemlyn, S. (2005) 'The social exclusion of Gypsy and Traveller children', in Preston, G. (ed), *At Greatest Risk: The Children Most Likely to be Poor*, London: CPAG.

Clark-Kazak, C. (2009) 'Towards a working definition and application of social age in international development studies', *The Journal of Development Studies*, 45(8): 1307–1324.

Cobbah, J. (1987) 'African values and the human rights debate: An African perspective', *Human Rights Quarterly*, 9(3): 309–331.

Coe, C. (2012) 'How debt became care: Child pawning and its transformations in Akuapem, the Gold Coast 1874–1929', *Africa*, 82(2): 287–311.

Coe, C. (2016) 'Orchestrating care in time: Ghanaian migrant women, family, and reciprocity', *American Anthropologist*, 118(1): 37–48.

Cooke, E., Hague, S. and McKay, A. (2016) *The Ghana Poverty and Inequality Report: Using the 6th Ghana Living Standards Survey 2016*, Accra: UNICEF, www.unicef.org/ghana/media/531/file/The%20Ghana%20Poverty%20 and%20Inequality%20Report.pdf (accessed 3 April 2023).

Corbett, B. (1985) '*Centuries of Childhood* by Philippe Aries', http:// faculty.webster.edu/corbetre/philosophy/children/aries.html (accessed 13 December 2022).

Crawford, G. (2009) '"Making democracy a reality"? The politics of decentralisation and the limits to local democracy in Ghana', *Journal of Contemporary African Studies*, 27(1): 57–83.

Cregan, K. and Cuthbert, D. (2014) *Global Childhoods: Issues and Debates*, London: SAGE.

Cunningham, H. (2013) 'Saving the Children c.1830–1920', in Morrison, H. (ed), *The Global History of Childhood Reader*, London and New York: Routledge.

Dadzie, C. (2009) 'Ghana at fifty: Reflections on the evolution and development of a culture of human rights in Ghana', in Tonah, S. (ed), *Contemporary Social Problems in Ghana*, Accra: University of Ghana.

Dako-Gyeke, M. (2019) 'Perspectives of key informants on child abuse: Qualitative evidence from northern Ghana', *Child and Adolescent Social Work Journal*, 36: 155–169.

Dei, G.J.S. and Simmons, M. (2011) 'Indigenous knowledge and the challenge for rethinking conventional educational philosophy: A Ghanaian case study', *Counterpoints*, 352: 97–111.

Dembour, M. (2001) 'Following the movement of a pendulum: Between universalism and relativism', in Cowan, J., Dembour, M. and Wilson, R. (eds), *Culture and Rights: Anthropological Perspectives*, Cambridge: Cambridge University Press.

Derrington, C. and Kendall, S. (2007) 'Challenges and barriers to secondary education: The experiences of young Gypsy Traveller students in English secondary schools', *Social Policy & Society*, 7(1): 119–128.

de Waal, A. (2002) 'Realizing child rights in Africa: Children, young people and leadership', in de Waal, A. and Argenti, N. (eds), *Young Africa: Realizing the Rights of Children and Youth*, Trenton and Asmara: Africa World Press.

Diptee, A. and Klein, M. (2010) 'African childhoods and the colonial project', *Journal of Family History*, 35(1): 3–6.

du Toit, L. (2013) 'In the name of what? Defusing the rights-culture debate by revisiting the universals of both rights and culture', *Politikon: South African Journal of Political Studies*, 4(1): 15–34.

Emiljanowicz, P. (2021) 'How Jerry Rawlings used democratic structures to legitimise military rule', *The Conversation*, https://theconversation.com/how-jerry-rawlings-used-democratic-structures-to-legitimise-military-rule-160714 (accessed 15 January 2023).

Ensor, M. (2012) 'Introduction – African childhoods: Education, development, peacebuilding, and the youngest continent', in Ensor, M. (ed), *African Childhoods: Education, Development, Peacebuilding and the Youngest Continent*, New York: Palgrave Macmillan.

Evans-Pritchard, E.E. (951) *Kinship and Marriage Among the Nuer*, Oxford: Clarendon Press.

Fapohunda, E. (1987) 'The nuclear household model in Nigerian public and private sector policy: Colonial legacy and socio-political implications', *Development and Change*, 18: 281–294.

Firestone, S. (1971) *The Dialectic of Sex: The Case for Feminist Revolution*, London: Jonathan Cape.

Fortes, M. (1949) *The Web of Kinship among the Tallensi: The Second Part of an Analysis of the Social Structure of a Trans-Volta Tribe*, London: International African Institute and Oxford University Press.

Fortin, J. (2009) *Children's Rights and the Developing Law*, Cambridge, New York and Melbourne: Cambridge University Press.

Foster, B. and Norton, P. (2012) 'Educational equality for Gypsy, Roma and Traveller children and young people in the UK', *The Equal Rights Review*, 8: 85–112.

Fottrell, D. (2000) 'One step forward or two steps sideways? Assessing the first decade of the children's Convention on the Rights of the Child', in Fottrell, D. (ed), *Revisiting Children's Rights*, The Hague: Kluwer Law International.

Franklin, B. (ed) (1986) *The Rights of Children*, Oxford: Basil Blackwell.

Freeman, M. (1992) 'The limits of children's rights', in Freeman, M. and Veerman, P. (eds), *The Ideologies of Children's Rights*, Dordrecht, Boston and London: Martinus Nijhoff.

Freeman, M. (2000) 'The future of children's rights', *Children & Society*, 14: 277–293.

Freeman, M. (2011) 'Children's rights as human rights: Reading the UNCRC', in Qvortrup, J., Corsaro, W. and Honig, M.-S. (eds), *The Palgrave Handbook of Childhood Studies*, Basingstoke and New York: Palgrave Macmillan.

Frimpong-Manso, K. (2014) 'Child welfare in Ghana: The past, present and future', *Journal of Education and Social Research*, 4(6): 411–419.

Gagnon, L. (2005) *Access to Justice by Children*, Accra: Judicial Service of Ghana, UNICEF-Ghana and CUSO.

Gathogo, J. (2008) 'African philosophy as expressed in the concepts of hospitality and Ubuntu', *Journal of Theology for Southern Africa*, 130: 39–53.

Gatsinzi, A. and Hilson, G. (2022) 'Age is just a number: Articulating the cultural dimension of child labour in Africa's small-scale mining sector', *Resources Policy*, 78: 102779.

Geoffrion, K. (2013) '"I wish our gender could be dual": Male femininities in Ghanaian university students', *Cahiers d'Etudes Africaines*, 53(209–210): 417–443.

Geoffrion, K. (2018) 'Homosexuality and religious fundamentalism in the Ghanaian mediascape: Clashes between an "un-godly" concept and lived practices', in Sow, F. (ed), *Genre et fondamentalismes/Gender and Fundamentalisms*, Dakar: CODESRIA.

Ghana National Commission on Children (2005) *Annual Report 2004*, Accra: Ghana National Commission on Children.

Ghana Statistical Service (2019) *Ghana Multiple Indicator Cluster Survey 2017/18: Snapshots of Key Findings*, Accra: Ghana Statistical Service, https://www.unicef.org/ghana/media/576/file/Ghana%20Multiple%20Cluster%20Indicator%20Survey.pdf (accessed 12 September 2020).

Ghana Statistical Service (2022) *Ghana 2021 Population and Housing Census Vol. 3*, Accra: Ghana Statistical Service.

Glozah, F.N. and Lawani, S. (2014) 'Social change and adolescent rites of passage: A cross-cultural perspective', *International Journal of Human Sciences*, 11(1): 1188–1197.

Goody, E. (1973) *Context of Kinship: An Essay in the Family Sociology of the Gonja of Northern Ghana*, London and New York: Cambridge University Press.

Goody, E. (1982) *Parenthood and Social Reproduction: Fostering and Occupational Roles in West Africa*, Cambridge and New York: Cambridge University Press.

Goody, J. (1989) 'Futures of the family in rural Africa', *Population and Development Review*, 15: 119–144.

Government of Ghana (1969) *Constitution of the Republic of Ghana*, Accra: Government of Ghana.

Government of Ghana (1979) *Constitution of the Third Republic of Ghana (Promulgation) Decree, 1979 (AFRC Decree 24)*, Accra: Government of Ghana.

Government of Ghana (1992) *The Constitution of the Republic of Ghana*, Accra: Government of Ghana.

Government of Ghana (1998) *The 1998 Children's Act of Ghana (Act 560)*, Accra: Government of Ghana.

Government of Ghana (2003) *Poverty Reduction Strategy 2003–2005: An Agenda for Growth and Prosperity*, Vol. 1, Accra: Government of Ghana.

Greene, S. (2009) 'Modern "*Trokosi*" and the 1807 abolition in Ghana: Connecting past and present', *The William and Mary Quarterly*, 66(4): 959–974.

Grier, B. (1992) 'Pawns, porters and petty traders: Women in the transition to cash crop agriculture in colonial Ghana', *Journal of Women in Culture and Society*, 17(2): 304–328

Grier, B. (2006) *Invisible Hands: Child Labor and the State in Colonial Zimbabwe*, Portsmouth: Heinemann.

Grover, S. (2004) 'On recognizing children's universal rights: What needs to change in the Convention on the Rights of the Child', *The International Journal of Children's Rights*, 12(3): 259–271.

Grugel, J (2013) 'Children's rights and children's welfare after the Convention on the Rights of the Child', *Progress in Development Studies*, 13(1): 19–30.

Grugel, J. and Peruzzotti, E. (2012) 'The domestic politics of international human rights law: Implementing the Convention on the Rights of the Child in Ecuador, Chile, and Argentina', *Human Rights Quarterly*, 34(1): 178–198.

Gugler, J. and Flanagan, W. (1978) *Urbanization and Social Change in West Africa*, Cambridge, London, New York and Melbourne: Cambridge University Press.

REFERENCES

Gyekye, K. (1996) *African Cultural Values: An Introduction*, Accra: Sankofa Publishing Company.

Gyekye, K. (2013) *Philosophy, Culture and Vision: African Perspectives*, Accra: Sub-Saharan Publishers.

Hale, C. (2013) *Asante Stools and the Matrilineage*, Doctoral Dissertation, Harvard University.

Hall, S. (1996) 'The West and the rest: Discourse and power', in Hall, S., Held, D., Hubert, D. and Thompson, K. (eds), *Modernity: An Introduction to Modern Societies*, Oxford: Blackwell.

Hanson, K. (2022) 'Reinventing children's rights', *Childhood*, 29(2): 149–156.

Hanson, K. and Nieuwenhuys, O. (2013) 'Introduction: Living rights, social justice, translations', in Hanson, K. and Nieuwenhuys, O. (eds), *Reconceptualizing Children's Rights in International Development: Living Rights, Social Justice, Translations*, Cambridge: Cambridge University Press.

Hardgrove, A. (2017) *Life After Guns: Reciprocity and Respect Among Young Men in Liberia*, New Brunswick, Camden, Newark and London: Rutgers University Press.

Harris-Short, S. (2001) 'Listening to "the other"? The Convention on the Rights of the Child', *Melbourne Journal of International Law*, 2(2): 304–351.

Harris-Short, S. (2003) 'International human rights law: Imperialist, inept, and ineffective? Cultural relativism and the UN Convention on the Rights of the Child', *Human Rights Quarterly*, 25(1): 130–181.

Hashim, I.M. (2005) 'Exploring the linkages between children's independent migration and education: Evidence from Ghana', *Working Paper T12*, Sussex Centre for Migration Research.

Hecht, T. (1998) *At Home in the Street: Street Children of Northeast Brazil*, Cambridge and New York: University of Cambridge Press.

Hendrick, H. (1997a) *Children, Childhood and English Society 1880–1990*, Cambridge: Cambridge University Press.

Hendrick, H. (1997b) 'The constructing and reconstructing of British childhood: An interpretative survey 1800 to the present', in James, A. and Prout, A. (eds), *Constructing and Reconstructing Childhood: Contemporary Issues in the Sociological Study of Childhood*, 2nd edn, Basingstoke: The Falmer Press.

Hepburn, S. and Jackson, A. (2022) 'Colonial exceptions: The International Labour Organization and child labour in British Africa c. 1919–40', *Journal of Contemporary History*, 57(2): 218–241.

Heywood, C. (2001) *A History of Childhood: Children and Childhood in the West from Medieval to Modern Times*, Cambridge: Polity Press.

Highmore, D. (2002) 'Introduction. Questioning everyday life', in Highmore, B. (ed), *The Everyday Life Reader*, London and New York: Routledge.

Hilson, G. (2010) 'Child labour in African artisanal mining: Experiences from Northern Ghana', *Development & Change*, 41(3): 445–473.

Hollos, M. (2002) 'The cultural construction of childhood: Changing conceptions among the Pare of northern Tanzania', *Childhood*, 9(2): 167–189.

Holt, L. and Holloway, S. (2006) 'Editorial: Theorising other childhoods in a globalised world', *Children's Geographies*, 4(2): 135–142.

Holzscheiter, A., Josefsson, J. and Sandin, B. (2019) 'Child rights governance: An introduction', *Childhood*, 26(3): 271–288.

Honwana, A. (2012) *The Time of Youth: Work, Social Change and Politics in Africa*, Sterling: Kumarian Press.

Honwana, A. (2014) 'Waithood: Youth transitions and social change', in Foeken, D., Dietz, T., de Haan, L. and Johnson, L. (eds), *Development and Equity: An Interdisciplinary Exploration by Ten Scholars from Africa, Asia and Latin America*, Leiden and Boston: Brill.

Hopkins, L. and Sriprakash, A. (2016) 'Unsettling the global child: Rethinking child subjectivity in education and international development', in Hopkins, L. and Sriprakash, A. (eds), *The 'Poor Child': The Cultural Politics of Education, Development and Childhood*, London and New York: Routledge.

Hountondji, P. (1996) *African Philosophy: Myth and Reality*, 2nd edn, Bloomington and Indianapolis: Indiana University Press.

Howard, R.E. (1986) *Human Rights in Commonwealth Africa*, Totowa: Rowman & Littlefield.

Howard, R.E. (1992) 'Dignity, community, and human rights', in An-Na'im, A. (ed), *Human Rights in Cross-Cultural Perspectives: A Quest for Consensus*, Philadelphia: University of Pennsylvania Press.

Hoyles, M. (1989) *The Politics of Childhood*, London: The Journeyman Press Ltd.

Inda, J.X. and Rosaldo, R. (2008) 'Tracking global flows', in Inda, J.X. and Rosaldo, R. (eds), *The Anthropology of Globalization: A Reader*, Malden, Oxford and Victoria: Blackwell.

IRIN (2002) 'Nigeria: IRIN focus on the challenge of enforcing children's rights', *IRIN News*, 12 November, www. reliefweb.int/report/nigeria/nigeria-irin-focus-challenge-enforcing-childrens-rights (accessed 13 November 2002).

Isiugo-Abanihe, U. (1985) 'Child fosterage in West Africa', *Population and Development Review*, 11(1): 53–73.

ISS Today (2022) 'Africa is losing the battle against extreme poverty – ISS Africa', 13 July, https://issafrica.org/iss-today/africa-is-losing-the-battle-against-extreme-poverty (accessed 12 March 2023).

James, A. and Prout, A. (eds) (1997) *Constructing and Reconstructing Childhood: Contemporary Issues in the Sociological Study of Childhood*, 2nd edn, London: The Falmer Press.

Jenks, C. (1996) *Childhood*, London and New York: Routledge.

Josefsson, J. and Wall, J. (2020) 'Empowered inclusion: Theorizing global justice for children and youth', *Globalizations*, 17(6): 1043–1060.

REFERENCES

Kaime, T. (2010) '"Vernacularising" the Convention on the Rights of the Child: Rights and culture as analytic tools', *The International Journal of Children's Rights*, 18(4): 637–653.

Kaime, T. (2011) *The Convention on the Rights of the Child: A Cultural Legitimacy Critique*, Groningen: Europa Law Publishers.

Kassa, S. (2017) 'Drawing family boundaries: Children's perspectives on family relationships in rural and urban Ethiopia', *Children and Society*, 31(3): 171–192.

Kaye, B. (1962) *Bringing up Children in Ghana: An Impressionistic Survey*, London: George Allen and Unwin.

Kayongo Male, D. and Onyango, P. (1984) *The Sociology of the African Family*, New York and London: Longman.

Kesby, M., Gwanzura-Ottemoller, F. and Chizororo, M. (2006) 'Theorising *other*, "other childhoods": Issues emerging from work on HIV in urban and rural Zimbabwe', *Children's Geographies*, 4(2): 185–202.

Kilson, M. (1974) *African Urban Kinsmen: The Ga of Central Accra*, London: C. Hurst and Co.

Kilkelly, U. and Lundy, L. (2006) 'Children's rights in action: Using the UN Convention on the Rights of the Child as an auditing tool', *Child and Family Law Quarterly*, 18(3): 333–350.

Kludze, A. (2008) 'Constitutional rights and their relationship with international human rights in Ghana', *Israel Law Review*, 41(3): 677–702.

Konadu, K. and Campbell, C.C. (eds) (2016) *The Ghana Reader: History, Culture, Politics*, New York: Duke University Press.

Koonar, C. (2014) 'Christianity, commerce and civilization: Child labour and the Basel missionaries in colonial Ghana 1855–1914', *International Labor and Working-Class History*, 86: 72–88.

Korbin, J.E. (2002) 'Culture and child maltreatment: Cultural competence and beyond', *Child Abuse & Neglect*, 26(6–7): 637–644.

Kurth, J. (2003) 'Western civilization: Our tradition', *Intercollegiate Review*, 39(1/2): 5–13.

Kuyini, A., Alhassan, A., Tollerund, I., Weld, H. and Haruna, I. (2009) 'Traditional kinship foster care in northern Ghana: The experiences and views of children, carers and adults in Tamale', *Child & Family Social Work*, 14(4): 440–449.

Kwaw, E. (2015) 'Colonial marginalisation of children and the denial of children's rights: The Ghanaian experience', *Centerpoint Journal (Humanities Edition)*, 18(1): 65–98.

Kwankye, S. (2012) 'Independent North–South child migration as a parental investment in Northern Ghana', *Population, Space and Place*, 18(5): 535–550.

Kyei-Gyamfi, S. (2011) 'Corporal punishment in Ghana', in Ame, R., Agbenyiga, D. and Apt, N. (eds), *Children's Rights in Ghana: Reality or Rhetoric?* Lanham, MD: Lexington Books.

La Ferrara, E. (2003) 'Kin groups and reciprocity: A model of credit transactions in Ghana', *The American Economic Review*, 93(5): 1730–1751.

Laird, S. (2002) 'The 1998 Children's Act: Problems of enforcement in Ghana', *British Journal of Social Work*, 32(7): 893–905.

Lambon-Quayefio, M.P. and Owoo, N.S. (2018) 'Child labour, future earnings, and occupation choice: Evidence from Ghana', *International Journal of Social Economics*, 45(12): 1596–1608.

Lancy, D. (2012) 'The chore curriculum', in Spittler, G. and Bourdillon, M. (eds), *African Children at Work: Working and Learning in Growing Up*, Berlin: Lit Verlag.

Lawani, S. (2016) 'The Master and Servant Ordinance and labour shortages in the Gold Coast', *Historical Research Letter*, 36: 44–51.

Levinson, M.P. (2008) 'Not just content, but style: Gypsy children traversing boundaries', *Research in Comparative and International Education*, 3(3): 235–249.

Liebel, M. (2012) *Children's Rights from Below: Cross-Cultural Perspectives*, Basingstoke: Palgrave Macmillan.

Liebel, M. (2020) *Decolonizing Childhoods: From Exclusion to Dignity*, Bristol: Policy Press.

Little, K. (1953) 'The study of "social change" in British West Africa', *Africa: Journal of the International African Institute*, 23(4): 274–284.

Locoh, T. (1994) 'Social change and marriage arrangements: New types of union in Lomé, Togo', in Bledsoe, C. and Pison, G. (eds), *Nuptiality in Sub-Saharan Africa: Contemporary Anthropological and Demographic Perspectives*, Oxford: Clarendon Press.

MacLean, L. (2011) 'Exhaustion and exclusion in the African village: The non-state social welfare of informal reciprocity in rural Ghana and Côte d'Ivoire', *Studies in Comparative International Development*, 46: 118–136.

Manful, E. and Manful, S. (2014) 'Child welfare in Ghana: The relevance of children's rights in practice', *Journal of Social Work*, 14(3): 313–328.

Markwei, U. and Tetteh, P. (2022) 'A study of alternative measures in resolving cases of child sexual abuse among the Ga Community in Accra, Ghana', *Child Abuse Review*, 31(1): 27–39.

Mazrui, A. (1986) *The Africans: A Triple Heritage*, London: BBC Publications.

Mbembe, A. (2001) *On the Postcolony*, Berkeley, Los Angeles and London: University of California Press.

Mbise, A. (2017) 'The diffusion of the UNCRC more than the African Charter on the Rights and Welfare of the Child in Africa: The influence of coercion and emulation', *International Social Work*, 60(5): 1233–1243.

McCrystal, P. and Manful, E. (2011) 'Ghana's Children's Act 560: A rethink of its implementation', *International Journal of Children's Rights*, 19 : 151–165.

McNee, L. (2004) 'The languages of childhood: The discursive construction of childhood and colonial policy in French West Africa', *African Studies Quarterly*, 7(4): 20–32.

REFERENCES

Mensa-Bonsu, H. and Dowuona-Hammond, C. (1996) 'The child within the Ghanaian family', in Ardayfio-Schandorf, E. (ed), *The Changing Family in Ghana*, Accra: Ghana University Press.

Merry, S. (1992) 'Anthropology, law and transnational processes', *Annual Review of Anthropology*, 21: 357–379.

Merry, S. (2006) 'Transnational human rights and local activism: Mapping the middle', *American Anthropologist*, 108(1): 38–51.

Miedema, E. and Oduro, G.Y. (2017) 'Sexuality education in Ghana and Mozambique: An examination of colonizing assemblages informing school-based sexuality education initiatives', in Allen, L. and Rasmussen, M. (eds), *The Palgrave Handbook of Sexuality Education*, London: Palgrave Macmillan.

Ministry of Gender, Children and Social Protection (Government of Ghana) (2018) *Corporal Punishment in Ghana: A Position Paper on the Legal and Policy Issues*, Accra: Ministry of Gender, Children and Social Protection.

Mizen, P. (2018) 'Bringing the street back in: Considering strategy, contingency and relative good fortune in street children's access to paid work in Accra', *The Sociological Review*, 66(5): 1058–1073.

Mniki, N. and Rosa, S. (2007) 'Heroes in action: Child advocates in South Africa', *Children, Youth and Environments*, 17(3): 179–197.

Myers, W.E. (2001) 'The right rights? Child labor in a globalizing world', *The ANNALS of the American Academy of Political and Social Science*, 575(1): 38–55.

Naftali, O. (2014) *Children, Rights and Modernity in China: Raising Self-Governing Citizens*, Basingstoke: Palgrave Macmillan.

Ncube, W. (1998) 'Prospects and challenges in Eastern and Southern Africa: The interplay between international human rights norms and domestic law, tradition and culture', in Ncube, W. (ed), *Law, Culture, Tradition and Children's Rights in Eastern and Southern Africa*, Dartmouth: Aldershot-Ashgate.

Nieuwenhuys, O. (2012) 'Embedding the global womb: Global child labour and the new policy agenda', in Aitken, S., Lund, R. and Kjorolt, A.T. (eds), *Global Childhoods: Globalization, Development and Young People*, Abingdon and New York: Routledge.

Nsamenang, A.B. (1992) *Human Development in a Cultural Context: A Third World Perspective*, Newbury Park: SAGE.

Nsamenang, A.B. (2002) 'Adolescence in sub-Saharan Africa: An image constructed from Africa's triple inheritance', in Brown, B., Larson, R.W. and Saraswathi, T.S. (eds) *The World's Youth: Adolescence in Eight Regions of the Globe*, Cambridge: Cambridge University Press.

Nsamenang, A.B. (2004) *Cultures of Human Development and Education. Challenge to Growing Up African*, New York: Nova Science Publishers.

Nukunya, G.K. (2003) *Tradition and Change in Ghana: An Introduction to Sociology*, 2nd edn, Accra: Ghana Universities Press.

Nyamekye, E. and Baffour-Koduah, B. (2021) 'The language of instruction dilemma in Ghana: Making a case for the various Ghanaian languages', *International Journal of Research, and Innovation in Social Science (IJRISS)*, 5(1): 146–150.

O'Brien, M. and Salonen, T. (2011) 'Child poverty and child rights meet active citizenship: A New Zealand and Sweden case study', *Childhood*, 18(2): 211–226.

Oestreich, J. (1998) 'UNICEF and the implementation of the Convention on the Rights of the Child', *Global Governance*, 4: 183–198.

Ofori-Attah, K. (2006) 'The British and curriculum development in West Africa: A historical discourse', *Review of Education*, 52: 409–423.

Ofosu-Kusi, Y. (2023) 'Deliberative disobedience as a strategy for claiming rights and representation in the family: The case of Accra's Street children', in Sandin, B., Hanson, K., Balagopalan, S. and Joseffson, J. (eds), *The Politics of Children's Rights and Representation*, London: Palgrave Macmillan.

Ofosu-Kusi, Y. and Mizen, P. (2012) 'No longer willing to be dependent: Young people moving beyond learning', in Spittler, G. and Bourdillon, M. (eds), *African Children at Work: Working and Learning in Growing Up for Life*, Berlin: Lit Verlag.

Okali, K., Boamah, E.F. and Sumberg, J. (2022) 'The quantification of child labour by Ghana's mass media: A missed opportunity?', *Africa Spectrum*, 57(2): 155–177.

Okonjo, U. (1970) *The Impact of Urbanization on the Ibo Family Structure*, Gottingen: Verlag U Berger.

Okyere, S. (2012) 'Re-examining the education–child labour nexus: The case of child miners at Kenyasi, Ghana', *Childhoods Today*, 6(1): 1–20.

Okyere, S. (2013a) 'Children's participation in prohibited work in Ghana and its implications for the Convention on the Rights of the Child', in Twum-Danso Imoh, A. and Ansell, N. (eds), *Children's Lives in an Era of Children's Rights*, Abingdon and New York: Routledge.

Okyere, S. (2013b) 'Are working children's rights and child labour abolition complementary or opposing realms?', *International Social Work*, 56(1): 80–91.

Okyere, S., Frimpong Boamah, E., Asante, F. and Yeboah, T. (2023) 'Children's work in Ghana: Policies and politics', in Sumberg, J. and Sabates-Wheeler, R. (eds), *Children's Work in African Agriculture: The Harmful and the Harmless*, Bristol: Bristol University Press.

Omoike, E. (2013) 'In the best interests of the child: The case of child domestic workers in Ghana and Nigeria', in Twum-Danso Imoh, A. and Ansell, N. (eds), *Children's Lives in an Era of Children's Rights: The Progress of the Convention on the Rights of the Child in Africa*, Abingdon and New York: Routledge.

Oppong, C. (1973) *Growing up in Dagbon*, Accra: Ghana Publishing Corporation.

Oppong, C. (2006) 'Demographic innovation and nutritional catastrophe: Change, lack of change and difference in Ghanaian family systems', in Therborn, G. (ed), *African Families in A Global Context*, Uppsala: Nordiska Afrikainstitutet.

Oquaye, M. (1995) 'Human rights and the transition to democracy under the PNDC in Ghana', *Human Rights Quarterly*, 17(3): 556–557.

Oquaye, M. (2000) 'The process of democratisation in contemporary Ghana', *Journal of Commonwealth and Comparative Politics*, 38(3): 53–78.

Orme, N. (2001) *Medieval Children*, New Haven and London: Yale University Press.

Oyowe, O. (2014) 'An African conception of human rights? Comments on the challenges of relativism', *Human Rights Review*, 15(3): 329–347.

Oxfam (2015) 'Africa: Rising for the few', *Media Briefing*, September, https://policy-practice.oxfam.org/resources/africa-rising-for-the-few-556037/ (accessed 1 December 2015).

Pakenham, T. (1991) *The Scramble for Africa: The White Man's Conquest of the Dark Continent from 1876 to 1912*, New York: Random House.

Pastore, M. (2022) 'Play, create, transform: A pluriverse of children and childhoods from southern Mozambique', *Journal of the British Academy*, 10(s2): 111–132.

Plumb, J.H. (1972) *In the Light of History*, London: Allen Lane the Penguin Press.

Pollock, L. (1983) *Forgotten Children: Parent-Child Relations from 1500 to 1900*, Cambridge and New York: Cambridge University Press.

Prout, A. (2005) *The Future of Childhood*, London and New York: Routledge.

Punch, S. (2003) 'Childhoods in the majority world: Miniature adults or tribal children?', *Sociology*, 37(2): 277–295.

Punch, S. (2015) 'Possibilities for learning between childhoods and youth in the minority and majority worlds: Youth transitions as an example of cross-world dialogue', in Wyn, J and Cahill, H. (eds), *Handbook of Children and Young Adulthood*, Singapore: Springer.

Punch, S. (2016) 'Cross-world and cross disciplinary dialogue: A more integrated, global approach to childhood studies', *Global Studies of Childhood*, 6(3): 352–364.

Pupavac, V. (2001) 'Misanthropy without borders: The international children's rights regime', *Disasters*, 25(2): 95–112.

Quarshie, E.N. (2021) 'Boys should not be overlooked: Sexual violence victimization and associated factors among school-going adolescents in urban Ghana', *Child Abuse and Neglect*, 120. 105227.

Renne, E. (2003) *Population and Progress in a Yoruba Town*, London: Edinburgh University Press.

Renteln, A. (2004) *The Cultural Defense*, New York: Oxford University Press.

Reynaert, D., Bouverne-De Bie, M. and Vandevelde, S. (2012) 'Between "believers" and "opponents": Critical discussions on children's rights', *The International Journal of Children's Rights*, 20(1): 155–168.

Reynaert, D., Desmet, E., Lembrechts, S. and Vandenhole, W. (2015) 'Introduction: A critical approach to children's rights', in Vandenhole, W., Desmet, E., Reynaert, D. and Lembrechts, S. (eds), *Routledge International Handbook of Children's Rights Studies*, Abingdon, Oxon and New York: Routledge.

Rich, J. (2010) 'Searching for success: Boys, family aspirations, and opportunities in Gabon, ca. 1900–1940', *Journal of Family History*, 5(1): 7–24.

Richter, L. and Dawes, A. (2008) 'Child abuse in South Africa: Rights and wrongs', *Child Abuse Review*, 17(2): 79–93.

Riisoen, K.H., Hatloy, A. and Bjerkan, L. (2004) *Travel to Uncertainty: A Study of Child Relocation in Burkina Faso, Ghana and Mali, Fafo-Report 440*, Oslo: Fafo.

Rizzini, I. and Barker, G. (2002) 'Promises kept, promises broken: Recent political and economic trends affecting children and youth in Brazil', in Hevener Kaufman, N., Rizzini, I., Wilson, K. and Bush, M. (eds), *The Impact of Global Economic, Political and Social Transformation on the Lives of Children: A Framework for Analysis*, New York: Kluwer Academic.

Robertson, C. (1984) 'Formal or non-formal education? Entrepreneurial women in Ghana', *Comparative Education Review*, 28(4): 639–658.

Rosemberg, F. (2005) 'Childhood and social inequality in Brazil', in Penn, H. (ed), *Unequal Childhoods: Young Children's Lives in Poor Countries*, Oxford and New York: Routledge.

Rwezaura, B. (1994) 'The concept of the child's best interests in the changing economic and social contexts of sub-Saharan Africa', in Alston, P. (ed), *The Best Interests of the Child: Reconciling Culture and Human Rights*, Oxford: Clarendon Press.

Sackey, E. and Johannesen, B. (2015) 'Earning identity and respect through work and study of children involved in fishing and farming practices in Cape Coast, Ghana', *Childhood*, 22(4): 447–459.

Sánchez Alonso, B. (2007) 'The other Europeans: Immigration into Latin America and the international labour market (1870–1930)', *Revista de Historia Economica-Journal of Iberian and Latin American Economic History*, 25(3): 395–426.

Sánchez-Cabezudo, S.S., Peláez, A.L. and Gilbert, N. (2016) 'Social work for the middle-classes', *Social Work & Society*, 14(1): 1–4.

Sandin, B. (2014) 'Children and the Swedish welfare state: From different to similar', in Fass, P. and Grossberg, M. (eds), *Reinventing Childhood After World War II*, Philadelphia: University of Pennsylvania Press.

Sarpong, P. (1974) *Ghana in Retrospect: Some Aspects of Ghanaian Culture*, Accra: Ghana Publishing Corporation.

REFERENCES

Sarpong, P. (1977) *Girls' Nubility Rites in Ashanti*, Tema: Ghana Publishing Corporation.

Save the Children (2019) *Closing the Gap: Our 2030 Ambition and 2019–2021 Global Work Plan*, https://resourcecentre.savethechildren.net/pdf/closing_the_gap_-_global_ambition_and_2019-21_global_work_plan.pdf/ (accessed 1 March 2022).

Schaumloeffel, M.A. (2008) *Tabom: The Afro-Brazilian Community in Ghana*, 2nd edn, Scotts Valley: CreateSpace Independent Publishing Platform.

Schildkrout, E. (1973) 'The fostering of children in urban Ghana: Problems of ethnographic analysis in a multi-cultural context', *Urban Anthropology*, 2(1): 048–073.

Schildkrout, E. (1978) 'Age and gender in Hausa society: Socio-economic roles of children in urban Kano', in La Fontaine, J.S. (ed), *Sex and Age as Principles of Social Differentiation*, London and New York: Academic Press.

Segado Sánchez-Cabezudo, S. and López Peláez, A. (2014) 'Social work with middle-class Spanish families: The challenge of the work–family conflict', *International Journal of Social Welfare*, 23(1): 100–111.

Serpell, R. (1993) *The Significance of Schooling: Life-Journeys in an African Society*, Cambridge: Cambridge University Press.

Seyram-Hamemoo, E., Apraku Dwomoh, E. and Dako-Gyeke, M. (2018) 'Child labour in Ghana: Implications for children's education and health', *Child and Youth Services Review*, 93: 248–254.

Shahar, S. (1992) *Childhood in the Middle Ages*, London: Routledge and Kegan Paul.

Shepler, S. (2005) 'The rites of the child: Global discourses of youth and reintegrating child soldiers in Sierra Leone', *Journal of Human Rights*, 4(2): 197–211.

Shepler, S. (2012) 'The rites of the child: Global discourses of youth and reintegrating child soldiers in Sierra Leone', in Twum-Danso Imoh, A. and Ame, R. (eds), *Childhoods at the Intersection of the Local and the Global*, Basingstoke: Palgrave Macmillan.

Smythe, K. (1997) *Fipa Childhood: White Fathers' Missionaries and Social Change in Nkansie, UFIPA 1910–1980*, PhD Thesis, University of Wisconsin.

Sommerville, C.J. (1982) *The Rise and Fall of Childhood*, Beverly Hills, London and New Delhi: SAGE.

Spronk, R. (2014) 'Exploring the middle-classes in Nairobi: From modes of production to modes of sophistication', *African Studies Review*, 57(1): 93–114.

Stahl, R. (2007) ' "Don't forget about me": Implementing Article 12 of the United Nations Convention on the Rights of the Child', *Arizona Journal of International and Contemporary Law*, 24(3): 803–842.

Steegstra, M. (2005) *Dipo and the Politics of Culture in Ghana*, Accra: Woeli Publishing Services.

Stephens, S. (1995) 'Introduction: Children and the politics of culture in "late capitalism"', in Stephens, S. (eds), *Children and the Politics of Culture*, Princeton: Princeton University Press.

Symonds, T. (2023) 'Nigerian street trader trafficked to UK in kidney donor plot', *BBC News*, 23 March, www.bbc.co.uk/news/uk-65015489 (accessed 1 May 2023).

Szulc, A. and Cohn, C. (2012) 'Anthropology and childhood in South America: Perspectives from Brazil and Argentina', *AnthropoChildren*, 1(1), www.popups.uliege.be/2034-8517/index.php?id=427 (accessed 1 May 2023).

Tafere, Y. and Chuta, N. (2020) *Transitions to Adulthood in Ethiopia Preliminary Findings: Summary and Policy Issues* (Young Lives 5th Wave Qualitative Study), Young Lives.

Tengey, W. (1998) *The Convention on the Rights of the Child Impact Study: The Study of Ghana*, Accra: Save the Children UK-Ghana.

Tetteh, P. (2011a) 'Child domestic labour in Accra: Opportunity and empowerment or perpetuation of gender inequality?', *Ghana Studies*, 14: 163–189.

Tetteh, P. (2011b) 'Child domestic labour in (Accra) Ghana: A child and gender rights issue', *International Journal of Children's Rights*, 19: 217–232.

Tine, N.D., the African Network for the Prevention and Protection against Child Abuse and Neglect, and Ennew, J. (1998) *The African Contexts of Children's Rights: Seminar Report*, Dakar: Global Gutter Press and CODESRIA.

Tsai, M. and Dzorgbo, D. (2012) 'Familial reciprocity and subjective wellbeing in Ghana', *Journal of Marriage and Family*, 74(1): 215–228.

Twum-Danso, A. (2008) *Searching for the Middle Ground in Children's Rights: Implementing the Convention on the Rights of the Child in Ghana*, PhD Thesis, University of Birmingham.

Twum-Danso, A. (2009) 'Reciprocity, respect, and responsibility: The 3rs underlying parent-child relationships in Ghana and the implications for children's rights', *The International Journal of Children's Rights*, 17(3): 415–432.

Twum-Danso, A. (2011) 'Assessing the progress of the 1998 Children's Act of Ghana: Achievements, opportunities, and challenges in its first ten years', in Ame, R., Agbenyiga, D. and Apt, N. (eds), *Children's Rights in Ghana: Reality or Rhetoric?* Lanham: Lexington Books.

Twum-Danso Imoh, A. (2012a) 'From central to marginal? Changing perceptions of kinship fosterage in Ghana', *Journal of Family History*, 37(4): 351–363.

Twum-Danso Imoh, A. (2012b) 'Rites vs. rights: Female genital cutting at the crossroads of local values and global norms', *International Social Work*, 56(1): 36–49.

Twum-Danso Imoh, A. (2013) 'Children's perceptions of physical punishment in Ghana and the implications for children's rights', *Childhood: A Journal of Global Child Research*, 20(4): 472–486.

Twum-Danso Imoh, A. (2016) 'From the singular to the plural: Exploring diversities in contemporary childhoods in sub-Saharan Africa', *Childhood: A Journal of Global Child Research*, 23(3): 455–468.

Twum-Danso Imoh, A. (2019) 'Terminating childhood: Dissonance and synergy between global children's rights norms and local discourses about the transition from childhood to adulthood in Ghana', *Human Rights Quarterly*, 41(1): 160–182.

Twum-Danso Imoh, A. (2020) 'Situating the rights vs. culture binary within the context of colonial history in sub–Saharan Africa', in Todres, J. and King, S. (eds), *Oxford Handbook on Children's Rights Law*, New York: Oxford University Press.

Twum-Danso Imoh, A. (2022) 'Framing reciprocal obligations within intergenerational relations in Ghana through the lens of the mutuality of duty and dependence', *Childhood*, 29(3): 439–454.

Twum-Danso Imoh, A. (2023) 'Adults in charge: The limits of formal child participatory processes for societal transformation', in Sandin, B., Hanson, K., Balagopalan, S. and Joseffson, J. (eds), *The Politics of Children's Rights and Representation*, London: Palgrave Macmillan.

Twum-Danso Imoh, A. (forthcoming 2024a) 'Challenging North South binaries and the implications for studies of childhood globally', in Wyn, J., Cahill, H. and Cuervo, H. (eds), *The Handbook of Children and Youth Studies*, Springer.

Twum-Danso Imoh, A. (forthcoming 2024b) 'Troubling the understanding of childhood competence in research ethics governance and its implications for research with children and their families', *Research in Education Journal (Special Issue: Democratic Methodologies in Education Research)*.

Twum-Danso Imoh, A. and Ansell, N. (eds) (2014) *Children's Lives in the Era of Children's Rights: The Progress of the Convention on the Rights of the Child in Africa*, Oxford: Routledge.

Twum-Danso Imoh, A. and Okyere, S. (2020) 'Towards a more holistic understanding of child participation: Foregrounding the experiences of children in Ghana and Nigeria', *Child and Youth Services Review*, 112: 104927.

Twum-Danso Imoh, A., Tetteh, P. and Oduro, G. (eds) (2022) 'Searching for the everyday in African childhoods (special issue)', *The British Academy Journal*, 10(2): 1–11.

Twum-Danso Imoh, A., Rabello de Castro, L. and Nsamali, O. (eds) (2023) 'Studies of childhoods in the Global South: Towards an epistemic turn in transnational childhood research?', *Third World Thematics*, 7 (Special Issue): 1–3.

Ugboajah, P. (2008) 'Culture-conflict and delinquency: a case study of colonial Lagos', *Eras*, 10, www.monash.edu/__data/assets/pdf_file/0007/1670623/ugboajah-article.pdf (accessed 10 April 2018).

UK Government (1933) *Children and Young Persons Act 1933*, www.legislat ion.gov.uk/ukpga/Geo5/23-24/12/part/II/crossheading/general-provisi ons-as-to-employment (accessed on 5 January 2023).

UN and Government of Ghana (2004) *Common Country Assessment (CCA) Ghana*, Accra: UN and Government of Ghana.

UNICEF (2018) *UNICEF Strategic Plan 2018–2021*, www.unicef.org/executiveboard/documents/unicef-strategic-plan-2018-2021 (accessed 1 March 2022).

UNICEF (2020) *UNICEF Launches First Ever Domestic Emergency Response Programme to Provide Food Support for Vulnerable Children Across the UK*, www.unicef.org.uk/press-releases/unicef-launches-first-ever-domestic-emerge ncy-response-programme-to-provide-food-support-for-vulnerable-child ren-across-the-uk/ (accessed 24 August 2020).

United Nations (1989) *The Convention on the Rights of the Child*, Geneva: United Nations.

Urch, G. (1974) 'Education and colonialism in Kenya', *History of Education Quarterly*, 11: 249–264.

US State Department (2001) *Ghana: Report on Female Genital Mutilation (FGM) or Female Genital Cutting (FGC)*, www.https://2001-2009.state. gov/g/wi/rls/rep/crfgm/10100.htm (accessed 31 March 2023).

Valentin, K. and Meinert, L. (2009) 'The adult North and the young South: Reflections on the civilizing mission of children's rights', *Anthropology Today*, 25(1): 23–28.

Valentine, G. (2003) 'Boundary crossings: Transitions from childhood to adulthood', *Children's Geographies*, 1(1): 37–52.

Vallgårda, K., Alexander, K. and Olsen, S. (2015) 'Emotions and the global politics of childhood', in Olsen, S. (ed), *Childhood, Youth and Emotions in Modern History: National, Colonial and Global Perspectives*, Basingstoke: Palgrave.

Van Bueren, G. (1995) *The International Law on the Rights of the Child*, Dordrecht, Boston and London: Martinus Nijhoff.

Van Hear, N. (1982) 'Child labor and the development of capitalist agriculture in Ghana', *Development and Change*, 13(4): 499–514.

Veerman, P. (1992) *The Rights of the Child and the Changing Image of Childhood*, Dordrecht, Boston and London: Martinus Nijhoff.

Verhellen, E. (1994) *The Convention on the Rights of the Child: Background, Motivation, Strategies, Main Themes*, Leuven and Apeldoorn: Garant Publishers.

Verhoef, H. (2005) '"A child has many mothers": Views of child fostering in Northwestern Cameroon', *Childhood*, 12(3): 369–390.

Wall, J. (2011) 'Can democracy represent children? Toward a politics of difference', *Childhood*, 19(1): 86–100.

REFERENCES

Weisberg, D. (1978) 'Evolution of the concept of the rights of the child in the Western world', *The Review of the International Commission of Jurists*, 21: 43–51.

Wells, K. (2015) *Childhood in a Global Perspective*, 2nd edn, Cambridge and Malden: Polity Press.

White, B. (1996) 'Talk about school: Education and the colonial project in French and British Africa (1860–1960)', *Comparative Education*, 32: 9–25.

Windborne, J. (2006) 'New laws, old values: Indigenous resistance to children's rights in Ghana', *Atlantic Journal of Communication*, 14(3): 156–172.

Woll, L. (2000) *The Convention on the Rights of the Child: Impact Study*, Stockholm: Save the Children Sweden.

Woodman, G.R. (2003) 'Family law in Ghana under the Constitution 1992', in Bainham, A. (ed), *International Survey of Family Law*, Bristol: Jordan Publishing.

Wyness, M. (2006) *Childhood and Society: An Introduction to the Sociology of Childhood*, Basingstoke: Palgrave Macmillan.

Yeboah, T. and Egur, I. (2023) 'Children's work in shallot production on the Keta Peninsula, South-Eastern Ghana', in Sumberg, J. and Sabates-Wheeler, R. (eds), *Children's Work in African Agriculture: The Harmful and the Harmless*, Bristol: Bristol University Press.

Zoller Booth, M. (2004) *Culture and Education: The Social Consequences of Western Schooling in Contemporary Swaziland*, Dallas: University Press of America.

Zuure, D. and Taylor, P. (2018) 'Legal framework for the protection of children's rights in Ghana', *Journal of Education & Practice*, 9(2): 50–55.

Index

31st December Women's Movement 109,
111, 114

A

abandonment/exposure to danger of a child,
criminalization of 92, 103–104
abduction of a child, criminalization
of 92, 104
Abebe, T. 11, 51, 59, 60, 148–149
abuse 102, 103, 119, 120
Addo-Fenning, R. 81, 83
Adichie, C.N. 13–14
Adjei, S.B. 155
Adomako-Ampofo, A. 155, 168
Adonteng-Kissi, O. 151, 157, 158, 162
adoption 93, 102
affluent families 4–5, 163, 165, 168–169,
182, 187
African Charter on Human and People's
Rights (the Banjul Charter) 151
African Charter on the Rights and Welfare of
the Child 61, 64–65, 151
age of consent (age of sexual
responsibility) 33, 103
age of criminal responsibility 44–45
age of majority 27–28, 61, 62
agriculture 83, 88, 89, 158, 160, 161
Akan 79, 129, 139, 141, 145, 149
Allman, J. 70, 71, 82, 83, 86, 134, 178
Andre, G. 171
An-Na'im, A. 68
anthropology 15, 73, 133, 167
apprenticeships 28, 102, 139, 160
Archard, D. 27, 29
Archibald, S. 66
Ardayfio-Schandorf, E. 76, 130, 133, 134,
135, 178
Ariès, P. 26, 27, 31
Armed Forces Revolutionary Council
(AFRC) 105, 111, 113
Asomah, J. 80
Assimeng, J.M. 128
Atiemo, A. 117, 128, 130, 131
autonomy, children's 49, 53, 70
Awedoba, A.K. 129

Awusabo-Asare, K. 128
Azu, D. 78

B

Balagopalan, S. 10, 11, 16, 45, 73
Barker, G. 7, 15, 187
Basel Mission 81, 82, 89, 144
Baughan, E. 41–42
Benwell, M. 9
Bernard, C. 182
best interest principle 66
Bilyeu, A.S. 80, 118
biological age, focus on 61, 62, 64
biological parents' responsibilities 76, 97, 100, 101
birth registration 87, 93, 102
Biswas, T. 59–60
boarding schools 5, 136
bonded children 79
Boyden, J. 34, 37, 38, 43, 57, 92
Bragoro 139, 141, 145
Brazil 7, 11–12, 187
'bred to work' 163, 167–168
bride price payments 70–71, 119
British colonialism 22, 44, 46, 83, 84, 88,
129, 130–131, 144
Brydon, L. 106
Buah, F.K. 105, 106, 109
Burr, R. 57, 58, 107, 163

C

Campbell, C.C. 83–84
capitalism 17, 69, 106
care, children in 84, 92, 101
'caregiver' as term 151
Carmi, E. 183
carriers/porters 85, 88, 160
cash, introduction of 70, 128, 134
cash crops 88, 160
Cemlyn, S. 20
character development 78
Cheney, K. 66
Child Cannot Wait 98
Child Care Society 84
child labour
affluent areas 169

INDEX

alongside education 154, 162
apprenticeships 28, 102, 139, 160
cash crops 88
cash economies 70
Children's Act 1998 102
colonial era 88–89
Ghana National Commission on
Children 98
global children's rights discourses 45
Gold Coast 84–85, 90–91, 93
health and safety at work 102, 160
house helps 6–7
middle-class activism 33, 34, 36
minimum age for industrial employment
(Gold Coast) 90–91, 93
and modern Western conceptions of
childhood 28, 32
paid work 70, 159–162
prohibited occupations 91
social inequality 148–172
work as form of learning 151–152
see also income-generating activity;
work, children's
child maintenance 93, 102
Child Panels 102–103
child pawning/debt bondage/pledging 79, 85
child protection 103, 182
child soldiers 19, 66
childhood, 'modern Western' conception
development 26–33
childhood studies 15, 73, 173–189
Children (Care and Reformation) Ordinance
1928 84
Children Act 1989 (UK) 101
Children and Young Persons Act of England
and Wales 1933 44, 45
Children's Acts 100–101, 101–103, 121–123
Children's Employment Commission 33–34
children's homes 84, 92
Children's Maintenance Act 1965 (Act
297) 93
chores
affluent areas 169–171, 187–188
colonial era 90
duties/responsibilities of children 153–154,
156, 157
low-income households 4, 8, 20
see also domestic labour/housework
Christianity
civil society 117
colonialism 69, 81–82, 130
marriage practices 131–133
middle-classes 33
and nuclear family 138
plural society 127, 128, 130
separate Christian communities 144
and traditional puberty rites 141–142
value system 132, 142–145
and 'the West' 176

chronological age 61, 62–64
Chuta, N. 63
citizenship 39, 66
civil and political rights 108, 124
civil society 66, 109, 117–118
'civilized knowledge' 81
'civilizing agendas' 35, 44, 69, 71, 81, 144
Clark, C. 20
Clark-Kazak, C. 61, 62, 64
class-based conceptions of childhood 35
clothing 27, 31
Cobbah, J. 59
cocoa farming 88
Code for Children (1922) 42
Cohn, C. 177
collectivism 8, 58, 78–79
Colonial Development and Welfare Act in
1940 84
colonization
Christianity 69, 81–82, 130
colonial authorities' role in welfare 84–87
education 71–72
Eurocentricity 64
interventions of colonial actors in
Ghana 81–92
introduction of cash 70, 128, 134
origins of global children's rights
discourses 10, 17–18, 39–40, 44–46,
67–68, 69
'scramble for Africa' 128–129
Commission on Human Rights and
Administrative Justice 99
Committee on the Rights of the Child 98
communalism 78, 138, 149
communitarianism 11, 20, 58, 149, 150
community-based learning 77
compulsory schooling 32–33, 34, 36, 92–93
concept versus conception of
childhood 27–29
Constitution 51, 94, 96–97, 99–100, 103,
109, 111, 113
continuum thinking 184–189
Convention on the Rights of the Child
(CRC)
as advocacy tool 53
children's participation in work 148
continuing development of 54
definitions of childhood 61, 63
dissemination 99
dominant children's rights discourses 21
drafting of 47–49, 98
focus on the poor 9
in Ghana's legislation 100–102
global ratification of 10, 49, 51, 61–62
granting of rights 50
implementation in Global South 51–52
individualism 58
influence on other systems of
governance 52–53

217

international lending agencies 113
international organizations drawing on 51
middle-class basis of 182
politics of ratification 114
preamble 58
ratification in Ghana 1, 49, 65, 97, 98,
110–111, 116–117
ratification in order to receive Western aid 64
research with principles as starting
point 14–15
role of Rawlings 110–112, 114, 115,
116–117
UN General Assembly adoption of 6
and UNICEF 50–51
United States 49, 124
Western bias 18
Cooper, A.A (Earl of Shaftesbury) 33, 34
coups d'état 93, 105, 107, 111, 115
COVID-19 10, 163, 164
Cowan, J. 16
criminal legislation 85, 92, 103, 105, 118
criminality 34, 80, 84, 92, 102–103, 118
Cudworth, R. 29
cultural essentialism 73
cultural fluidity 69–70, 72
cultural imperialism 57, 65–68
cultural markers determining end of
childhood 62–63
cultural relativism 16, 186
'culturalist paradigm' 73
Cumberland, R. 29
Cunningham, H. 37, 38, 39, 40, 41, 43
custody 102, 103
customary law 106, 131, 133, 152
customary obligation 70

D

Dadzie, C. 94, 99
Dagbon 76–77
day-care centres 102
de Waal, A. 61, 62, 63, 64, 114
decentralization 99, 103
Declaration on the Rights of the Child
42–43, 46–47, 53, 54, 94, 97, 175
Defence for Children 48
deficient/inferior, children seen as 37–38
deficit childhoods, focus on 8–10, 11–21, 57,
183, 189
definitions of adulthood 62
definitions of childhood 25, 27, 44, 61, 62,
100, 101
definitions of 'Western' and
'non-Western' 175–181
delinquency 34, 84
Dembour, M. 186
democracy 99, 108, 109, 110, 113, 115
Department of Children 104, 114
Department of Social Welfare 84, 103,
105, 121

deprived areas 3–4, 8–9
destitution 101, 162
development assistance 13, 62, 64, 107, 112
Dickens, Charles 34
differentiation from adults 27, 28, 30,
36–37, 43
Dipo 140, 141, 146
Diptee, A. 69
disabled children 82, 84
discipline 78, 121, 154
see also punishment
discrimination 94, 97, 102, 187
District Assemblies 98, 103, 122–123
divorce 132
domestic labour/housework 4, 8, 20, 89, 90,
149, 152, 153, 156, 167
domestic service 6, 161
domestic violence 104, 105
double shifts at school 4
duties/responsibilities, children's 148–172
Dzorgbo, D-B. 134

E

early marriage 19, 31, 119
economic recovery program 106, 107,
112, 114
education
affluent families 5, 166
child labour laws 32
children's work interfering with 154, 162
co-generational understandings 60
compulsory schooling 32–33, 34, 36,
92–93
deficit childhoods, focus on 13
domestic skills 72
early modern period 30–31
effect on kinship bonds 135
Europeanization 178
Free Compulsory and Universal Basic
Education policy 97
free education 92–93, 97
in Ghana's Constitution 100
Gypsy, Roma and Traveller
communities 20
in household chores 154
institutionalization of children 35
legislation 32–33, 105
missionaries 71, 89, 178
National Commission for Civic
Education 99
poor areas 4
post-independence 92–93
post-ratification of CRC changes 119
pre-colonial Ghana 76, 77, 78
reform 97, 115–116
right to 47, 101, 185–186
transitions to adulthood 145
work as form of learning 151–152
see also schools

INDEX

Ekweremadua, I. 165–166
electricity 5, 107, 162
Emile ou Traite de l' Education (Rousseau, 1762) 29–30
Emiljanowicz, P. 108, 115
employment laws 32–33
English language 179
Enlightenment 30, 176
Ensor, M. 8–9
errands 153–154
Ethiopia 51, 60, 63, 164
ethnic groups in Ghana 128–130, 178–179
Eto 145
Eurocentricity 10, 57–65
Europeanization 18, 127, 128, 130, 178
Ewe 79, 99, 129
extended family 4, 8, 76–78, 133, 134–135, 136–137

F

Factory Acts (UK) 32, 34
Family Tribunals 102, 103
fathers 70–71, 93, 122
female genital cutting 16, 19, 100
fieldwork 22
Firestone, S. 29, 30, 31, 34
First Republic of Ghana 93
Flanagan, W. 83
food 27, 31, 33
forced labour 88
  see also slavery
forced marriage 19, 104
Fortes, M. 133
Fortin, J. 47, 49
fosterage 76, 77, 78, 102
Free Compulsory and Universal Basic Education policy 97
freedom of expression 109
Freeman, M. 19, 40, 50, 54
Frimpong-Manso, K. 82, 84, 122

G

Ga 99
Ga-Dangme 78, 129, 130, 145
gambling 28, 31, 33
games 27, 28, 29, 31
Gathogo, J. 59
gender differences
  chores 4, 156–157
  definitions of adulthood 62
  domestic labour 156
  exclusion of girls from conception of childhood 31
  gender equality 104
  girls as cheaper compensation for crimes than cattle 80
  socialization 155–157
Geneva Declaration *see* Declaration on the Rights of the Child

Germany 41, 42
Ghana Bar Association 115
Ghana Education Service 97
Ghana Institute of Journalism 98
Ghana National Commission on Children 97, 98–99, 100, 104, 111, 114–115
Gini coefficient 164
girls
  chores 4, 156–157
  education 104
  exclusion from early conceptions of childhood 31
  inclusion in education provision 93
  puberty rites 139–141, 146
  Science, Technology and Mathematics Education clinic 97–98
  socialization 155–157
global children's rights discourses 18–19, 25–40, 41–55, 57–65
global economic crisis (2008) 164
globalization 67, 128, 131
Gold Coast 44, 79, 81, 82, 83–84, 128, 129, 130
Gonja 77
Goody, E. 77, 78
grandparents 76–77, 135–136
Grier, B. 70
Grover, S. 61
Grugel, J. 52, 66, 117–118
Gugler, J. 83
Gyekye, K. 149, 150
Gypsy, Roma and Traveller communities 19–20, 174

H

Hall, S. 176, 179
Hammond, J. 68
Hanson, K. 174
happy childhood, right to 36, 37
Hardgrove, A. 154–155
Harris-Short, S. 47, 48, 57, 58, 64, 66, 72
Hausa 99
Hebdige, D. 180
Hecht, T. 15, 187
Hendrick, H. 33, 34, 35–36
Hepburn, S. 46
Heywood, C. 26
Hilgers, M. 171
holistic approaches to study of children's rights 21, 183–184
Hollos, M. 15, 18
home education 20
homeless children 101
Homowo 192n4
Honwana, A. 63, 167
Hountondji, P. 15, 72, 73
house helps 5
housework/domestic labour 4, 8, 20, 89, 90, 149, 152, 153, 156, 167

219

Howard, R.E. 70, 71, 146
Human Development Strategy and Vision 2020 98
human rights
  children's own claims of 66
  civil society 117–118
  cultural relativism 186
  democracy 109
  Eurocentricity 57–58
  evolution of 17, 18, 25
  in Ghana's Constitution 94, 97, 99
  Ghana's revolution 108
  and the Global South 175
  Rawlings, Jerry John 111
  violations 108
Human Trafficking Act (2005) 105
hybrid culture 131, 146, 147, 177, 179

I

illiteracy 119
incest 104, 121
income-generating activity 3–4, 152, 153, 159–162
incremental competence in tasks, children's 60, 157–159
Inda, J.X. 180
independence, children's 57, 150–151
independence, Ghana's 44, 65, 92–94, 99
Indigenous people
  changing economic roles of women and children 83
  colonization 18
  education 179
  ethnic groups in Ghana 129–130
  hybrid culture 131
  leaders and rules 87, 88
  learning through work 168
  migration 83
  plurality of childhoods in sub-Saharan Africa 127
  pre-colonial Ghana 76–81
  puberty rites 139–141
  traditional values 19
  understandings of childhood 101
  values 179
  worldviews marginalized 57, 59
individualism
  collective prized over individual 79
  cultural shift to 178
  dissonance in global rights discourses 66
  encouraged through colonial education 71
  human rights 58, 60–61, 64
  individualized wealth 70
  in sub-Saharan African societies 60
industrialization 25, 33
infant mortality 82
infant welfare centres 82
inheritance 101, 103, 106, 134
initiation rites 139

innocence of childhood 29–30, 34, 38
institutionalization of children 35, 39, 77, 102
Inter-Agency Committees 104–105
interdependence 59–60, 78–79, 133, 149, 150, 151
intergenerational relations 59, 71, 80, 149–155, 166
  see also extended family
international charities 42
International Labour Organization (ILO) 45, 100
international law 9, 10, 21, 49–50, 61–62, 63, 66–67, 182
International Monetary Fund 107, 112, 164
International Needs Ghana 117, 118
international schools 4, 5, 168
International Union for Child Welfare 46
International Year of the Child 9, 47, 96
internationalization of discourse around children's rights 41–55
intestacy 106, 112
inverted duties 43, 50
Islam 18, 127, 128, 130

J

Jackson, A. 46
James, A. 73
Jamestown 130
Jebb, E. 41, 42
Jenks, C. 30
jobs, choice of 71–72
Johannesen, B. 152, 157
juvenile justice system 33, 84, 102, 105

K

Kaime, T. 11, 58–59
Kaye, B. 71, 134
Kesby, M. 16, 17, 18
Kilkelly, U. 50
kinship fostering 76, 77, 78, 102, 135
kinship groups 59, 60, 76–77, 133–135, 136–137, 138
Klein, M. 69
Kludze, A. 115
Konadu, K. 83–84
Koonar, C. 89, 144
Krobo 140, 141, 146
Kuffour, John A. 104
Kumasi 86
Kurth, J. 176
Kwaw, E. 78, 84, 85, 88, 92, 94, 97

L

Labour Decree Act of 1967 93
Laird, S. 113, 162
Lambon-Quayefio, M.P. 160
Lancy, D. 158
Latin America 14, 36, 43, 45, 66, 177–178

INDEX

Lawani, S. 82
League of Nations 43, 45, 46, 88
leaving the community 71
Legge, K. 106
legislation
  anti-child labour 84
  child-focused laws 51, 53, 62, 92
  children's rights language in Ghana's
    laws 96–126
  colonization 69
  criminal legislation 85, 92, 103, 105, 118
  education 32–33, 105
  Factory Acts (UK) 32
  Nigeria 63
Legislative Instrument for the Children's Act
  (LI 1705) 100–101
Levinson, M.P. 20
liberalization 107
Liebel, M. 16, 38, 53, 68, 69, 175
life history approaches 135
Limann, Hilla 105, 111
lineage-based child rearing 76–77, 78–79
literacy 119
literature, children's 29
'living rights' 174
living standards 164
loan security, children as 79
loans, foreign 107, 112
local chiefs 87–88
local languages 99, 129, 179
Locke, J. 29–30
Locoh, T. 131, 132
Lundy, L. 50

M

Manful, E. 78, 84, 99, 100, 101, 125
map of Ghana 2
marriage
  autonomy in choice of partners 70
  customary and civil law 131, 133
  early marriage 19, 31, 119
  forced marriage 19, 104
  learning the skills for 141, 168–169
  legal minimum ages for 63–64
  marking transition to adulthood 62–63
  polygyny 131–133, 145
  and waged labour 70
matrilineal societies 79
maturity, work as measure of 157–159
Mazrui, A. 18, 128
Mbembe, A. 9, 15–16, 17
Mbise, A. 49, 64–65, 112, 113
McCrystal, P. 84, 99, 100, 101, 125
media images 13, 109
medieval concepts of children 26, 27
menarche rites 139–141, 145–146
Mennonite communities 19
middle-classes 33–38, 40, 171,
  181–183

migration 83, 107, 130–131, 138, 160, 177,
  179–180
military take-over 96, 105–106, 110, 113
Ming-Ching Tsai 134
Ministry of Gender, Children and Social
  Protection 104, 105, 114, 121
minor crimes committed by
  children 102–103
minority status of children 27
missionaries
  child welfare cases 81
  Christianization 128
  contact with Europe 17, 18
  dominant children's rights discourses 68,
    69, 72
  early children's rights discourses 44
  export of new understandings of
    childhood 89
  'mission houses' 137
  role of hard work 89–90
  transitions to adulthood 144
  use of child labour 89–92
Mole-Dagbani 129
morality of duty 149
motherhood 62–63, 76, 86–87
multi-ethnic societies 128–129
multiple childhoods 73
Multiple Indicator Cluster Surveys 121
multi-sectoral taskforces 98, 104–105
music 5
Mutua, M. 175
mutual aid 59, 78–79, 133, 134
mutual obligations 60, 78, 134,
  149–155, 168

N

Naftali, O. 67
National Children's Day 99
National Commission for Civic Education 99
National Council on Women and
  Development 104
National Democratic Congress (NDC) 109,
  110, 113
National Development Policy Framework 98
National Multi-Sectoral Committee 104–105
National Plan of Action (NPA) 98
Ncube, W. 37, 38
neglect, protection from 101
New Patriotic Party 104, 105
Newspaper Licensing Law 109
NGO Ad Hoc Group in the Drafting of
  the Convention on the Rights of the
  Child 48
NGOs (non-governmental
  organizations) 48, 117
Nieuwenhuys, O. 45, 90, 174, 185
Nigeria 60, 63, 106, 165
Nkrumah, Kwame 65, 92, 93
non-discrimination principle 97

221

Nsamenang, A.B. 62, 77, 139
nuclear family units 71, 134–137
Nyame 149

O

Oestreich, J. 48, 49, 50
official development assistance (ODA) 112
Okyere, S. 159–160, 161
Open-Ended Working Group on the
   Question of the Convention on the
   Rights of the Child 47–48
Oppong, C. 76–77, 158
opposition to children's rights 123–124
Oquaye, M. 106, 108, 109
oral traditions 20, 139
Organization of African Unity 64
Organization of Arab Petroleum Exporting
   Countries 106
Orme, N. 27, 28
orphaned children 82, 101
Osu Children's Home 84, 92
over-18s still in need of parental support 101
overcrowding 3, 4
Owoo, N.S. 160

P

parental authority 122
parental property, rights to 101, 103
parental responsibilities 76, 97, 100, 101
parent-child relationships 136
passive, children as 47
paternalism 10, 50, 53, 94
pawning 79, 85
personhood 40, 59–60, 78, 149–155
Persons with Disability Act (2006) 105
Peruzzotti, E. 66, 117–118
philanthropy 34, 37, 38–39, 44
philosophy 29–30, 59, 149
play 4, 37
Plumb, J.H. 28–29, 30, 31, 36, 39
Poland 47, 49
police 83, 104, 105, 109, 121
political rights 108, 124
polygyny 131–133, 145
Population and Housing Census 2021 120
porters/carriers 85, 88, 160
Portuguese colonialism 82–83, 177
poverty 8, 13, 31–32, 162–171, 182
power 38, 68–69, 71, 79, 112–113
pre-colonial societies 18, 23, 68, 73, 75, 76–81
preschools 112
prevention of cruelty to children 33
primary education 92–93, 97, 115
private property 70
productive members of society, children as 60
property 28, 101, 103, 106
protection, children viewed as in need
   of 37–38, 43, 47, 62, 94, 100, 102,
   103, 120, 182

Prout, A. 13, 73
Provisional National Defence Council
   (PNDC) 106, 108, 109, 110, 113, 115
puberty/puberty rites 27, 62, 139–141,
   145–146
public health 86–87
Punch, S. 9, 11
punishment
   affluent families 169
   communal 80
   physical punishment 8, 36, 121, 122,
      169–170
   right to protection from 185–186
   'slave of the gods' (*trokosi*) 79–80, 104,
      117–118, 160, 161
   when running errands 154
Pupavac, V. 10, 53

Q

Quarshie, E.N. 121

R

race 43–46, 187
Ragged Schools Union 33–34
rape 103, 120, 121
Rawlings, Jerry John 100, 105, 106, 107,
   108, 109, 110–111, 113–114
Rawlings, Nana Konadu Agyemang 109,
   111–112
reciprocity 78, 123, 133, 134, 138, 150, 152
Regional Houses of Chiefs 98
regions in Ghana 2
relationality 59, 76, 78
religion 59, 81, 109, 127, 130, 137,
   149–150, 178
   see also Christianity; Islam; missionaries
removal from families 39
Renteln, A. 69
research methods 22–23
resource extraction 84
'revolution' 107
Richards, P. 66
rights discourse, development of 40, 41–55
Rio de Janeiro 7
rites of passage 27, 139–140, 145–146
ritual bathing rites 140, 141
ritual servitude 79–80, 104
Rizzini, I. 7, 15, 187
Robertson, C. 93
Rosaldo, R. 180
Rosemberg, F. 11–12
Rousseau, J.J. 29–30
rural/urban distinctions 35, 71, 159, 165

S

Sackey, E. 152, 157
sacralization of culture 72
'sacrificial lambs' 80, 118
Salvation Army 87

INDEX

Sarpong, P. 153
Save the Children 10, 41–42, 46
'saving' children 38–39, 40, 41–42, 43, 44
Schildkrout, E. 60, 62
School Health 104
schools
  boarding schools 136
  children not in school 120, 160
  'civilized knowledge' 81
  'civilizing' children 35
  as disguise for labour exploitation 90
  history of British schools for poor
    children 33–34
  international schools 4, 5, 168
  medieval concepts of children 28
  missionaries 44, 71, 81, 89
  school fees 71, 97
  school food 31, 33
  school leaving age 61, 116
  teacher power 119
  see also education
Science, Technology and Mathematics
  Education clinic 97–98
secondary education 115, 136
security guards/watchmen 5, 6
Selwyn-Clarke, Dr 87
semi-legal personhood 40
settler colonies 45, 67
sex 30, 37, 61
sexual abuse 120, 121
sexual exploitation 119, 160, 161
sexual violence 121
  see also rape
Shelter for Abused Children 104
Shepler, S. 66
siblings of parents, sending children to
  76–77, 79
Sierra Leone 66
single story, danger of the 14
Slave Dealing Abolition Ordinance of
  1874 82
'slave of the gods' (*trokosi*) 79–80, 104,
  117–118, 160, 161
slavery 17, 79, 82, 83, 85, 130, 177
Smythe, K. 71
social media 120, 166
social parents 77
social welfare offices 121
social workers 101, 121, 182
socialization 7–8, 77, 78, 151, 152, 155–157,
  167–169
socioeconomic rights 106–108, 124
Sommerville, C.J. 29, 30, 34, 36
South Africa 9, 51
Spence, T. 190n2
Stahl, R. 50
state roles 27, 39, 101, 115
Steegstra, M. 141
Stephens, S. 17, 18, 69

Strahan, George Cumine 82
street children 102
Structural Adjustment Programme 107
subjects of law, children as 50
Swaziland 45
Szulc, A. 177

T

Tabom 130
Tafere, Y. 63
Tanzania 71
Tefera, T. 51
Tine, N.D. 125
Togo 131
toilets 3
torture 100, 101, 108
toys 29
trade (international) 83, 130
trade, learning a 76, 78
  see also apprenticeships
'traditional society' 15–16, 18, 72
traffic 4, 6
transitions to adulthood 62–63, 70, 138–147,
  155–157, 166–167
'triple heritage' 18, 128
trokosi 79–80, 104, 117–118, 160, 161
trotros 6
tutors 5
TV 166
Twi 99
Twum-Danso, A. 28, 29, 33, 63, 64, 69, 101,
  102, 121, 122, 146, 151, 153, 157, 186
Twum-Danso Imoh, A. 8, 9, 10, 11, 15, 16,
  17, 18, 21, 25, 50, 51, 52, 53, 58, 59,
  60, 61, 62, 64, 66, 67, 68, 69, 71, 78, 79,
  118, 121, 134, 147, 150, 151, 152, 153,
  154, 159, 164, 166, 171, 175, 184, 185,
  186, 187, 188

U

Ubuntu 59–60
Uganda 66
UN (United Nations)
  Committee on Human Rights 49
  Development Programme (UNDP) 107
  Economic and Social Council
    (ECOSOC) 46, 48, 49
  Open-Ended Working Group on the
    Question of the Convention on the
    Rights of the Child 47–48
  Standard Minimum Rules for the
    Administration of Juvenile Justice 100, 101
  Sustainable Development Goals 163
  Temporary Social Commission 46
  UN Commission on Human Rights 47
  UNICEF (United Nations Children's
    Fund) 10, 47, 48, 50–51, 113, 121
  see also Convention on the Rights of the
    Child (CRC)

unfit parents 101
universalism 186
university education 115
upper-class elites 31, 33, 35, 40, 171
urbanization 17, 84, 132, 134
US (United States) 19, 49, 113, 124

V

Van Beuren, G. 151
Van Hear, N. 88, 89
Veerman, P. 42, 43, 47, 49, 50
Verhoef, H. 76
Vietnam 163
village, returning to 135–136, 138
virginity 80, 140
voluntary sector 87
vulnerability 51

W

'waithood' 63, 167
Walker-Hall, N. 183
waste disposal 3, 5
'web of kinship' 133
welfare, historical approaches to 75–95
wellbeing/health, right to 101

Wells, K. 37, 38, 39, 40, 47, 53
'West' as analytical lens 175–181
Western childhoods, normativity of 19
White, B. 77
White privilege 187
Windborne, J. 79, 113
women
  forced labour 88
  women's movements 109, 111, 114
  women's rights 112, 117
  see also gender differences; girls
work, children's 4, 37, 46, 60, 148–172,
  187–188
  see also child labour; domestic labour/
    housework; income-generating activity
working alongside adults 20, 28
working hours 32
working-class children 31, 36
World Bank 107, 112, 117
World Declaration and Plan of Action 98
World Summit on Children 1990 98
Wyness, M. 61

Z

Zimbabwe 16, 70